The Labour of Obedience

Petà Dunstan is Librarian of the Faculty of Divinity in the University of Cambridge, where she supervises in modern church history, and is a Fellow of St Edmund's College. She is editor of *Anglican Religious Life*, the bi-annual directory of Anglican Religious communities worldwide.

The Labour of Obedience

*The Benedictines of Pershore, Nashdom
and Elmore – A History*

Petà Dunstan

CANTERBURY
PRESS
Norwich

in association with
The Anglo-Catholic History Society

© Petà Dunstan 2009

First published in 2009 by the Canterbury Press Norwich
Editorial office
13–17 Long Lane,
London, EC1A 9PN, UK

Canterbury Press is an imprint of Hymns Ancient and Modern Ltd (a registered
charity)
St Mary's Works, St Mary's Plain,
Norwich, NR3 3BH, UK

www.scm-canterburypress.co.uk

British Library Cataloguing in Publication data

A catalogue record for this book is available
from the British Library

978 1 85311 974 3

Printed and bound in Great Britain by
CPI Antony Rowe, Chippenham, Wiltshire

Contents

Acknowledgements

I owe a tremendous debt to Prior Simon and the monks of Elmore Abbey for their kindness and encouragement as I have worked on this book, and for their generous hospitality during the periods I have researched in the community's archives. Elmore Abbey is a beautiful and restful place to stay, and the warm welcome and support of the monks made it also an enjoyable location.

My thanks go to the Anglo-Catholic History Society, and particularly Michael Yelton and the committee, for their enthusiastic support for this venture, and whose financial support has been invaluable. Also thanks to Christine Smith for her kindness and advice, and for facilitating the book's publication.

I am grateful to the staff of the libraries and archives I have visited, and to all those who granted me personal interviews to share their recollections.

For members of my family and my friends, who never fail to encourage me, I give heart-felt thanks to you all. Especial thanks go to my parents, Cynthia and Roy, who listened patiently as I tried out drafts of chapters upon them, and gently urged me forward. My father's passing before this book is published has been a great sadness, but it has made me all the more appreciative of the blessing of his love and presence through so many years. May he rest in peace and rise in glory.

The idea of researching this history followed fascinating conversations in the mid-1990s with the late Dom Augustine Morris. I was blessed to call him a friend in his last years and grateful for all he shared and gave to me. His long life of over ninety years was spent from the age of eighteen in the Nashdom/Elmore community, and his personal history was entwined with the story related here. So I dedicate this book to his memory.

Key to Abbreviations

AC	Aelred (Benjamin) Carlyle OSB
AH	Anselm (Humphrey) Hughes OSB
AidH	Aidan (Harold) Harker OSB
AM	Anselm (Charles) Mardon OSB
Anson1	Peter Anson, *The Benedictines of Caldey*, Catholic Book Club, London 1940, new rev. edn, Prinknash Abbey, Gloucester, 1944
Anson2	Peter Anson, *Abbot Extraordinary: A Memoir of Aelred Carlyle, Monk and Missionary, 1874–1955*, Faith Press, London, 1958
Anson3	Peter Anson, *Building Up the Waste Places*, Faith Press, Leighton Buzzard, 1973
Anson4	Peter Anson, *Fashions in Church Furnishings, 1840–1940*, Faith Press, London, 1960, 2nd edn, Studio Vista, London, 1965
AR	Athelstan Riley
AugM	Augustine (David) Morris OSB
Bailey	Simon Bailey, *A Tactful God*, Gracewing, Leominster, 1995
BC	Bernard (William) Clements OSB
Bel	Bell Papers, Lambeth Palace Archives
BKB	Bernard Kenworthy Browne, sometime N/OSB
BL	Benedict (Cyril) Ley OSB
BR	Benedict (Richard) Reid OSB
CC	Peter Anson, *The Call of the Cloister*, SPCK, London, 1955
CG	Charles Gore CR
CGL	Cosmo Gordon Lang, Archbishop of York and then Canterbury
CHBH	C. H. Bickerton Hudson
CHC	Community of the Holy Cross
CM	Chapter minutes

ConfM	Minutes of the daily community conference
CR	Community of the Resurrection
CSC	Community of the Sisters of the Church
Dav	Davidson Papers, Lambeth Palace Archives
DP	Denys (Gostwyck) Prideaux OSB
DS	Darwell Stone
EA	Elmore Abbey Archives
EP	Ernest Pearce, Bishop of Worcester
FV	Frederick Vasey
GB	George Bell, Bishop of Chichester
GD	Gregory (George Eglinton Alston) Dix OSB
GM	Gerald Maxwell SSJE
GS	Godfrey Stokes OSB
HB	Hubert Burge, Bishop of Oxford
JA	John Aglionby, Bishop of Accra
James	Bruno S. James, *Asking for Trouble*, Darton, Longman & Todd, London, 1962
JP	Jessie Prideaux
Jub	*The Jubilee Book of the Benedictines of Nashdom, 1914–1964*, Faith Press, London, 1964
KCA	King's College Cambridge Archives
Kemp	Eric N. Kemp, *The Life and Letters of Kenneth Escott Kirk*, Hodder & Stoughton, London, 1959
KK	Kenneth Kirk, Bishop of Oxford
Kollar1	Rene Kollar, *Abbot Aelred Carlyle, Caldey Island, and the Anglo-Catholic Revival in England* (American University Studies, Series 7 Theology and Religion, Vol. 177), Peter Lang, New York, 1995
Kollar2	Rene Kollar, *A Universal Appeal: Aspects of the Revival of Monasticism in the West in the 19th and Early 20th Centuries*, International Scholars Publications, San Francisco, 1996
Laing	G. E. F. Laing, *Dom Bernard Clements in Africa*, SCM Press, London, 1944
Lan	Lang Papers, Lambeth Palace Archives
LH	Charles Lindley Wood, 2nd Lord Halifax
LPL	Lambeth Palace Archives
MA	Malling Archive
Marr	Andrew Marr and Abraham Newsom, eds, *Singing God's Praises: The First Sixty Years*, St Gregory's Abbey, Three Rivers, Michigan, 1998

MC	Martin Collett OSB
NC	Niall Campbell (Duke of Argyll from 1914)
NAL	*Notes from the Abbey* (supplement to Laudate)
NAR	*Nashdom Abbey Record*
OHP	Order of the Holy Paraclete
OSB	Order of St Benedict
PA	Peter Anson (sometime Richard Whiting OSB)
PH	Peter (William) Harris OSB
RD	Randall Davidson, Archbishop of Canterbury
SC	Congregation of the Servants of Christ
SG	Samuel Gurney
SGS	Society of the Good Shepherd
SHT	Society of the Holy Trinity
SPB	Society of the Precious Blood
SSF	Society of St Francis
SSJE	Society of St John the Evangelist
SSM (men)	Society of the Sacred Mission
SSM (women)	Society of St Margaret
SSP	Sisters of St Peter
SSPP	Society of St Peter and St Paul
Tem	Temple Papers, Lambeth Palace Archives
TS	Thomas Strong, Bishop of Ripon, subsequently Bishop of Oxford
VR	Victor (Thomas Victor) Roberts OSB
WF	Walter Frere CR, Bishop of Truro
WS	Walter Seton
WT	William Temple, Archbishop of Canterbury
WW	Michael (William) Warner OSB

Introduction

During the twentieth century, the Anglo-Catholic movement played a significant part in Anglican history. It is often associated in the popular mind with liturgy and the revival of Catholic ceremonial, but this was only one, outward and less important aspect of its influence. In theology and spirituality, and in social action and church politics, it has played an influential and decisive role in shaping Anglican identity.

For the Anglo-Papalist wing of the movement, considered the most pro-Roman Catholic and also the most radical, one dominant focus was ecumenism, and the reconciliation of all Christians back into one church under Papal leadership. It was also concerned with the return of the Church to what its followers saw as the authentic spiritual depths of Christian tradition, away from the political and secular entanglements of state-influenced 'established' religion. The Religious life was a necessary component of this return – not only for the social action of apostolic communities, but also for the prayerful witness of more enclosed monks and nuns.

The *Rule of St Benedict* offered those drawn to Religious life a discipline, rhythm and focus for this renewal of Christian life, with communities being the centre of a movement of oblates, associates and others whose stability of purpose would help transform the Church. Of all ancient rules for monasticism, it seemed the best to fit the Church of England, which, during the centuries since the Reformation, had retained much of the Benedictine ethos in both its structures and worship. Some women Religious in the Anglican fold had successfully embraced the *Rule of Benedict*. For Anglo-Papalists therefore, establishing a parallel Benedictine community for men became crucial. After false starts, the community at Pershore and then Nashdom came to fulfil this need and vision.

The history of these monks is therefore of wider significance than a mere charting of the course of one Religious community. Especially after its move to Nashdom in the 1920s, the very name of the striking house (designed by Lutyens) in which they resided became associated with a set of principles that ultimately shaped the sense of identity of Anglo-Papalists, lay and clerical, setting them apart even from other Anglo-Catholics.

The community, originally developed under the leadership of Denys Prideaux, went through tough and discouraging years after its foundation, but gathered strength and vitality in the 1920s when a group of remarkable and talented men were professed. Astonishingly, by the community's Silver Jubilee, it was already a force to be reckoned with in the debates within the Church of England.

The story begins, however, with the crisis of conversion amidst a previous attempt at establishing the Benedictine life for men among Anglicans; the curious and exotic monastic community on Caldey Island in Wales.

I

The Legacy of Secession

It was a sensation. The press, both national and provincial, blurted out the event in dramatic headlines. Roman Catholics were triumphant. Anglo-Catholics were despondent. Evangelical Protestants rejoiced at the news. Some commentators said it did not matter, others thought it was the beginning of the end for the 'Anglo-Catholic' wing of the Church of England. The event in question was the decision taken early in 1913 by Abbot Aelred Carlyle and a majority of the Benedictine monks on Caldey Island, off the Pembrokeshire coast, to leave the Church of England and be received into the Roman Catholic Church.[1]

That it was such an 'event' to contemporaries was partly because it was a colourful story. Aelred Carlyle was a flamboyant abbot, charming and charismatic, who had not been shy to court publicity. Since 1906, he had raised much money to build on Caldey Island an elaborate monastery with turrets and gables, and fulfil his own and many other people's rich fantasy of a Religious house. He had endured privations and tribulations in establishing the Benedictine abbey, and had shown unflagging determination to build a committed community of monks in the Church of England, despite scorn and scepticism from some quarters. Novices came and went. Some of those professed were not able to remain faithful to the monastic vocation. Yet, others did stay, and, by 1913, Aelred had a community of over thirty. It had required persistence and integrity as well as charisma. This was no small achievement and could only have been expedited by someone of vision and substance.

However, many had noticed that, as the monastery became more established, Aelred had lived with greater flamboyance, despite being a monk vowed to poverty. His achievements brought him into contact with the wealthy and powerful, and perhaps this changed his perception of his own status. His style developed accordingly. So, while his monks lived frugally, the abbot's personal quarters were generously appointed, with much of it done in marble and oak. He had a boat for 'private pleasure'. He owned a Daimler car for chauffeur-driven trips on the mainland. He had holidays on the continent, ostensibly for his 'health'. On the railways, he was said to travel first class, and when in London would hire a private suite at a hotel. For all the pressures and sacrifices of his life (and there certainly were many), there appeared also to be numerous perks and privileges, although it is not easy to separate fact from hyperbole in the numerous stories of his activities.

Some visitors may have been embarrassed, although others were perhaps refreshed, by the less reticent atmosphere compared to many communities. Anglican communities of men tended to be dominated by priests educated at Oxford and Cambridge, most of whom had been inculcated with the sense of reserve preferred by many in the British upper classes. For them, drawing attention to yourself or being 'showy' was inappropriate, especially for men, and was not considered good manners. Aelred did not go to Oxbridge[2] and in any case did not share these instinctive inhibitions. He had not encouraged such men to join him either: hardly any of those who had entered the Caldey community had been to university or to public school. The result was a less formal atmosphere than might have been expected. In addition, there was an overt sensuousness about the lush ecclesiastical trappings at Caldey, and also some undemure practices, such as nude bathing in the sea, which the abbot insisted upon as a regular activity for the whole community, compulsory even for the shyest monks. The atmosphere all this engendered attracted some, but repelled others, who came into contact with the monastery.

Aelred had therefore become controversial, especially to existing and potential benefactors: a figure who might inspire devotion or distrust, admiration or disapproval, both inside and outside the Church. It is on the antics (whether true or false) of such 'colourful' characters that many pages of newsprint will always be sold. In an era where denominational allegiance still had strong political and cultural resonances, a dramatic gesture by such a person, in this case deserting the Established Church for the Roman Catholic Church, inevitably made startling headlines for a few days.

But more seriously, it was also newsworthy because of what it represented in ecclesiastical terms. Since the days of the Tractarians in 1830s Oxford, there had been a steady growth in the number of Anglicans who believed that the Church of England was a 'branch' of the Catholic Church, which, although severed from the Roman Church, was nevertheless an equal heir to the doctrine and practice of the early church. They considered its position similar to that of the Orthodox Churches of Eastern Europe and Asia Minor. They believed the Church of England should therefore acknowledge and embrace this Catholic identity rather than being content to be bracketed with the Protestants. But among those who held this view, sometimes collectively referred to as Anglo-

Catholics, opinions differed and shifted, and the arguments could be as heated between their internal factions as they could be with those outside who scoffed at the whole idea of a Catholic Church of England. Some Anglo-Catholics believed in being loyal to the *Book of Common Prayer* and the structures of the Church of England, but within those boundaries using a Catholic interpretation of doctrine and a more ceremonial Catholic liturgical expression. They were sometimes known as 'Prayer-Book' Catholics. For others, it meant affirming a range of Catholic doctrine while seeking to revive the Sarum Rite, one of the liturgies commonly used in England in the medieval period, which they believed would thereby establish authentic 'English' Catholicism. By so doing, they would declare themselves Catholics, yet (they believed) be properly distanced from what they judged to be the post-Reformation errors of Roman Catholicism, such as Papal Infallibility.

For a third group, the scandal of disunity among Christians was the most important obstacle to the proclaiming of the Christian Gospel to the world, and the principal reason for promoting Catholic doctrine and worship in the Church of England was reunion with Rome. By pushing for Anglicans to embrace their rightful heritage as members of the Catholic Church in its widest sense, they would be bringing closer the day when that corporate reunion – church uniting with church – was not just possible but became inevitable. The Church of England had separated from Rome in the sixteenth century as a body, not as individuals one by one; reunion could only be successfully expedited therefore by a reverse of that *corporate* separation, and not by individuals converting piecemeal. To achieve this, the doctrine and liturgical practice of the Church of England needed to be brought as close as possible to that of contemporary Roman Catholicism. As Pope Leo XIII had declared Anglican orders 'utterly null and void' in the encyclical *Apostolicae Curae* issued in 1896, their only major disagreement with Rome was over the validity of the orders of Anglican priests. Those who followed this line of reasoning were sometimes termed Anglo-Papalists. Some used this term originally in an abusive sense and so not all those to whom it refers have been content with it as a descriptor. Anselm Hughes in his book *Rivers of the Flood* preferred the term 'papistical' to 'papalist'.[3] However, 'Anglo-Papisticals' sounds clumsy, so for the purposes of this study, Anglo-Papalism is employed to distinguish this particular group of Anglo-Catholics from others.[4]

The position of Anglo-Papalists was a difficult one to hold and proclaim because of the scorn it roused in others. From two opposite sides, the Anglo-Papalist position was ridiculed and condemned. To many Roman Catholics, it was contradictory to say you believed everything they did and yet not submit to the authority of the Pope. To believe in Catholicism yet not seek admission to the Roman fold was, in their view, to put your soul in peril, and an Anglo-Papalist was either naively foolish or else even cynically wicked to adopt such a position. Why settle for a hollow pretence, they argued, when you could have the 'fullness' of the 'real thing'? On the other side, many Anglicans saw the Anglo-Papalists as at worst a 'fifth column' of Romanists trying to subvert the integrity of the Church of England from inside, fatally weakening its theological truth by spreading 'Roman errors': or at best, a group of misguided dreamers advocating an unreachable vision. Unity, they insisted, could only take place when *Rome* reformed and discarded the accretions with which the Papacy had distorted Christian truth, not by Anglicans becoming imitation Roman Catholics.

But to those convinced of the Anglo-Papalist position, the opposition merely served to fire their commitment to greater heights. They were enthusiastic ecumenists in an age when Catholics in general were not ecumenical. For them, corporate reunion was the only way forward, not a stream of individual conversions. However, each time their wing of the Church of England 'lost' members to Rome, their strength appeared diminished – and so, in the opinion of their critics, was the force of their argument. Therefore as they won support person by person on one side among their fellow Anglicans, they were faced with a steady erosion of existing supporters on the other. Each conversion to Rome appeared to all shades of opinion among their opponents as evidence of the flawed nature of the Anglo-Papalist position.

When the conversions were among Religious – monks and nuns, friars and sisters – the impact was even greater. For the revival of Religious communities in the Church of England had been one of the most notable achievements of Anglo-Catholicism. Since its controversial beginnings in the 1840s, this revival had evolved into a movement shown respect and even admiration in many parts of the Church. The Lambeth Conferences of Anglican bishops in 1897 and 1908 had given some approval.[5] For the Anglo-Papalists, too many of the new communities were insufficiently Catholic, trimming and cutting their beliefs and practices to suit bishops. They believed Religious should be at the forefront of the fight for the reunion of Christendom, leading the transformation of Anglican worship and doctrine. In the Benedictine monks of Caldey Island, many had seen the ideal they were seeking. The adherence of the community to Roman liturgical forms, and particularly to Roman doctrines such as the Immaculate Conception and Assumption of the Blessed Virgin Mary, was a model for the whole Church of England. The submission of this group to Rome in 1913 was then a real disaster for their hopes. The view was well

4

expressed by Niall Campbell, who would later inherit the Dukedom of Argyll, and one of the leading lay Anglo-Papalists of the time, in a letter written in early 1912:

> That the Reunion of Christendom, East and West alike – of all, that is who see the Divine Necessity of the Episcopate – is to come at some not very far off time, is a belief to which all Catholics increasingly cling. That the Monastic System as revived in the English Church will enormously hasten on that event has long been clearly seen by me, and many others – as clearly as that a secession prematurely and at this juncture, and for absolutely no adequate or apparent reason, on the part of a community, either as a whole or in part, might retard not only the Revival of Contemplative Life in our Land, but also that Great Reunion itself to which the whole movement should be directed ...[6]

When that secession came therefore, it was a significant – and newsworthy – event in the ongoing struggle for the future direction of the Church of England, and also in the struggle in the wider Church for what the real definition of a Catholic was. Could you be a Catholic outside the Roman fold? The Caldey story suggested 'no'; yet many remained convinced that the answer was still 'yes' and they were determined to rebuild the witness of a Religious community such as the one Aelred Carlyle had created.

This was especially so as there were those who believed Carlyle's decision to lead a majority of his monks to Rome was not a theological decision at all. Some believed it to be an economic one. Various Anglo-Catholic donors had begun to withdraw their continued support from the Caldey Island monastery some years before the secession, upset by the abbot's extravagances, both in his building projects and his personal life-style, both of which had led to him increasing demands and begging letters to his wearied sponsors. Going over to Rome, claimed the sceptics, was about economical survival not theological understanding.[7] Rumours of Aelred's secretive contacts with Roman Catholic Benedictines prior to the secession added to the sense of a covert advance 'deal' being done, and his extraordinarily rapid progress through a 'novitiate'[8] and ordination studies in the Roman Catholic Church added yet more to the cynicism about his underlying motives. The correspondence with Archbishop Davidson[9] of Canterbury and the subsequent invitation to Bishop Gore[10] of Oxford to perform a Visitation to Caldey in the latter part of 1912 looked like manoeuvres to create a quarrel, which in turn could serve as an excuse for rejecting the Church of England. Was this not an exercise in ecclesiastical politics, nudged by economic factors, instead of a principled theological decision?

Others, however, defended Carlyle, even some who thought his decision wrong. Gore had sent two emissaries to visit the monastery in late 1912, and Gore's response to their report was to insist the Benedictine community adhere to the *Book of Common Prayer* in celebrating the Eucharist and abandon expression of and support for various doctrines considered Roman Catholic. To his defenders, Carlyle had no option but to convert or else betray his principles and beliefs. Blame for the catastrophe could be laid at the door of the intransigence of Bishop Gore.

The arguments of the sceptics could also be counter-balanced by other parallel events, which indicated there was a crisis of confidence in a section of the Anglo-Papalist movement. Aelred Carlyle was not only the Abbot of Caldey but also the head of a 'Congregation' of Anglican Benedictines. Two communities of nuns were associated with Caldey and his leadership. One community was based at Baltonsborough in Somerset.[11] The other had been resident at Malling Abbey in Kent but had moved to Milford Haven in Wales in 1911.[12] This second community of nuns, led by Abbess Scholastica Ewart[13] and a part of Aelred's 'congregation', converted to Rome at the same time as the Caldey monks. (Whether Scholastica influenced Aelred or the other way round was a topic of speculation at the time.) Although individual Anglican Religious had become Roman Catholics throughout the history of the revival of communities, it has to be noted that corporate conversions were already not unknown. A branch house of the Society of St Margaret in Bloomsbury had 'gone over to Rome' in 1908.[14] A small Franciscan order in the Episcopal Church of the United States had converted in 1909.[15] Most of the fledgling Community of St Francis in London had followed their Reverend Mother to Rome in 1910.[16] If Religious communities were 'hasteners' of the Anglo-Papalists' vision, as Niall Campbell had suggested, these secessions were a brake on their ambitions. This was why the Caldey secession mattered so much.

At an even deeper level, the question was raised about the specific presence of contemplative communities, and more specifically the Benedictine contemplative life, for men in the Church of England. Once the Caldey monks had become Roman Catholics, there were none. This was surprising given the foundational place of the *Rule of St Benedict* in the history of Religious life in Western Europe. Many Anglican Religious were influenced by Benedictinism – indeed some would have judged that the liturgical life of English cathedrals, as well as aspects of collegiate tradition in Oxford and Cambridge universities, still echoed much of Benedictine ethos and practice, and that the Church of England as a whole owed much to the same.

This dearth of male Benedictines was not for want of effort by a handful of pioneers. Joseph Leycester Lyne, known as Father Ignatius, spent several decades in what proved to be abortive, and somewhat amateurish, attempts to revive the Benedictine life in the Church of England, beginning in 1863. He was an exciting and energetic preacher, who attracted inquisitive crowds wherever he went, trying to raise funds for his monastic experiments. But his Benedictine foundation failed to flourish, despite a series of locations: Claydon in Suffolk, then Norwich, Laleham-on-Thames, and finally Llanthony in Wales. Ignatius's eccentricities and the lack of stability in the way of life in his monasteries sadly undermined the genuine aspirations he longed to fulfil.[17]

Benjamin Fearnley Carlyle began his Benedictine journey in the 1890s, when he was a medical student in London, by being an extern oblate brother of the Anglican Benedictine nuns then at Twickenham,[18] before then founding a monastery. His small community also migrated several times, finally settling on Caldey Island in 1906. By 1913, Caldey was a unique effort in establishing a community of Anglican Benedictine monks in Britain, Llanthony having faded away after Ignatius's death in 1908.[19] For any good Anglo-Papalist therefore, the secession of the Caldey monks was a severe blow. The absence had to be remedied and quickly.

Hence, while the sensation of the 'conversion' was still being debated in the press and among church people, some minds were already turning to keeping a Benedictine presence in the Church of England. Leading Anglo-Catholics such as Niall Campbell,[20] Athelstan Riley,[21] Dr Darwell Stone,[22] Lord Halifax[23] and Father Henry Mackay[24] began conferring both by letter and in meetings. Campbell wrote to Riley on 7 March,

> I dined with Lord Halifax last Monday & saw Hubert Miller[25] there and have been in touch with Howell over this provoking Caldey business. However, it is no use now to weep over them or S. Brides and fresh Plans must be made for all interested in the Movement …
>
> Cyril Howell,[26] I, Gurney[27] & many others have been thinking over matters in connection with getting the shattered residue of the 4 or 5 monks (which include Dom Anselm the cantor who is in solemn vows, and Br David who is a priest now & in simple vows) to collect together and in some quite [sic] country place, continue unbroken the divine Offices. Fr Mackay is I hear in touch with them as they all come to personally interview him.[28]

Stone reported to the Bishop of Oxford, Charles Gore, that Halifax and Mackay were trying to organize a new foundation almost immediately.[29]

They too believed any 'continuing' community should be built around the 'remnant', the members who had not converted.

Anselm Mardon was the one solemnly professed monk from Caldey who was still loyal to Anglicanism. He had believed a plea for further negotiation with the Anglican authorities was the proper response to the pressure put on the Caldey community to modify their practices. At first he had agreed to sign the community's letter to the Bishop of Oxford, which defied the episcopal commands, but then he had decided against. Abbot Aelred's version of Anselm's change of heart was articulated in a letter to the bishop,

> One monk in Solemn Vows first gave his signature, but afterwards withdrew it; he had been a Nonconformist for many years, and felt that as far as the community was concerned we could not come to any other conclusion, but that for himself his personal convictions would not allow him to associate himself with the actions of the community.[30]

When he had left the island, he had gone to stay with Father John Lopes,[31] the parish priest at St Francis, Saltley, in Birmingham. Mackay wrote to Lopes, and Anselm then agreed to see Darwell Stone on 4 March 1913, and Lord Halifax and Mackay in London the day after. This was the same day the formal reception of Abbot Aelred Carlyle and the majority of his community into the Roman Catholic Church took place on Caldey Island.

Anselm had been born Charles Newt Mardon in Plymouth in 1879, the son of a naval seaman. He had been brought up in later years in Birmingham. He had been in the choir at St Jude's in that city, and so, after joining the Caldey community in 1907, he was soon given the job of chief cantor in the monastery chapel. His 'fruity tenor voice' was remembered as 'lush' when singing solos. Peter Anson recalled him possessing 'considerable charm of manner' and noted also that he was 'prematurely obese'. This was possibly the reason that Abbot Aelred's strictly enforced rule that community bathing was done in the nude was relaxed only in Dom Anselm's case.[32]

Being the only Caldey monk in solemn vows who was still an Anglican, his presence was important if the new Anglican foundation was to be seen as a 'continuation'. To the disappointment of many, he seemed reluctant to take on the task of leading a community. He was not intellectually confident, perhaps because, like most of the Caldey monks, he had not had a university education. But as the urgings from eminent Anglo-Catholics besieged him, he began to waiver from his initial refusal. He wrote in some confusion to Father Vasey,[33] the chaplain of the Anglican Benedictine sisters at Baltonsborough, on 18 April 1913:

When I left Caldey my one idea was to try to find some congenial work of a Religious nature which would enable me to live a quiet life and keep as far as possible my rule – I find now that this idea of mine does not at all meet with the approval of those who were interested in Caldey, and all agreed that the Benedictine Life for men must not be allowed to die out and that I must do what I can to get men together and prevent it. I have opposed this from the first because I felt most strongly my own incapacity for such work. But deep down in my heart I do feel that God is calling me through these people to take up this cross and I am much concerned to know what I ought to do. I have had many letters from all kinds of people but all are agreed on this one point. Lord Halifax has most kindly offered a house and says there would be no financial difficulties. What ought I to do? I have not sought this rather I have tried to evade it and yet the call still comes. I *know* I am not the man to do *great* things but is this sufficient reason for refusing to co-operate with others in just living the Common life.[34]

Father Vasey's reply was unequivocal:

There is, in my opinion, no shadow of a doubt as to what you ought to do. I think it would be an unpardonable error of judgement on your part to take up any other kind of work whatsoever in preference to this burden which now rests upon your shoulders.[35]

But who would join him? Of the other monks who remained Anglicans, there seemed little enthusiasm in trying to continue Religious life. Of the priests, Augustine Jones, who was a novice brother, declined to stay on Caldey, but nevertheless soon after did become a Roman Catholic at Downside Abbey.[36] David Tugwell[37] (in simple vows) was an indecisive man (and considered by Anson to be 'silly, and temperamental, riddled with scruples'),[38] so this may be the reason he was not pressed to join any new venture. He instead took a curacy at St John's, Southwark, and remained in parochial work until his retirement. One simply professed brother (Placidus Cooper)[39] and one novice (Michael Barton)[40] both pursued ordination and became priests, but in the Episcopal Church in the USA. According to Aelred at the time, there was also a 'brother Giles and an old Br William' who left the community, while Brother Henry went back after a few weeks away.[41]

The community also included intern oblates, those who lived alongside the community but who did not have the obligation of saying all the Offices in choir with the monks or of taking the full set of vows. Of the priest oblates, John Blaker[42] had already left the island in 1912. The

9

senior of the lay oblates, Charles Hutson, though remaining on the island to continue his help in the vestment-making department of the monastery under Dom Samson Carrington, did not become a Roman Catholic. Born in Kent in 1861, he was the son of a blacksmith, and Peter Anson, who only knew him in his Caldey days, recalled him as a 'simple soul much loved by all his brethren'.[43] Once the new Anglican community was gathered, he left Caldey to join them.

Yet, according to an anonymous letter published in the *Church Times* on 7 March 1913, there was another figure of far greater importance than any of those already mentioned.

> It should be a very great relief and encouragement (to those who loved Caldey) to know that the one man who, by common consent, stood – as theologian, historian and scholar – like a giant above the heads of all the Community, and who is widely recognized outside its ranks as an exceptionally able and intellectual writer and thinker (especially on ecclesiastical history), has refused to secede to the Roman Communion. I do not mention his name, but no one who has been in touch with the life at Caldey will fail to know to whom I refer, ...

According to the writer, this man was the 'brains of the Community'. He was referring to Denys Prideaux, the most significant of the oblates throughout the last Anglican years of the Caldey community. It seems everyone working towards a refoundation of Anglican Benedictinism saw Denys as the essential presence to give both intellectual weight and stability to any new venture. It was his encyclopaedic knowledge of Benedictine history, and his academic prowess in arguing convincingly for the validity of the Benedictine life among Anglicans, which made him such a pivotal figure. He was a man with an unusual history.

2

The Journey to Pershore

Denys was Prideaux's monastic name. Following his birth on 16 September 1864, he had been christened William Gostwyck Charles, with the middle of those three being the name by which he was known. He was the second of five children[44] born to William Gostwyck Prideaux (1835–1875) and Jessie Forbes Prideaux (née Jackson) (1840–1925). Gostwyck's name was a family one, borne not only by his father but also by his grandfather.[45] This paternal grandfather had inherited a considerable property in Devon and Cornwall, the cornerstone of the family's income, and after ordination, he had settled in Kent, where he had two livings. Family tradition suggests he wished his son and heir William to follow him into the Church, but for whatever reason this hope proved unfulfilled.

In 1861, the son married Jessie, the daughter of Charles Forbes Jackson (c.1810–72), a Major General in the British army, who had had a colourful career in India. There General Jackson had displayed both great courage and also at times dissolute behaviour, a man gifted yet undisciplined. Jessie was the product of an affair, and her motherless childhood was a mosaic of experiences: looked after at first by a servant in her father's quarters at the fort of Mhou; later by her paternal grandmother,[46] first in England and then in France; then by an aunt,[47] with visits to other relatives in places such as Egypt and Italy. The background was cosmopolitan, multilingual and restless.[48] Jessie could not be 'launched' in London society as she was illegitimate, and so, as a young woman, the social world in which she could take part was restricted to Kent, where her aunt was now living. Here she met her husband.

Jessie's soldier father had come from a family which had made its living from a coffee plantation in Mahogany Vale in Jamaica, and, having made his fortune in India, that is where he had decided to return. Jessie and her new husband went with him, and hence Gostwyck and his siblings were born in the West Indies. But the context was not conducive to the young couple's happiness. William had no productive employment and boredom set in. He embarked on a relationship with a servant woman and spent periods living away from his family. He also served for a time as a merchant seaman. Despite their estrangement, which eventually became permanent, Jessie could not contemplate the scandal of a divorce, but the humiliation of her husband's behaviour must have been a tremendous stress to a proud woman, and his early death from typhoid in his fortieth year in 1875 must have been a release as well as being a bewildering shock.

This marital tragedy proved an emotionally unbalanced background for the young Gostwyck. What information survives suggests he was a shy child, often unwell, somewhat overshadowed by his adored younger brother, who was the maternal favourite. His unhappiness was perhaps best reflected in his reticence later in life to discuss his family background. In his last years, when his mental faculties were loosened by illness, he was troubled by the belief that his community 'despised' him because of his 'origins'. In fact, they knew hardly anything of his personal history, as he rarely discussed it. It can be judged that he had absorbed his mother's sense of shame and anxiety over both her illegitimacy and marital failure, and this possibly led to a damaged self-esteem, evident later in his life in his over-sensitivity to criticism or perceived rejection.

Following her father's death in 1872, Jessie had inherited sufficient money to be financially independent, and, before her widowhood, she sent Gostwyck to a preparatory school in Ipswich, back in England, in 1874. But he was soon to move again, as his mother decided against continuing to run the plantation in Jamaica, and in 1876 she moved the whole family, including Gostwyck, to continental Europe instead. In the autumn of that year they settled in Geneva, Switzerland, for three years, spending the following three in Leipzig in Germany.

Such locations for his education meant Gostwyck became fluent in several languages and gained a broad European perspective on politics and religion. He met a wide circle of European intellectuals, and family tradition has the teenage boy on one occasion debating with German atheists while his sisters hid under the table.[49] He was introduced to a range of traditions, from Calvinism to Eastern Orthodoxy. Part of this stemmed from his mother's religious search. The unhappiness of her marriage and then the tragic death of her younger son Charles in 1877, during the family's stay in Geneva, meant she sought solace in her faith, and trailed the family around to services in many different traditions. She became a friend of Père Hyacinthe,[50] the ex-Roman Catholic priest, who preached a 'liberal' Catholicism at his church in Geneva. Here he advocated a reconciliation of science and religion and the abandonment of literal interpretations of biblical texts. All these early influences on Gostwyck explain his breadth of interests, and his intellectual ability to see above denominational antagonisms and pursue an ecumenical approach to Catholicism. Returning to London in 1882, the Prideaux family finally found a religious home in Anglo-Catholicism, first at St Andrew's, Willesden, and then at St Cuthbert's, Philbeach Gardens.

In 1885, Gostwyck went to Clare College, Cambridge, to read German, and in his finals took a first-class degree. The ill-health of his childhood seems to have been conquered too as he played several sports, and coxed the winning Clare boat two years running. After a short stint of teaching, he trained at Cuddesdon Theological College, near Oxford, before being made deacon in 1892, and ordained priest the following year. The most significant parochial experience he had in succeeding years was as a curate at St Margaret's, in the Toxteth area of Liverpool, from 1896 to 1904. There were both social problems in the area facing the clergy, and also a significant number of wealthy parishioners, whose sense of superiority aggravated the new curate. Senior laymen of the Anglo-Catholic party also visited the church and Gostwyck met notables such as Lord Halifax, Athelstan Riley and the Duke of Newcastle.[51] As the curacy progressed, he became noted as an intellectual and powerful preacher, and his academic abilities were widely respected. It seems his view of the Church of England crystallized during these years and can be seen in letters to his family, as well as his surviving sermons. In 1899, he wrote to his mother,

> Yes, I agree with what you say about the English Church and it[s] wondrous revival. What I object to is its 'cocksureness' and its 'respectability' – alas its ingratitude to its 'Mother'. It really sprang from St Augustine's mission, ... it borrows largely from Rome in ritual, in theological works, in the ethos of its 'advanced' clergy – and it showers abuse upon her.[52]

His European background meant he did not have the ingrained prejudice and fear of Roman Catholicism prevalent in much of the Church of England, including the 'high church' wing. To Gostwyck, the Church had eventually to be one, although he recognized that the Anglo-Papalist vision was a long-term goal. He reflected on this when there was antagonism to his parish priest[53] over the latter's support for a particular catechism,

> I look upon it as an instance of that narrowness, that spirit of Obscurantism which seems to be at work in certain sections of the Catholic party, and which always proved itself an enemy of the Church in the long run. Surely we of the Church need to recall more frequently than we do that patience is the secret of all true success ...[54]

He was tolerant of the same priest's use of the medieval Sarum Rite, which Gostwyck termed a 'fad'. Yet he was content to go along with this, because to him the main task was theological and spiritual. The Catholic faith was not about ceremonies but about a 'life'. As he put it in a Christmas Day sermon in 1896: 'Religion ... is a devotion to a living person, Christ.'

Gostwyck had been influenced by such Anglican thinkers as Charles Gore, Henry Scott Holland and J R Illingworth. These theologians had published a book of essays in 1889 entitled *Lux Mundi*, in which they had accepted many of the developments of biblical criticism and science. Faith centred on the personality of Christ and could accommodate new ideas and discoveries while still maintaining the essentials of the Christian faith as handed down through the generations. Catholicism to these thinkers – and to Gostwyck – was a living tradition, not merely a loyalty to any particular set of theological propositions and ecclesiastical duties. For this reason, Gostwyck was also critical of the position of the contemporary Roman Catholic Church, which would, for example, oppose biblical criticism until the middle of the twentieth century. He did not accept the 'neo-scholasticism' then dominant in Roman Catholic intellectual life. As he wrote once to his mother, he was '... realizing more than ever that modern Romanism stands and falls with Jesuitism'.[55] This is perhaps one underlying reason why Gostwyck would never choose to convert to Roman Catholicism, despite his belief in the necessity of the Papacy and of a unified Catholic Church. He was comfortable with the intellectual freedom that being an Anglican afforded him.

The Liverpool years were also ones in which he first considered a vocation to Religious life, and he had become an authority on monastic history, Orthodox as well as Catholic. He had been aware of the existence of Anglican communities certainly since arriving back in England in 1882. His oldest sister had been educated by the sisters of the Community of St Mary the Virgin at Wantage, and had considered joining that community at one time. His mother became attached to the Benedictine sisters at Malling Abbey, where she would visit regularly. In his Liverpool parish, Gostwyck acted as chaplain to two sisterhoods. Fathers of the Society of St John the Evangelist (SSJE), the longest-established men's community among Anglicans, also visited the parish.[56] The first glimpse we have of his own possible vocation, however, came in 1898, in a letter to Jessie, where he hinted at a future entry into the Community of the Resurrection, founded by Gore.

I have a great deal to write about, for Canon Gore has been staying with us lately, and I have had a long talk with him about my future. He

... has allowed me to correspond with him, and has promised to take me into his community, should I desire it.[57]

A commitment to celibacy had emerged for Gostwyck by this time. Rumours of an unhappy romance were part of family tradition handed down to the next generation,[58] but how deep such a possible attachment was is now impossible to establish. Certainly, Gostwyck's demanding and dominant mother had little appetite for any of her children marrying. Her own unhappy experience meant she used all her influence to keep them single. In the end, only the youngest daughter, Ada, managed to defy the maternal veto.[59] Gostwyck was close to his mother to the end of her life, deeply attached, yet also chaffing at her strictures, as their correspondence revealed. One niece remembered the 'stupendous hysteria' that could result when 'Uncle Gos' visited her grandmother and aunts, and how the rows were usually conducted in German, with Gostwyck speaking in French.[60] He had inherited his paternal grandfather's estate but it was his mother who continued to administer it with the help of her lawyer, and most letters Gostwyck sent to her are peppered with urgent exhortations to 'send money'. This background made him somewhat wary of feminine influence in his life, so that, despite his evident love of children, he avoided matrimony and having a family.

Gostwyck had to work extremely hard as a curate, with very few days off. It was something of a 'treadmill' for him, not allowing him the luxury of considering alternatives for the future. He found some of his parochial activity a frustration too, especially with the more wealthy section of the congregation, as he indicated in this extract from a letter of 1900,

> I am so 'moidered', as they say in Lancashire, i.e., upset and worried in general. I have run down badly, but is any work so disheartening as trying to infuse some vitality, some reality into a Church that is a martyr of respectability?[61]

His health was again beginning to trouble him.[62] With a private income from the family investments, a stipend was a preference rather than an absolute necessity economically, and so in 1904, having it seems reached breaking point at the age of forty, he resigned his position. Whether this was a full nervous breakdown, or more simply intense fatigue, or the result of a specific illness, is impossible to establish. Whatever the cause may have been, by early 1905 Gostwyck was in Llanfairfechen in north Wales relaxing, going for walks and clearing his head. Once he was feeling better, he found a position as an honorary curate at St Cuthbert's, Philbeach Gardens, one of the churches his family attended in the early

1880s. By now his mother was living in Devon so Gostwyck lodged at the clergy house. The vicar at St Cuthbert's[63] was one of the Westall family who he had known since the days when both families lived in Leipzig.

St Cuthbert's was one of the most notorious Anglo-Catholic churches in London. In an era when Catholic practices were a controversial issue in Anglican churches, some parishes almost competed to be, in the contemporary term, more 'advanced' than others. St Cuthbert's was so 'advanced' that it was under the censure of the Bishop of London and so Gostwyck's appointment could only be 'honorary' and without the episcopal licence. It was essentially a 'stopgap' for Gostwyck while he looked for another position. This soon came in the form of an invitation from the Abbot of Caldey to live alongside his community.

Gostwyck knew of Aelred Carlyle's Benedictine community in the late 1890s. His mother's association with Malling Abbey brought contact with the sisters' chaplain there, Morley Richards,[64] who had received Aelred Carlyle's solemn vows as a Benedictine monk in February 1898. Richards was concerned at the lack of historical perspective and knowledge among the Anglican Benedictines and so he visited Gostwyck in Liverpool in the autumn of that same year to consult him. By 1906, Aelred had moved the community to Caldey. He preached at St Cuthbert's on 24 November 1906 and we can assume this is when the Abbot probably met Gostwyck, who he must have regarded as a valuable resource with regard to the history of Religious life. On that occasion or later, the Abbot invited Gostwyck to move to Caldey Island, which he did in the summer of 1907.

Peter Anson suggested that Aelred made this invitation because the Abbot had taken Gostwyck on as one of his 'cases'. Aelred had become involved with the Guild of Health movement, which sought to help the sick with faith healing, verbal suggestion and hypnosis.[65] Anson himself did not join the community until 1910 so this explanation did not come from first-hand knowledge. Indeed, Anson reported that it came from his conversations with George Chambers,[66] who in 1907 was a professed monk of the Caldey community, but who was released from vows in 1912. However, at the time of Gostwyck's arrival, Chambers was serving a curacy at Dalston in London, and so he too was unlikely to be remembering from first-hand experience: he may well therefore, when advancing this suggestion, have been merely repeating speculative gossip. The theory that Gostwyck went to Caldey for Abbot Aelred to practise 'healing' on him is clearly suspect. Gostwyck was an exceptionally private man and there is no evidence that he discussed his inner thoughts and emotions with anyone beyond his closest family. It would have been completely out of character for him to allow someone to hypnotize him.

He was also a lifelong and uncompromising opponent of things psychic or mystical, and the Abbot's belief in such phenomena[67] were something of which he would have strongly disapproved. It is far more likely that Gostwyck went to Caldey to put his great knowledge at the service of the community, and because it provided him with a quiet and healthy place in which to read and study, and go swimming for exercise, all away from the pressures of city parochial life which so tired him.

In 1908, Aelred clothed Gostwyck in the black habit of a Benedictine oblate and gave him the name Denys. He also gave him a job: warden of the guesthouse. This meant Denys did not reside in the monastery itself, but in a large room in the guesthouse, its floor littered with papers and books. A short, round figure, with a large bald head, he was frightening to some, intriguing to others, but memorable to those who engaged him in serious conversation. There was a good cook-housekeeper, who dealt with domestic matters, so Denys's duties as warden were not onerous, and he gave most of his time to writing articles and reviews for the community's regular publication, *Pax*. Indeed, it was he who, almost single-handed, gave the Caldey Island monks an intellectual reputation and attracted scholarly visitors. Peter Anson has left the impression of Denys as a respected but remote figure to the monks,

> Br Denys ... was little more than an erudite Anglican clergyman leading his own life on the island, with few contacts with the Abbot or the monks. In fact he was virtually a hermit, living in the upper room of the Guest House, buried in his books – aloof and mysterious.[68]

However, even if this proved to be true after 1910, the year Anson joined the community, other evidence would suggest it was not the case in the first years of Denys's stay on the island. He wrote to his mother less than a year after his arrival on the island,

> Since Easter, the Abbot has been away, and practically everything has been in my hands, and I have now so much writing to do. They seem to look upon me as a kind of Theological Encyclopedia, which may be flattering, but is a nuisance.[69]

Even later, Niall Campbell reported after a visit to Caldey during Holy and Easter weeks in 1911 that it was Denys who 'had presided in the most admirable manner' over 'all the cycle of solemn ceremonies', as the Abbot was then absent.[70]

This suggests involvement with the community, with a role as Aelred's deputy when the Abbot was away. It is probable that Denys withdrew more from the community as the years went by, perhaps finding the Abbot's charismatic personality too overbearing, or the 'expectation' placed on his academic expertise by the monks irritating. According to Anson, Denys still attended community recreation every Sunday, even after 1910.[71] If Denys was tiring of the Abbot, he did not articulate his views. Ronald Knox,[72] during one of his stays on the island, asked Denys his view of Aelred's actions, and the oblate merely shrugged his shoulders and pointed to the motto 'Pax' on the wall.[73]

Aelred's concern was to have someone who would impress those *outside* the monastery – potential donors, influential clergy, educated laypeople. In that sense, placing Denys in the guesthouse was a shrewd gesture by the Abbot – he had put the oblate in exactly the right place to influence visitors. However, even if Aelred did not take much notice of Denys, others did, especially the devout young men, most from universities, who had stimulating discussions with the warden. They were reassured by the confident reasoning, backed by a barrage of factual information, of the opinions that Denys expressed. Aelred may have excited their enthusiasm but Denys gave them confidence their stance was sound and intellectually defensible.

Some of these young Anglo-Catholics founded the Society of St Peter and St Paul to further the cause of Anglo-Papalism, a public announcement being made at a meeting on 24 February 1911 in London.[74] The established organs of the Anglo-Catholic party, such as the English Church Union, seemed to lack the radical edge, which some of the younger generation craved. If the conversions to Roman Catholicism were to be halted, a more urgent agenda had to be embraced so that corporate reunion could be seen to be only a few years away. The waverers would then hold off from individual secession and continue to work for the Anglo-Papalist cause. One of the first tasks was to convince all the Catholic-minded in the Church of England to adopt the full Anglo-Papalist vision. The SSPP saw liturgy as key. The Church of England must be transformed into what it would have been had the negative aspects of the Reformation not taken place. Returning to medieval forms was counterproductive. What was needed was the baroque style of *modern* Roman Catholicism.[75]

If they could demolish the arguments and justifications for the use of the Sarum Rite and Gothic decoration, a whole swathe of Catholic-minded Anglicans would be convinced to adopt the Roman-style Mass, with the public words of the *Book of Common Prayer* being retained, the Roman canon in Latin could still be said *sotto voce* by the priest. Worshipping in a baroque style would clarify and instil important doctrine: how you worship both affects and reflects what you believe. The Anglo-Papalist position would then be consolidated and provide a united Catholic front to challenge (successfully, the enthusiasts believed) the other parties in the Anglican fold: the Evangelical wing; the Establishment-minded 'broad church'; and what they regarded as the 'heretical' liberals and modernists. A triumphantly united Catholic Church of England could then negotiate for reunion with Rome. At least that was the theory.

Even some of the older, more cautious supporters began to agree that Anglo-Papalists had to seize the initiative and offer more energetic leadership to the whole Catholic movement. Lord Halifax organized a conference at his home at Hickleton in Yorkshire in August of 1911. Abbot Aelred attended on behalf of Caldey. Although the main item on the agenda was reform of the Prayer Book, the need to establish strong arguments for remaining in the Church of England was also paramount. Aelred was a particular anxiety for the conference and the other attendees must have been relieved when the Abbot pledged to remain an Anglican.

Denys was consulted much through these events and the subsequent appeal to the Archbishop of Canterbury for a regularization of the Caldey community's place in the Church of England. It is in his writings in *Pax* that we find the clearest articulation of Denys's view of the intellectual underpinnings to Anglican Benedictinism. For him, the Council of Chalcedon of 451 AD, an ecumenical council recognized by all parts of the Christian Church, was key. Its fourth canon stated that any monastery or house of prayer had to have the approval of the bishop of the city. This proved to Denys that the validity of a Benedictine foundation came at diocesan level and was not dependent upon papal approval. It was therefore quite possible for the Church of England bishops to approve Benedictine foundations in their dioceses. He explained in an article in *Pax*,

(a) that the Benedictine life was founded in the early church before the main divisions of Christendom, and cannot, therefore, belong to the Roman Catholic Church only; (b) that the Benedictine life is not an 'order' in the sense of a close corporation with a line of succession. It is an independent life under the sanction of the Diocesan Bishop. The fact, then, that there was no succession in Benedictinism in the English Church at the Reformation does not prevent its being introduced into the English Church now.

As Catholics we are only concerned with Benedictinism as St. Benedict, its founder, intended it to be and as the Oecumenical Council of Chalcedon, in accordance with whose enactments it was founded, ordered it to be. Thus the Benedictine Rule is part of our Catholic heritage and appeal to the Early Church.[76]

But did all Denys's writings have any effect on Abbot Aelred? They certainly helped him frame his approach to Archbishop Davidson and Bishop Gore, as is revealed in their surviving correspondence of 1911–12. But in the overall forging of the Caldey community's identity, Aelred's own long-standing vision remained paramount. His was a more Cistercian concept of an abbey standing alone, a community self-sufficient as an example to the rest of the Church, a place apart. It did not bother him that Caldey Island was 'extra-diocesan' and self-regulating. Denys in contrast believed in a locally-rooted Benedictinism, interacting far more with the society around it. Ironically, it was Denys's view that a monastery must have diocesan backing that led Aelred to seek formal recognition by the Church, the very process that triggered the community's eventual secession.

By 1911, it is probable Denys was tiring of life on Caldey Island. Perhaps he believed secession was now inevitable and he was too retiring a figure to want to be mixed up in any impending controversy. He went to the continent in the spring of that year, travelling to various destinations. At the close, he spent Christmas in Rome, and did not arrive back on the island until January 1912. He gave some addresses to the community during the following Lent, recalled by one who heard them,

> ... [his] erudition was so profound that most of the monks failed to understand what he was driving at, unable to see the wood for the trees. He hinted at mysterious conversations going on between Rome and Eastern Orthodox theologians in the Balkans; of secret meetings under the shadow of the Vatican. He backed up the arguments by quotations from French, German, and Russian theologians whose names meant nothing to the majority of the community.[77]

Anson's memories may be exaggerated, but this account does suggest a gulf between Denys and the community, which accords with the evidence of the oblate distancing himself from Caldey Island. He packed up his books, which were finally delivered to London in July 1912,[78] and then left the guesthouse.[79] He returned to Caldey in November 1912, at the Abbot's request,[80] to prepare for when Dr Stone and Father Trevelyan visited on behalf of Bishop Gore of Oxford on 2–3 January 1913. Denys talked with the emissaries on 2 January and took them to the boat on their departure next day.[81] Soon after the visit, he left for good to return to St Cuthbert's Clergy House in London, and was on holiday in France when news of the secession reached him.

The previous year, in the face of the persistent rumours that the Caldey monks would 'go over to Rome', one of the founders of SSPP, Niall

Campbell, had speculated as to how Anglican Benedictinism could be maintained after such a catastrophe. He had written to Denys in February 1912,

> ... I do not for one moment believe that such an Act of Faith as the Abbot undoubtedly engaged on in his youth, and what he has brought to so fair a fruition up till the present, is destined to be the last monastic Revival in our Church, or that the movement towards it will be killed even if the step contemplated in regard to Roman claims should take place.
>
> Even if a secession of the greater part of the Community were to happen, a remnant might yet not see their way to take up the step spoken of, and if such remnant continued their rule in however humble a manner in communion with Canterbury, friends would not be found lacking to help them.[82]

If the secession should happen, Denys decided he would help form another Benedictine community. On returning from France he entered the negotiations, which, as we have seen, included Dom Anselm Mardon. By late April 1913, after giving a retreat for the Society of St Margaret sisters at East Grinstead, he could write to his mother,

> The Mother here seems pleased with my work and has offered me the refusal at *any time* of the Assistant Chaplaincy here, which will, I suppose, in time lead to the Chaplaincy. ...
>
> The Benedictine Life is to be carried on. ... I am to be a kind of Assistant Superior and Visitor, as I have been asked to be. This work I can do from London, so it will not interfere with my work at S[t]. C[uthbert]'s.
>
> Should the assistant Chaplaincy fall vacant here this year or at any time, I propose coming here (I want to be connected to the Religious Life) and giving up my work at S. C's and directing the Benedictine life from here.[83]

The implication is clear: Denys was to be a *non-resident* assistant to Anselm Mardon, advising the new foundation from either East Grinstead or London. He had no desire to be a monk himself, only to put his expertise at the service of the Religious life. However, in the event, he did join Anselm, as a resident oblate. Several reasons present themselves to explain this change of plan. With none of the other Anglican monks from Caldey willing to continue, Anselm required another senior presence in the new monastery. The monastery also needed a priest, and as no priest from 'the remnant' would participate, Denys had to fill the gap. In addition,

Anselm felt ill-equipped to teach new postulants and novices who joined, and Denys was the only person available to educate them in matters such as the history of the Religious life.

A home was found for the new community: the Abbey House, Pershore. This was a large residence, built in the 1830s by the Bedford family on old monastic land, with considerable grounds bordering the parish church which had once been the ancient abbey church. Abbey House had been put up for sale in 1910 and bought by a Mr Henry Wise.[84] Immediately after the purchase, he had donated it to the Caldey Island community as a possible 'branch house'. However, it had never been used for that purpose and had stood empty for three years. In the agreement over assets after the secession, Caldey Island was transferred to Roman Catholic hands and the Abbey House, Pershore, left in Anglican. It was returned to the ownership of Henry Wise.

By August 1913, this house in Pershore had become the preferred location for continuing the Benedictine life in the Church of England, and it was agreed it could be rented from the owner. But Denys was concerned about the bishop, for, wherever the community settled, he felt it imperative to have episcopal sanction from the beginning. Yet, he feared the bishops were not sympathetic because of the influence of Bishop Charles Gore of Oxford.

> Pershore Abbey, Worcester, has been transferred from Caldey and offered to me for the Continuation of the Benedictine Life, but the Bishop of Worcester raises objections to having us in his Diocese. I am in correspondence about the matter.
>
> I had a long talk with the Bishop of Oxford the other day. He is against any continuation of the Benedictine Life. He said (1) 'The multiplication of Religious orders in the Church of England is a danger.' (2) 'The English character does not make for Contemplation & does not need it.' (3) 'Cowley[85] sufficiently supplies the Contemplative side.' The Bishops all follow Bp. Gore blindly on this point, and we shall have difficulty with any Diocesan. If they all object, Athelstan Riley may give us something in Jersey, and I may go and stay with him in a few weeks to talk over matters.[86]

Whatever influence Gore may or may not have had with the Bishop of Worcester, Dr Yeatman-Biggs,[87] the latter became more sympathetic after the intervention of James Peile,[88] the Archdeacon of Warwick, who met with Denys and Anselm, probably later in August 1913. Anselm moved to the Abbey House in September, followed by Denys in October 1913, as Campbell noted in a letter:

I had an interesting letter from Dom Anselm in reply to one of enquiry from me, and I am delighted to hear that the regular life will restart 'ad multos annos' as I trust upon the Hallowmass, and that he is now at Pershore getting the house ready and so forth and that Brother Denys will join him before the end of this month. Though they may be a handful at the start, I do not doubt but that a great future will be in store for them, built on a calm life of true recollection and prayer.[89]

The house was large but not in prime condition. There was no electricity or water supply, whatever was required of the latter having to be pumped manually to the house each day. The large reception rooms on the ground floor were transformed into a library, a guest sitting room, and a refectory, along with another room that Anselm used as his office. Upstairs, the master bedroom became the chapel, its small adjoining dressing room making a cosy sacristy. An altar complete with curtains on three sides, a robed Christ on a cross, six candlesticks and a hanging pyx for the reserved sacrament were the focus of the room, while choir stalls furnished its main body.[90]

Once the recitation of the Offices was begun, the Benedictine Office and liturgy in Latin were used. This was partly because the Anglo-Papalist supporters themselves saw this as essential – they wanted a community expressing full Catholic ideals as they saw them. It was also because Aelred Carlyle's second community of nuns, the ones at Baltonsborough in Somerset, who had not followed the St Bride's sisters to Rome, used the *Breviarium Monasticum* and *Missale Monasticum*. Their chaplain, Father Vasey, was anxious that these sisters 'came under' the new foundation at Pershore – in other words that the congregational structure created by Abbot Aelred remained in place to give the sisters legitimacy. As their bishop (in the diocese of Bath and Wells) would have nothing to do with giving permission for professions, Father Vasey required them to have an alternative source of authority. The new community at Pershore was the obvious successor to Abbot Aelred and the Caldey monks, and Anselm therefore the new head of the congregation. Had the Pershore monastery decided not to use the same Office as these sisters, it would have put the Baltonsborough community in a difficult position.

Although negotiations with the bishop were not complete, Denys was confident his own intellectual arguments and loyalty to the Church of England would overcome any doubts. This is indicated early in December 1913 in a letter to his mother. Amidst pleas for her to send rugs and furniture, he wrote,

A friend of the B[isho]p of Worcester ... was here yesterday. He tells me the B[isho]p is quite keen and will allow the Breviary (Benedictine) & Missal.[91]

Again, a few days later,

We have started here, though we still have to arrange details with the Bishop. But I fear little from him: he is most sympathetic.

Money, however, was a problem, and he continued,

We have no money in hand and live on the barest food. ... The little I have I have been obliged to hand over to keep the House going, ...

The money already given to the <u>Community</u> has had to go in paying for the repairs of the Abbey, bills, etc. ... and we cannot appeal for more until matters are finally settled with the Bishop.[92]

Settling the Church's recognition was therefore crucial economically as well as ecclesiastically. By February, Anselm could write confidently to Lord Halifax,

Both Br Denys & I gathered from our last interviews with him [Archdeacon Peile of Warwick] that we had the Bishop's sanction & approval for the use of the Breviary so long as we were willing to omit the observance of certain 'feasts'.[93]

The Bishop of Worcester met the Archbishop of Canterbury on 19 February 1914, after which the latter noted in a memorandum,

Full talk with the Bishop of Worcester ... about the problem of Pershore and the residuum of the Caldey monks.

He seemed to me to have the matter well in hand and to see his way to some arrangement for securing that these men, who apparently do want to be loyal, shall not find themselves cold-shouldered by the Church of England even if they are difficult to fit in to our ordinary system.[94]

The 'well in hand' meant specific proposals agreed by both bishop and community on liturgical practices, and as long as these proposals were followed, the Bishop of Worcester agreed to be the community's official Visitor, a recognition which Denys believed to be crucial. The agreement included the statement that the community chapel was a private chapel and not one for the public: even retreatants staying in the monastery were to be directed to the parish church for Morning and Evening Prayer, and all services for them were to be in English. The Latin *Brevarium* was for the use of the brethren only, and was authorized on the condition that they omitted 'modern innovations and accretions and all that is distinctively Papal or in any way casts doubt on the Catholicity of the Church of England.' Reservation of the Blessed Sacrament was to be allowed, provided it was not kept in a tabernacle on the altar but elsewhere. There was to be no benediction or exposition. The Virgin Mary's prayers could be asked for in the third person but not invoked directly in the second,[95] and the Marian feasts of the Immaculate Conception and the Assumption were to be left unobserved. A Latin translation of the *Book of Common Prayer* could be used at Holy Communion.[96] This showed much flexibility on the part of both the Archbishop of Canterbury and of Bishop Yeatman-Biggs. They were prepared to grant to the 'remnant' far more than Bishop Gore had been to the Caldey monks. Something had been learned on both sides: the bishops wanted to demonstrate they could be very tolerant in exchange for loyalty, the monks wanted to show they were good enough Catholics to respect episcopal authority if shown understanding.

The community could now appeal for financial support and on 1 May 1914, the Bishop of Worcester formally blessed the house. A 'Wickcliffe Preacher'[97] from Birmingham turned up to protest – presumably about 'Papism' – and an infuriated former owner of the house and local squire, Colonel Hudson, offered to eject the unwanted intruder by force. But the bishop decided to hear the protest out and then resume his solemn blessing.[98]

The community was still fragile: one professed, two oblates and some aspirants/postulants. Yet a beginning had been made on a sound footing. But this disguised an unresolved issue. Apart from the matter of loyalty to the Church of England, what sort of Benedictine foundation was this new community to be?

3

Struggling to Survive

In May 1914, there was a distinct choice. The foundation at Pershore could be either a fresh start or it could aim to be a 'continuation' of Caldey. Denys and Anselm each worked for one of these goals, and so their joint leadership of the new venture was effectively a stalemate. It was a clash that threatened fatally to weaken the fledgling community from its very inception.

Denys's position was rooted in an intellectual approach. For him, the word 'Order' in the Order of St Benedict did not represent a 'corporation', dependent on a 'line of succession' or an historical 'continuity'. In the early church, the word 'order' meant a 'state of life', just as 'clerical order' in those times meant the 'clerical state'. This was what he termed the 'catholic' interpretation of Benedictinism as distinct from the 'papal' form, the latter having developed after 1215.[99] To Denys, founding a Benedictine community did not require the copying of any particular pattern, but instead meant living the Christian life as guided by the *Rule of St Benedict*, interpreted in accordance with the current era. For Denys, the mistake of Caldey had been to try to mimic Roman Catholic models too closely. That inevitably led to an inauthentic community within the Anglican fold, and the consequence was either dissolution or conversion to Rome, as you could not have a Roman Catholic community in the Church of England; that would be an unviable contradiction. This is where he insisted Carlyle had gone wrong.

It was not Abbot Aelred's original intention to copy Roman Catholic Benedictinism either at Painsthorpe or Caldey. He once told me, for instance, that he would be willing to have the services in English not Latin. But owing to pressure of circumstances, he eventually took over the Roman Catholic constitutions of Buckfast [Abbey] … and during the last 3 years of Caldey's Anglican existence, it became more and more Romanized.[100]

For Denys, there was no point in repeating this mistake. As novice master of the new community, he taught this view to postulants who entered the monastery. The community's purpose was to restore 'the Contemplative Life, on the basis of St Benedict's Rule …' There should be no attempt to model the community on Cistercian or other particular Benedictine traditions: instead, the tradition would evolve through living the life. It would not necessarily be enclosed either. Indeed, Denys believed the true contemplative life could only grow out of the active.

> One common mistake is to consider, as most people do, the Bene-dictine Life a Contemplative Life. Benedictinism is not a Contempla-tive Order, in the sense in which the Carthusian & Carmelites are Contemplatives. Benedictinism is more like the Dominicans, a <u>mixed</u> life, that is, active as well as contemplative. The history of Bene-dictinism will show that the Benedictines were always missionaries, scholastics, students etc. St Benedict himself was a missionary in the Campagna.

Denys quoted Eastern Orthodox sources and also Father Benson,[101] founder of the Society of St John the Evangelist, as other supporters of this view that contemplation grows out of action. The new community must therefore be open to opportunities for ministry and activity outside the monastic enclosure. Any move to enclosure would be a long-term evolution, and could not be part of a restrictive blueprint laid down in advance. One reason for this was because of Denys's rejection of what he termed 'mysticism' or any other form of 'spirituality' which was de-tached from the rhythms of everyday life.

> Again, in any attempt to restore the Contemplative Life in the Church of England, we have to be on our guard against the present *wave of mysticism*. A great deal of this mysticism is purely sentimental, or un-dogmatic, or theosophical. … Contemplation is not mysticism, or any form of transcendental or 'other' *thinking* at all. Contemplation is not *meditation*; nor is it primarily *intellectual* or reflection on bible texts. Contemplation is primarily harmonized personality; …

In other words, contemplation was living a Christian life, being an 'extension of Christ's personality', and it could take a variety of forms. The Pershore community must therefore be free to evolve along these lines.

The problem for Denys was that he was an oblate not a full member of the new foundation. There were many historical examples Denys could provide of oblates being significant influences on – or even founders of – Benedictine communities. Indeed Aelred Carlyle was a Benedictine oblate (of the Twickenham community of nuns) when he founded his Religious community. As Denys regarded Benedictinism as a life, it did not matter to him that as an oblate he was exempt from obligations such as saying all the Offices in choir. He was still a Benedictine.

Denys's reasons for not seeking profession as a Religious can be judged to be twofold. First, he was concerned about his health: he did not feel strong enough physically (or perhaps even emotionally and psychologically) to cope with the rigours of, for example, rising each night for the Office at 2 a.m.[102] The warning of his 1904 breakdown made him fearful of putting himself under too much pressure. What energies he had, he wished to put into intellectual pursuits. For him, he could serve the community best as an intern oblate. The other reason was that he was wary of swearing a vow of obedience to anyone, a vow which profession would involve. He saw the excesses in a charismatic man like Aelred Carlyle and the limitations of a less-educated monk like Anselm Mardon. He could not put himself in a position of complete obedience to such leaders. This might blunt or even curtail the contribution he could make.

However, spending most of his time in his room, going to chapel only to say the daily mass and for perhaps just two of the seven Offices, while contributing little to the housework, he became an isolated figure. Denys was brought up a gentleman, and had some of the manners and aura of his class. He was used to being supported by servants and had perhaps too little awareness of how much was done for him domestically. Yet, he may have felt unconsciously entitled to such service, as it was essentially his allowance from Prideaux family money that paid a share of the running expenses of the monastery.

In contrast, Anselm was neither of the gentry class nor was he an intellectual. He organized the house very well, and was a competent cook. He began growing produce in the large garden, some for sale. Animals such as pigs were also introduced and the community in effect began the hard work of running a small farm. For all this Anselm had essentially sole responsibility. He was also the mainstay of the round of services in chapel. From his point of view, he was the only professed monk, the person in charge, and his choice was to live the Religious life as he had been taught it at Caldey. Denys's intellectual monologues and writings meant little to him, for Anselm was approaching the task of community from a more emotional perspective. Caldey had to be his model. Aelred was still his friend and mentor in many ways, and the two maintained a correspondence. Anselm was faithful to the rigorous timetable of the Office in Latin, and any postulants and novices were expected to adhere to the same. But as he attempted to pass on to them all he had learned on Caldey Island, it must have seemed that the reclusive novice master was influencing them in a very different direction. The novices sided with Denys, and Anselm must have felt his being 'Head' of the new foundation was undermined on a daily basis. To Dom Anselm, it must have seemed as if Denys was trying to run the community without being of it, acting like an interfering lodger disrupting the household.

This clash was played out against the background of the First World War, which broke out in August 1914, and this added to the pressures. The financial situation of the community was already precarious as Denys reported to his mother in January 1914,

> And you must, please, try and send the quarterly amount you said you would let me have *regularly*. You know I have given all I had to the Community here, as funds are not coming in well, and I regret [that I] make very little by writing. If I cannot depend on your allowance *regularly*, it will be rather difficult to get on here.[103]

But his income was adversely affected by the war, as some of Denys's money was invested in a German bank and it could no longer be accessed.[104] War also affected many publications, and Denys had even fewer opportunities to make any money from writing articles and reviews. The restrictions of wartime also reduced donations from supporters. With many men volunteering for the Forces, possible vocations to Religious life were put on hold and the possibilities of growth halted.

With all these additional pressures, a crisis was inevitable and it began to break within a year of the blessing of the monastery. Its focus remained the clash of aspirations. Denys claimed that Anselm had been open to having the Offices in English in 1913–14, but that the 'Baltonsborough problem', referred to in the last chapter, meant that he could not be persuaded to abandon the congregational model. According to Denys, Anselm decided to adopt the congregational model officially in May 1915. This was another step in the power struggle between the two for the direction of the community.

At this time, there were two novices: Clement (Clement Carter) and Martin (Thomas Chaplin). Other aspirants had it seems come and gone, without staying more than a few weeks, but these two men had persevered and received the habit. There is a photograph of Anselm, Charles Hutson (the oblate) and two novices, using a fishing rod by a pond, and it may well be that Clement and Martin are the two novices in this picture.[105] These novices were understandably unsettled by the antagonism between Denys and Anselm, as the former noted.

The novices ... objected to Dom Anselm's going back on his original intention of the Contemplative Life on the basis of the Benedictine Rule, and the policy of Pershore being dictated by Baltonsborough. They also lost confidence in Dom Anselm through his 'Romanizing', his defects of character, training etc.

This account is backed up in a surviving letter from one of the novices sent to Fr Maxwell,[106] the superior of SSJE at Cowley.

On my return to Pershore in May [1915] after seeing you, I could see quite plainly after a few days that it would be impossible to remain there if one had to accept the line of action Dom Anselm was bent on following. So I told him that I could not see my way to continue there & must withdraw once more. However, in a subsequent conversation I pressed very strongly that you should be consulted, so that if possible the Community at Pershore might be advised & guided by your Society.

... it appeared to me almost impossible for anyone who had been trained & influenced by the Abbot of Caldey as Dom Anselm had been, to unlearn that training and begin again. ... and I am afraid too, that the link with Caldey was never absolutely & entirely broken.[107]

Father Maxwell SSJE was, at that time, advising the former superior of a Franciscan community in Plaistow, Father William Sirr of the Society of the Divine Compassion, who felt drawn to a contemplative, possibly Cistercian, life. Maxwell suggested William could join forces with Pershore, and that this might help to establish greater stability.[108] The novices agreed to stay while this possibility was explored. However, according to Denys, Anselm wrecked the plan.

The amalgamation really fell through because in the beginning of May [1915] Dom Anselm had openly said in Birmingham and to me that he was going over to the Church of Rome. This report reached Cowley and Plaistow, and Fr. William naturally fought shy of Pershore.

By June 1915, Denys was on the verge of giving up, as he wrote wearily to his mother,

I am also sorry to say that it is more than probable that this Community will cease, as I told you in my last letter. The monk in *solemn vows* here – he is the only one and nominally head – is quite incapable of carrying on this work. ... we are calling in the help of Cowley or

Plaistow (I tell you this in strict confidence), but I doubt very much if this will save matters.

It is probable that I shall have to leave here either this summer or autumn.[109]

In August 1915, the two novices finally made their exit, both volunteering for the army.[110] Anselm went secretly to see Abbot Aelred on Caldey, returned on 21 August and announced he was converting to Roman Catholicism. He indicated he would return money deposited in the community accounts to the donors and intended to close the house. He was said to have offered all the vestments and chapel stalls to a local Roman Catholic priest. His argument (possibly pressed upon him by Aelred Carlyle) was that his departure brought an end to the community and therefore the house should be disposed of, most probably returned into the ownership of the Roman Catholic monks on Caldey Island. However, Denys persuaded Anselm to leave for Caldey immediately and leave him (Denys) to wind up the house. This Anselm did and he was subsequently received back into the Caldey community.[111] To Denys, the blame for the collapse was entirely Anselm's.

> Having no reserve strength, and refusing to take advice from Cowley or Plaistow or myself, Dom Anselm let the thought of the ordered and peaceful monastic life of Caldey dwell more and more in his mind, and *Caldey* became eventually the *sole* refuge from a series of blunders for which he alone was responsible. Hence Rome.

Denys was a prickly insecure man, sensitive to criticism throughout his life, and he was reluctant to acknowledge his own share in the breakdown when writing his memorandum. To retain the confidence of possible backers for a continuation of the new foundation, he needed to establish his own lack of culpability for the events of August 1915.

Anselm has left no letters or papers putting his side of the story. Some indication of his mindset, however, can be found in two memoranda written for the Baltonsborough nuns by their chaplain, Father Vasey. Anselm had visited Baltonsborough regularly as the 'head' of the congregation of Anglican Benedictines. Father Vasey was a natural person in whom the troubled monk could confide. It would be reasonable to judge we can hear something of Anselm's own voice from those conversations coming through Vasey's report.

> Dom Anselm was surrounded by difficulties at Pershore: in particular he mentioned to me on his visit here the immense amount of house-work

he had to do, the strain of keeping the Office going, the sense of un-fitness & incompetence when interviewing the men – and there seem to have been a not inconsiderable number – who went to there with the idea of trying their vocation, but who seldom stayed long: you see Dom Anselm was not well equipped in the matter of education & felt it rather bitterly. Then also, as I gathered from him, he greatly missed ever hearing the Office and especially the Mass sung. And last but not least he did not feel he was at one with the priest holding the Bishop's authority – Brother Denys.

... the attraction to his warm heart of the thought of companions in the Life he wanted and escape the burden of responsibility which lay *very* heavy upon him overcame his patience & perseverance with the result that he quite suddenly collapsed & fled back to Caldey. It was, as you will see, not a question of Rome but of home.

And again, in a second memorandum,

Before Dom Anselm came to visit us some time ago, he & Brother Denys had not been pulling together: (with a single eye to the end in view) they may have meant to pull together: but they didn't, or at all events neither of them thought the other free of ambition-for-power. Each thought the other was hankering to be Head of the whole work not for God's glory but out of that strange snare the lust of power and success.

... Of course Dom Anselm was Head of the Congregation, but as such he told me he felt very grievously the want of more education than he had, & the want of spiritual training. I tried to cheer him up & strengthen his trust in God to supply all his defects if he went on steadily and patiently: but his patient enduring seems to have just ... fallen short of enough.[112]

The unsevered link with Caldey was perhaps the most significant fac-tor. There are extant letters Abbot Aelred wrote to Anselm through the twenty months the latter was at Pershore: sympathetic and warm, they encourage Anselm to return to the community on Caldey. Certainly, we know Peter Anson, then Brother Richard Whiting at Caldey, visited Per-shore during this time, as he remembered forty years later:

My only visit to Pershore was in the late summer of 1914. A very mis-erable Dom Anselm entertained me to tea. It was obvious that he was home-sick for Caldey. Br Denys struck me as just as lost and somewhat overwhelmed with everything. ... I came away with the feeling that the whole thing was rather a muddle, and badly needed the dynamic personality of an Aelred Carlyle to wake it up.[113]

He gave a similar account in another letter written in 1972,

> When I called at Pershore it was fairly obvious that Anselm felt he was a square peg in a round hole, and that he yearned to be back on Caldey with his former brethren. So we were not surprised when he came back.
> D[om]. A[nselm]. would have been right out of his depth with the Dionysian erudition, and a conception of Benedictine life utterly different to what he had loved at Caldey, which was all jam and no bread![114]

Whatever the inner motivations may have been for Anselm leaving, his departure appeared at first to bring an end to the community. Denys was still there, so was the other oblate, Charles Hutson, but there was no professed monks. There was one postulant, a young priest who had arrived just three weeks before Anselm departed. He was called Bernard Browne.[115] In the 1960s, he wrote some private reminiscences about his time at Pershore[116] and he claimed that he had had an argument with Anselm, insisting that his (Bernard's) presence as a postulant meant the community still existed and that he would work for its continuation. He also claimed he was the one who persuaded Denys not to give up the house. However, letters from the time, which he sent to Father Maxwell SSJE, indicate a more nuanced story. In these, it seems evident that *both* Denys and Bernard *initially* had no confidence to continue. Bernard wrote on 22 August,

> I am afraid I have bad news to tell. This house has come to an end. ...
> I am writing to ask a favour, whether you could see your way to take me in at Cowley.[117]

Bernard then added that he would have to wait a few weeks 'to help fix things up' but could then go to SSJE.

Denys's inclination to give up the monastery must have motivated the natural supporters of the community to press for a continuation. Alban Baverstock[118] wrote to Vasey,

> Have you heard that Anselm decided definitely last week to go over to the Roman majority? Allan, who has just been here, with a message from Br Denys asking my advice, gives me the impression of a difficult situation and much perplexity. ... Anselm seems rather bent on wrecking

any attempt at a continuance of an Anglican Community. And Denys, though he is resisting attempts to give away the furniture, seems very undecided what to do. I am suggesting he convenes a gathering of a few friends to take counsel, Halifax, Argyll, yourself, one at least of the London clergy etc.[119]

Among those London clergy, Father Cyril Howell of St Mary's, Graham Street, also wrote to Vasey,

Letters are flying about in regard to Pershore. I hope Br. Denys will go straight on with the business of slowly forming a Community, on Benedictine lines, such as will continue.

The Bp. of Worcester has written most warmly to Lord Halifax, saying he wishes this to be done, and that all will have his support and blessing.

... What a chance of distinction and nobility he [Dom Anselm] throws away! It is like a man abandoning his post in the trenches, and coming home to beg for a special constable's place in Brixton.

We must back up Br. Denys in every possible way.[120]

The immediate show of high profile support from the Bishop of Worcester and the Anglo-Catholic leaders, almost certainly given even before the two letters above were sent, must have changed Denys's mind. On 24 August, Bernard Browne wrote again to the superior of SSJE,

The developments here within the last few days have been very favourable, & there need be no necessity to close this house.

Dom Anselm decided to leave at the earliest opportunity, & to place the correspondence in the hands of the sollicitor [sic]. We had a meeting yesterday afternoon, at which he (the sollicitor [sic]) was present, with the Archdeacon, & the Vicar of the Parish, & they thought that if Bro. Denys and myself as representatives of the Benedictine Community, could stay in the house for the present, it would be by far the wisest thing to do ...

As you know, the house was only given for the purpose of the Benedictine life. If that were to cease with us, it would very likely be given to the Abbot of Caldey.[121]

What seems apparent is that it was the Church – the bishop, Archdeacon Peile, the local vicar, and Anglo-Catholic supporters – who inspired the continuation. The remnant of the community had been prepared to bring it to an end. This is not to cast any aspersion on Denys, but to show

how significant the Benedictine witness had become to a range of church people. The immediate response safeguarded the possession of the house, and gave Denys the reassurance that he would be supported if he persevered. The Bishop of Worcester made him 'warden' of the community and for the first time Denys was in charge of it as well as its intellectual guide. There would be no clash of authority. The link with Baltonsborough was not mentioned again.[122] It gave him hope that the community had the possibility of an independent future. There were even some aspirants enquiring about the life,

> We go on well here, and have now received 7 applications for the postulancy since the recent secession. The Life will be refounded, and I may myself now enter the *full* Religious Life.
> In the meantime, the Bishop of Worcester has formally appointed me Warden and acting Head here.[123]

Bernard Browne's reminiscences written in the 1960s suggest that things were haphazard in the monastery, and that Denys did not say the Offices with him (even though the 2 a.m. Office had been abandoned). Bernard had responsibility for the cooking (the local Vicar's wife and her 'admirable cook' gave him lessons), the growing of food in the kitchen garden, and also the care of animals (he was taught how to milk a cow). The impression is of a 'one-man band', but again from the contemporary correspondence a different account emerges,

> We are once more peaceful at Pershore, & as quiet as if nothing had happened. I have returned to the rule again, as best I can, & Bro. Denys says the office with me. Besides us two there are four other men living in the house, so that I have none of the responsibility, & I am able to keep strict silence. There are, therefore, facilities for developing a possible vocation, for it is a complete retirement from the world.[124]

In later letters he speaks of having to cope with his 'self-will running riot' because Denys, not being a practical man, left much of the organizing of the house to him, and he had to make his own decisions.[125] He still wanted to know if a vocation at Cowley was a possibility in the event of Pershore closing.[126] In the autumn of 1915, there were eight people living at the monastery. Apart from Denys and Bernard, Charles was making vestments and earning about £50 a year for the community. The rest were seculars or long-term guests. A man called Andrews, in exchange for board and lodging, cared for the poultry and pumped the water.[127] A cockney lad from London, called Charlie also stayed with them and he was very helpful. In his mid-teens, he had been sent there from his parish in Cable Street, London: whether this was to improve his health, or to keep him out of trouble, or because he had no family, is not clear. He worked hard for his lodging, milking the two cows, driving the donkey[128] and cart to market every week to sell garden produce, and caring for the lawns, again with the help of the donkey and a 'mowing machine'. There was also the help of a gardener once or twice a week, arranged by a friend of the community in Evesham. From time to time priests in difficulties, perhaps under episcopal discipline, some with alcohol problems, spent periods at the monastery. They helped with finances and the garden and housework, although they could be a disruptive presence. With all these extra hands, the community was impressively self-sufficient, despite the wartime conditions, growing all types of fruit, including grapes and figs. There was a hay crop harvested each summer. The poultry produced eggs; the cows produced milk, from which the community also made its own butter; pigs were kept for bacon. In 1918, hares, rabbits and ducks were added to the farm. The same year, more land was added and a new gardener taken on.[129] All these activities provided income as well as food for the refectory table, although in winter rations were more frugal. It was not a lavish life, yet there was sufficient money to buy such extras as a portable altar and relics, a sanctuary lamp, mugs from Harrods, a typewriter, an oil stove, and fish from Grimsby.[130]

The monastic community itself was not static. With the monastery now more stable, postulants arrived to test their vocations, although many did not stay for more than a few months. It was probably Denys's health worries that still prevented him from taking the step of being professed himself. So it is probably true that Bernard was left to say the Office alone in the autumn of 1915. But from the spring of 1916, others began to arrive. William Evans was the first, described by Bernard as 'an earnest young man from Leytonstone, but not strong'. It seems he occasionally suffered epileptic fits, but he had no difficulty with the Latin of the Office and took over some of the cooking from Bernard. He was still there when Denys began to record the minutes of a regular house meeting[131] in September 1916, but seems to have left before the end of that year.

Another priest arrived in the summer of 1916. He was called George Withers.[132] He was certainly there until February 1917, and his duties included washing up, sweeping and tending the stove. Bernard recalled that Father George 'was quite incapable of keeping the silence' and we have to assume that to be one of the reasons he stayed only a matter of months, and then left to be a chaplain in the forces.[133] Other postulants took the names Donovan, Henry, Basil, Dominic and Francis. They and all the seculars made a motley group, and the notes of the house meetings hint at

Denys's struggle to enforce a monastic demeanour and atmosphere. He pleaded that members of the community were not to 'perambulate with the hands in cassock pockets at any time', while the use of slang in recreation was to be 'shunned' (16 September 1916). The warden asked to be addressed as 'Father' not 'sir' (18 September 1916). If the monks went out of the enclosure they were not to look in shop windows unless they had been sent to make a purchase, and they should aim to restrict conversation with townsfolk to 'the bare necessities of common politeness' (20 September 1916). 'Felt slippers' were to be worn in chapel and the refectory (2 October 1916). Doors should not be slammed and must be shut quietly even in windy weather (5 October 1916). Boots, presumably muddy from the garden, should not be changed in the back kitchen but in the 'slip room' (3 October 1916). Greater care was to be observed with regard to the rule of silence (27 November 1916). Perhaps to facilitate this, Denys 'felt it expedient that the Community should be apart from the Oblates' (3 October 1916), except himself of course!

There must have been times when Denys tired of the lack of affective maturity and intellectual depth among those who had assembled at the monastery. No wonder that he stayed in his room with his books much of the time. In 1916, however, someone who was potentially a more appealing companion arrived at Pershore. This was Father C F Hrauda. He had an unusual background for a priest in the Church of England because he was Austrian on his father's side and it appears he was brought up (at least some of the time) as a Roman Catholic. However, he was an Anglican when studying theology at Keble College, Oxford, taking his degree in 1906 at the age of twenty-five, prior to being ordained in the Church of England.[134] He was ardent for the Anglo-Papalist tradition, completely in sympathy with Roman Catholicism in all his beliefs, except that he still believed unswervingly in the validity of his orders as an Anglican priest.

The story of how Hrauda came to Pershore has only one source: a letter from a cousin of his sent to the community in 1962, seventeen years after the priest's death. There are no other records to back it up, but it seems reasonable to accept that the explanation told there is plausible.[135] At the outbreak of war in 1914, Father Hrauda was a curate at St John's, Waltham Green. He opposed Britain's entry into the First World War, and, being partly Austrian, he objected to having to say prayers after Mass for an Allied victory, given that his own countrymen were on the opposite side. Already at loggerheads with Bishop Winnington Ingram of London over his Anglo-Papalist views, Hrauda's stance enraged the bishop, the latter being known for his 'jingoistic' view of the conflict. The curate was sacked in 1915 and the bishop would not give him another job. Father Thornewill[136] at the clergy house in St Mary's, Cable Street, invited him to stay there, but eventually local hysteria about the war meant slogans were painted on the clergy house walls, such as 'A German is hiding here.' Feeling he was embarrassing his friend, Hrauda needed to find another refuge. Thornewill knew the Pershore community; indeed he had been the priest who had sent the teenager Charlie to work at the monastery. Presumably he suggested Hrauda wrote to Denys, who in turn agreed to let the priest stay at Pershore in return for his help.

In the minutes of the daily meeting at the monastery, Denys recorded the expected arrival of Father Hrauda on 18 September 1916, saying the visitor may be made 'Master of Studies' and could even become a postulant. His exact date of arrival is not recorded, but he was certainly present by that December and in January 1917 was made sacristan.[137] Bernard remembered him as 'an intensely humorous fellow' and a 'great exponent and defender of the Anglican claim to valid orders'. Indeed, Bernard, who became a Roman Catholic soon after he left the Pershore community, claimed that it was Hrauda who had taught him the Roman version of the Christian faith.[138]

How long Hrauda stayed is not entirely clear, but it can be assumed he left by the end of the war in 1918.[139] If Denys was hoping to instil a more Anglican view of Benedictinism, Hrauda can hardly have been of assistance. According to the cousin, Hrauda undermined Denys's authority, as he spoke of Denys's learning as being 'so muddled up that it came out of his brain in great disorder', and claimed that he had told the Warden that 'the end of your sentences never seems to have any connection with the beginning'. It was claimed he regarded Denys as neurotic and felt very sorry for him. Instead of providing support, Hrauda must have disappointingly exacerbated Denys's anxieties over establishing the community.

Anxieties there certainly were: the Warden bemoaned to his mother in 1918,

The war becomes more and more trying to an Attempt like this ....[140]

The most worrying development was that the postulants and novices did not stay: there were no professions. Part of this may have been due to the introduction of conscription to the armed forces in 1916. Many communities did not stand in the way of any member who wished to enlist, but the role of some brothers in pastoral or social work was so crucial that their withdrawal would have jeopardized vital projects. The ordained were automatically given exemption from the call-up, but lay monks had to struggle for similar consideration, as witnessed by the struggles of the

Society of the Divine Compassion and the Society of the Sacred Mission. The War Office would accept their exemption only if the Archbishop of Canterbury personally sanctioned it, and while sympathetic to the professed, he was less accommodating about postulants or novices. The Pershore community was especially vulnerable as there were no professed members. Any general call-up would have left Denys unable to maintain the Pershore house and estate.

Lord Halifax wrote on the community's behalf to the Archbishop of Canterbury, but Randall Davidson was cautious about making any general statement on the matter and would only consider individual cases.[141] Denys made the case for the two lay novices resident, Dominic and Francis, in a letter to Davidson in July 1917, as the pair had been ordered to appear at a recruiting station early in August.[142] He pointed out that they were doing mainly agricultural work in the gardens and growing food (and not just for themselves), so they were clearly contributing to the war effort. Lord Hugh Cecil backed Denys and put forward another significant point in his letter to the Archbishop.

> ... I cannot help feeling that it would have a mischievous effect if the State disregarded the monastic vows and vocation of Anglicans while they respect such vows and vocation in the case of Romans.[143]

Cardinal Bourne[144] had been unequivocal in fighting the cause of Roman Catholic monks. Davidson was now challenged to show the same consideration and he agreed to see Denys personally on 4 August.[145] By the end of August, the matter was settled: Dominic and Francis were granted exemption.[146]

Yet conscription was not the sole reason for the lack of growth in the community. Denys's approach to leadership must also bear some of the responsibility. His convoluted presentation of his intellectual approach, whatever truth it contained, was out of reach of the less-educated postulants: while those who could understand his teaching criticized his semi-detached position as an oblate, not fully participating in the Offices. Bernard claimed Denys 'took no part in our life', which may be judged an exaggeration, but nevertheless must indicate some neglect of leadership by the Warden.[147] Bernard took on outside ministries, including being chaplain to St Christopher's Home in the town.[148] He also went out on Sundays, to Old St Martin's, Worcester, to preside and preach at services, and (he recalled) by 1918 was living 'less and less' a community life. He left the monastery intending to return to parochial ministry that same year.[149] Although Bernard believed the Warden was glad to see him go, the departure of the only other priest in the community must have created some doubt in Denys's mind about the future. It was perhaps the lessons that were learned in this period that influenced Denys to consider a different approach if he should ever manage to assemble a group of novices again.

Despite the trials and tribulations of the war period, there were some small encouragements, in particular small tokens of recognition from the Church. The Bishop of Worcester had moved to Coventry for the duration of the war and made the parish church there his pro-cathedral.[150] He invited Denys to give a series of sermons there in Advent 1917, and the significance of the gesture excited the Warden.

> I don't consider the personal recognition in the Diocese that this invitation gives me. You will see that it means far more than that. It means the first Diocesan recognition of a monastic order since the Reformation – a recognition that neither Llanthony nor Caldey ever had. It is the bringing of Monasticism again into the historical life of the Church in England. So this is something to have done, whatever may happen to our venture here.[151]

A year later, he was flattered to have his name put forward as one of an ecumenical team to discuss reunion with the Archbishops of Athens and Belgrade, then visiting England.[152]

But such gestures were of little lasting value if the community itself did not grow. The armistice of November 1918 brought a new context. Denys was now fifty-four and not in the best of health. If he was ever to succeed in building a Benedictine community for men in the Church of England, he was now surely approaching his final chance. Would the new peace allow the Benedictines at Pershore to attract committed vocations?

4

Growing under Pressure

Denys still had hope at the end of the First World War in November 1918, but he was not full of optimism that peace would bring a revival in his fragile community's fortunes or for the Church in general,

> One thing I am inclined to believe is that this war is not going to make England a bit religious.[153]

Nor did the better conditions of the peace, when it came, improve his health. In December 1919, he complained of the 'swamp' like climate in Pershore, blaming the monastery's location in lowland.

> It is not easy to keep well in a spot like this. When I go to London, I hope to see whether it is not possible to have our head-quarters elsewhere.[154]

If he did search for alternative premises, nothing came of it, and April 1920 saw him emerging from illness once again,

> I am better but the doctor tells me it will take 6 months before I am myself again. I was badly run down, had fever and was at times delirious. I have got very thin ... I hope to get away for a change when I can, but at present I am the only priest here, and I must carry on the services.[155]

He may have been exaggerating some of his symptoms to win his mother's sympathy in this letter, but he was certainly at this juncture heavily committed. Not only was he running the community, but he was also committed to writing for various publications, both to earn money and to help the community be known. The pressures eventually became too great and, in 1920, he gave up the editorship of the journal *Caritas*, refused the joint-editorship of *Christian Warfare*, and began to cut down on reviewing. He was also in demand for conducting retreats, preaching, giving papers at conferences (few of which he had sufficient time to accept) and especially for spiritual direction, although some of those sent to him were an irritation.

> Cowley has now taken to sending some of its penitents to me for direction – which is of course a compliment, but means extra work. If the English clergy would only read they wouldn't need to bother me with questions they could very well answer for themselves.

The stress he felt under because of all the demands was neatly summed up by a sentence in the same letter to his mother,

> People seem to think I have nothing to do but to be at their beck and call.[156]

The outside contacts did make Pershore Abbey known, however. This in turn brought visitors and retreatants, and to Denys's relief some men asked to test their vocations. What was different from previous years about the new aspirants was that a majority were priests, some into their forties. Aelred Carlyle had been successful with younger less educated men, his strong charismatic leadership instilling in them a sense of purpose in the Religious life, but Denys was not able to emulate such a centralized role. It was as if Denys needed postulants and novices who were able to chivvy him into leading them, and also that they be men with the maturity to create a tradition alongside him instead of waiting for him to make every decision. The community had not been without novices in the period 1918–20, but the only one to stay for a considerable time was Dominic Carter. (The other novice exempted from the military in 1917, Francis Phillips, had left.) When Bernard Kenworthy Brown withdrew in 1918, he judged it was Dominic who was 'more or less ruling the roost'.[157] Denys leaned on the young novice somewhat in the maintenance of the house and gardens, yet Dominic was like many before him: eager to please, but young and relatively inexperienced, and in need of teaching about the faith and Religious life.

In contrast, the priests who presented themselves for the postulancy from 1920 on were not in need of teaching in the way that the young laymen were. Most of them had Oxbridge degrees and had pastoral experience in parishes. As one of his later monks noted, Denys was 'eminently qualified, admirably helpful' on spiritual matters, but less good as a tutor day by day. He was not so capable in communicating his knowledge and vision of the Religious life as he was at guiding the individual through times of spiritual and psychological hardship.[158] Therefore, because the priests who arrived at Pershore were seeking spiritual leadership from him, Denys could respond constructively. In this regard – through direction and confession – Denys was at his best. Several of the priests who entered had been extern oblates, and so it was Denys's qualities as a spiritual director which brought them originally to the Abbey and then later to join the community. Victor Roberts was a curate in Wolverhampton and became an extern oblate in 1919, coming to live at Pershore in February 1921. William Clements, a naval chaplain both before and during the war, stayed at Pershore in 1919, the same year he became vicar of St Michael and All Angels, Portsea. He too became an extern oblate, wearing a scapular in the monastery and sharing in the enclosure housework during his regular visits.[159] He joined the community as a postulant in November 1921 and took the name Bernard.

The first of this group of priests to enter (in mid-1920) was forty-year-old Martin Collett, a stubborn gritty Yorkshireman, who had administrative and organizational skills, but who could be aloof. Some (including it is said Denys) even thought him pompous. He had been a lecturer in physics at Birkbeck College, London, before training for the priesthood. He maintained that he did not consider his vocation to be primarily monastic, but instead he had felt a specific call to help Denys in the restoration of the Benedictine life.[160] Along with Victor Roberts, early the following year came Sandys Wason,[161] a priest in his fifties, who took the name Placidus. A monocled eccentric, he had been deprived of his living in Cornwall in May 1919, after years of antagonism with the more Protestant of his parishioners, and censure from two successive bishops of Truro. His refusal to abandon the service of benediction had finally led to his deprivation, followed in October 1919 by violent eviction from the vicarage by some burly Cornish farmers. Pershore was therefore partly a refuge as well as a possible future for the persecuted priest, although in the end Father Placidus did not stay long a monk. At the same time as these two priests arrived, so did Francis Wheeler, who was clothed a couple of weeks before his seventeenth birthday, joining Dominic and Antony as a lay novice.

With a novitiate of six assembled, and others expected later in the year, Denys must have realized that he had to take a different course as superior from the one he had previously taken. He had come to believe that the best chance of forging a committed community identity was for him to become a professed Religious and then to become abbot. As early as 6 February 1921, before all the new postulants had been clothed as novices, he wrote to his mother,

... fresh men are beginning to join us, and it is possible that I shall be elected Abbot some time this year. It is to be done quite constitutionally by the Bishop or his delegate the Archdeacon. Of this I am determined, there shall be no question about the validity and legality of the step. We have now two Charters from Diocesan Bishops – the last and present Bishop of the Diocese – and we have also the tacit sanction of the Archbishop. And this means that monasticism must now be constitutionally recognized in our Church, and no other attempt at it has ever yet been formally and constitutionally recognized. I do not yet know when the election and installation will take place. I have still some preliminary measures to deal with before the whole matter can be properly actualized.

The reasons why Denys contemplated becoming a full Religious are clear, but making himself abbot – for in any 'election' there was no other possible candidate but him – was a less obvious step. Most communities only have an abbot once there is a core of life-professed members, the abbacy being a sign of an attained stability. Here Denys was suggesting being an abbot in order to encourage and inspire the formation of a community. It was about providing spiritual fatherhood rather than reaching some milestone in numerical growth.

Some believed pursuing this idea was the result of pressure from leading Anglo-Catholics such as Lord Halifax and Athelstan Riley.[162] However, such men had wanted a replacement Anglican 'abbot' ever since Aelred Carlyle's secession, and yet Denys had not obliged their hopes in previous years. So his change of mind in 1921 cannot be put down purely to outside pressure. Partly it may have been to do with the challenge, as well as the opportunity, that the new more mature ordained postulants posed. They were not likely to tolerate half-measures and a semi-detached superior. Their presence must surely have demanded an authority figure to whom they could hold allegiance. Having an oblate with the position of Warden as superior could not possibly have been adequate for them. In addition, the novices wanted to make their professions when the time came to an abbot; otherwise they would have to be made to a bishop and Anglo-Papalists tended to be wary of bishops. To men like Martin Collett, the election of an abbot also gave the community a sense of permanence; it would be a sign that Pershore monastery was no longer a tentative experiment.

Equally, Denys was concerned, as the last quotation above demonstrated, about the Church's view of the community. Being an abbot would certainly give him greater recognition and status, and he was not averse to wearing a mitre. He wrote more than once in letters to his mother of 'making' the Prideaux name in the English Church,[163] and he believed that an elevated status for him would reflect well on the community's reputation outside. In 1919, he had joined the committee of the Anglo-Catholic Congress and was well regarded there. He must have been anxious to show them that progress was being made in restoring the full Benedictine monastic life to the Church of England. It may be added here that Denys regularly overstated the size and growth of the community over the years, sometimes assuming that someone who had merely asked to visit would automatically be joining the novitiate. Becoming an abbot when there were only a few novices is another example of his inflation of where the community had reached. He felt himself getting old, and he had limited time, so he decided to accelerate the pace.

Denys believed he had lived 'morally' the three vows of poverty, chastity and obedience, his obedience having been to the bishop. For Denys to be professed without living a novitiate year was acceptable, he claimed, in the exceptional circumstances in which he found himself. There was nowhere he could serve a novitiate, as any other community such as Cowley would not be Benedictine. So, canonical law could not be strictly adhered to in this case. After all, he argued, St Benedict had never technically been a novice; neither for that matter had Aelred Carlyle when he founded his Anglican community. According to Denys's understanding of Benedictine history, if the bishop and the community desired it, the diocesan bishop could receive a profession and then install that monk as abbot. All Denys's consultations with canonists and others convinced him this was a legitimate way to proceed.[164]

However, there was a problem with this way forward. The diocesan bishop was no longer the sympathetic Dr Yeatman-Biggs, who had been translated to the new See of Coventry in 1918. Since 1919, the Bishop of Worcester had been Dr Ernest Pearce.[165] The new bishop had far less interest in the Religious life, and although he had renewed the Charter issued by his predecessor, he had a different view of being Bishop Visitor and might not have read the Charter's 'small print', which contained a section about installing any future abbot. Pearce was temperamentally and theologically not inclined to facilitate the community but more to limit it. He made a note in a memo in September 1919 that he was not happy about the community reserving the sacrament, although in the end he did not pursue this issue, and was doubtful about giving Denys a priest's licence in the diocese.[166] When he invited Denys over to see him on 7 October 1919, they managed a 'long, amicable conversation', but one in which he urged Denys to produce a revised Benedictine breviary in English, and insisted he could not consider ordaining any monks without consulting the Archbishop of Canterbury.[167] The Archbishop counselled caution,

I do not think that the 'Monkery' of Pershore fits in readily with our Prayer Book as it is, or with the Elizabethan settlement, but I do think that we should be making a stupid blunder if we peremptorily ruled it out from our system. There are elements in the Church spirit of today which find expression in the sort of Community life which might I think be quite wholesomely revived among us on primitive Benedictine lines.

I do not think that what your Pershore men now want is necessarily incompatible with a reasonably wide interpretation of loyalty to the Church of England.[168]

Archbishop Davidson had no intention of making the same mistake with Denys as he had with Aelred. The Bishop of Worcester heeded the coded archiepiscopal warning and backed down. Denys retained his preacher's licence[169] and the community was left alone, at least for the time being.

However, when Denys contacted Bishop Pearce about installing him as abbot, the episcopal doubts and scruples resurfaced. The novices had eventually elected Denys their abbot at a meeting on 2 October 1921, and so Denys had written to the bishop the following day asking him to perform the installation or nominate someone else to do it. The bishop had replied immediately, saying he would take advice and asked for the names of the 'electors'. Denys did not help his cause by exaggerating, claiming there were five men 'ready' for profession, which was not strictly true as none of the priest novices had completed a year since clothing. Of the other names on the list that Denys sent to the bishop, not all were yet resident at the monastery. The Bishop of Worcester wrote to the Archbishop of Canterbury giving his opinion that the community did not 'warrant' an abbot, it being too small. The Archbishop agreed and so Bishop Pearce declined to take any responsibility for the installation.

For Denys, who had staked his community's legitimacy on diocesan recognition, this was a threatening blow. It seemed he could not proceed; yet he could hardly now retreat and not be an abbot. This latter course would demolish his strategy for the community and some of the novices might be less inclined to commit to the life. He was saved by the intervention of Dr Arthur Chandler, the former Bishop of Bloemfontein in South Africa.[170] Chandler had returned to Britain in 1920 and become a parish priest in Hampshire. In his near two decades as the head of a South African diocese, he had established a reputation as a strong Anglo-Catholic. He had great respect for Denys, who he knew through the Anglo-Catholic Congress, and a desire to promote the Religious life: so he stepped in and agreed to receive Denys's solemn vows and install him as Abbot of Pershore. The solemn vows were received privately on 18 February 1922, the abbatial blessing being a slightly grander affair, held the next day, Sexagesima Sunday, with ceremonies beginning at 7.30 a.m. and lasting two hours. In the intervening months between the October decision and the ceremony itself, three more priests had arrived to try their vocations: William Clements, already mentioned, who was known as Bernard, William Harris who took the name Peter and Cyril Henslow. Bernard described the installation day in a letter written that same evening.

> The great day has come & gone – Fr Denys was installed as Abbot of Pershore by Bishop Chandler this morning. The mitre was actually placed on his head at 9am, & we rang our bells such as we have, as a very little sign of all that it means to us. ... Br Peter and I did chaplaincy to the Bishop ... Br Martin and Br Victor did 'assistants' to the Abbot-Elect. At the end the Abbot gave his solemn pontifical blessing from the Altar in full pontifical vestments (with the beautiful red cope you know of) and his mitre and pastoral staff. Tonight we sang a solemn Te Deum after Vespers ...
>
> It makes already a great difference to the feel of the place ... To our personal affection and devotion to Fr Denys is now added something which I can't size up yet, but which I think will turn out to be a great sense of stability & permanence.[171]

Archdeacon Peile attended from the diocese, but it seems the Bishop of Worcester had not even been informed. He wrote in some irritation to the Archbishop of Canterbury, and in a later letter insisted that his letter to Denys criticising the 'election' of an abbot had only had a 'holding reply' from Martin. This reply said that Denys had to go to a conference and would write later. According to the bishop, no further letter had arrived, 'In actual fact, no word of any sort has come to me since.' Even Bishop Chandler had not written to him: he had learned of the installation only from newspapers.[172]

The Archbishop was again wary and offered to write to Bishop Chandler himself and in doing so took the matter out of the angry diocesan's hands. Chandler was puzzled by the surprise at his action.

> ... [Fr Denys] told me that he had been in communication with the Bishop of Worcester, who said –
> a) that he did not see his way to take the service himself – but
> b) that he had no objection to my taking it.[173]

There would have been no reason for Bishop Chandler to make this up. Denys therefore had misled him, as the Bishop of Worcester's letter had been unequivocal. After giving his reasons for declining to preside at the installation, Pearce summed up his position in his letter of October 1921,

> I know that this letter will be a keen disappointment to you personally but you will agree that open & official action such as you ask me to take should be the result of a full inward conviction, and it is for lack of this conviction that I now say with much regret that I do not feel free to install an Abbot for the Pershore Community. Nor by consequence can I ask anyone else to do for me what I do not feel free to do in my own person.[174]

Denys's defence for his subsequent action would have been that while the letter stated that the bishop could not ask someone else to preside for him, it said nothing about the *superior* not being allowed to invite someone else. However, such subtleties cannot disguise the reality of the situation. Denys had blatantly defied the will of the bishop from whom he claimed his community's legitimacy. Instead of seeing the bishop's letter as a sign that it was not yet the right time to elevate the Pershore monastery to an abbey, the community had refused to change course. The pressures of the Anglo-Papalist position meant that on occasions a Catholic proclamation of obedience to authority had to be tempered with the rider 'whenever possible'. On this occasion, obedience was not possible for Denys.

The friction was diffused once more, however, because Bishop Pearce, guided by Archbishop Davidson, decided not to retaliate against this slight to his diocesan authority. Yet Denys had taken a risk, for he had crossed the boundary of his own belief that a Benedictine community took its authority from the diocesan bishop. Had the bishop reacted badly and withdrawn any remaining goodwill and tolerance, Denys's position and his credibility would have been seriously undermined. He may not have realized that it was the Archbishop of Canterbury's intervention that had helped calm the potential storm.

Unfortunately, another different storm did begin to break not long before the installation. Henry Wise, the owner of Abbey House, had fallen into financial difficulties during the First World War, and had used the deeds of the monastery house as security for an overdraft facility with his bank in 1917. Wise's personal affairs had fallen even further into difficulty: a week before his abbatial blessing, Denys received the news that the house would have to be sold. The money would have to be raised to purchase it or else the community had to move out. It threatened the real yet fragile progress the community had made and Denys was plunged into despair, writing to his sister,

... we may have to leave this house or buy it. There is, apparently, some legal flaw in the tenure, ... I am very anxious and worried, as if we have to buy it will practically run into thousands, and sweep away much of our capital and my own. ... It is one of the hardest blows we have had since we started here, and I don't see my way clear yet. ... it makes my life a positive burden to me. I shall never be myself again. ... I have the moral courage, but I have no longer the nerve-power. Advancing age and other things are sapping it.[175]

And again similarly to his mother,

I go forward to the installation with great misgivings as to the future of my work, ...unless the Church will come forward with a few thousands, our work will be crippled for years. ...

In fact, it means that we shall practically have to begin all over again. Personally, I think nothing of becoming an Abbot. I did before this blow fell, but now I shall simply have to become a man of affairs again and devote myself to the business side of things here.

At the most, the English Church does not want the Benedictine Life, and her condition, as a Church, seems to become more farcical with every year.[176]

The enraged comment at the end was typical of Denys under pressure. It could lead to others misunderstanding Denys's relationship to Anglicanism. He was a man who expressed his frustrations and irritations by taking it out on those he loved. So, for example, his commitment to his mother was never in doubt, and yet his letters to her are full of criticisms and laments, and when he met up with her he would become embroiled in arguments. In a similar way, he reacted to his other 'mother', the Church of England, regularly expressing exasperation and scorn, but this was not an indication of disloyalty. In this case, we see another example of this frustration boiling over into barbed comments. Denys was anxious and could not see a way forward; he had to blame someone, so he wrote a jibe at the Church of England.

In the end, a way forward was found. The new abbot raised a loan of £3,500 from Father Philip Bartlett,[177] which would take thirteen years to repay. The Pershore property was however secured, even if precariously.

Yet more men arrived to try their vocations, including: William Warner, a young man from Father Bernard's old parish in Portsea, who took the name Michael; and Humphrey Vaughan Hughes, a priest in his early forties who took the name of Anselm, and who was a distinguished musicologist. The community now had a member who could teach them a high standard of plainchant. On the debit side, Placidus and Antony had left, while Cyril withdrew but then returned again in the summer.

Even before the new entrants arrived, Denys had pushed forward very quickly after his abbatial installation with professing some of the novices. Yet again, he was not cautious. In later years, the postulancy, the very first stage of formation in the monastery, would last between three and six months before 'clothing' in the habit when the postulant became a novice. This was a fair test of whether the new member could live amidst the community before the deeper training of the novitiate began. In the early to mid-1920s, several *weeks* became the norm for the postulancy. For some like Victor Roberts (three weeks) and Bernard Clements (six weeks) this was perhaps justifiable as they had been extern oblates for some years prior to entry, and were experienced priests. But the same haste was applied to the twenty-one-year old William Warner in the summer of 1922, when he spent a mere five weeks in the monastery before his clothing as Brother Michael.

When it came to profession, Abbot Denys was equally precipitate in his actions. Novitiates lasted only just over the minimum year. After such a short period, it might have been prudent practice to profess the novices in vows for a proscribed period only, such as three years. These would be 'temporary vows'. The other alternative might have been to profess the monks in simple vows. This would mean a life-long intention but with the vows to the community, so that there was a possibility of release, rather than solemnly to the Church as a whole, in which case the vows were deemed by any good Catholic to be like marriage vows and hence indissoluble. Denys was cautious with the very young Francis Wheeler, who was simply professed at the age of eighteen in July 1922, taking his solemn vows three years later in March 1925. However, with others, Denys was determined to rush his new recruits through to solemn profession as quickly as possible. The priests who had joined him – Martin Collett, Victor Roberts, Bernard Clements, Peter Harris and Anselm Hughes were all *solemnly* professed, after novitiates lasting the bare minimum of a year, during the fifteen months March 1922 to June 1923. This was done solely on Denys' authority for, as we have seen, the diocesan bishop had remained distant and there was no other Bishop Visitor from whom permission or approval could have been sought.

The first two solemn professions took place on 21 March 1922 and the two monks concerned were Victor and Martin. Victor, not yet thirty, had already proved adept at gaining the abbot's attention. Denys enjoyed anyone 'fetching and carrying' for him, and so any brother who acted as his 'right-hand man' might attain a greater share of his good will. Dominic held this position for some years, then young Francis, but the slightly older and canny Victor may be judged to be the first to have used this position more politically. He was the only brother who had a prear-ranged dispensation to go away from the monastery twice a year to visit family.[178] A few years later, Victor claimed he was

> ... more and more drawn into the Abbot's confidence and identified with his methods. ...[179]

He asserted too that he had not felt ready to be solemnly professed in 1922, owing to the deficiencies in his training, but that Denys had pres-sured him. Victor was correct in recalling that he had not had an enclosed year of preparation in the novitiate. The Chapter minutes confirm that, as a novice, he was permitted to go away for some weeks to be chaplain at a retreat house,[180] and he also acted as chaplain at regular intervals for two women's communities. He also preached and led retreats. This cer-tainly did not add up to an enclosed period of reflection and testing.

Denys was very keen to have *solemn* professions. The two that were celebrated in March 1922, a month after his own, made a total of three monks in solemn vows, the canonical minimum for a community. This was a legitimacy of great importance to the abbot. Victor knew this and he manipulated this situation so that he was professed in the ceremony before Martin, although the latter had been in the community longer. This ensured Victor was second in seniority after Denys. The threat of re-fusing to be solemnly professed may have been used by Victor to influence the abbot. Whether Victor's additional claim was true that his vow of obedience was agreed by Denys to be 'conditional' is impossible to con-firm.[181] The change of order in the profession was clearly a controversial step, which led to an underlying rivalry. As Bernard related in a letter,

> The natural temptation to resentment when he has been passed over in favour of someone junior to him had always been, I think, a greater difficulty for Fr Dom Martin than it would be to most men, and I hon-our him very greatly for the fight he has always put up against this. I was honoured by his confidence at the time when Fr Dom Victor was made senior to him at his profession, and I shall never forget how tre-mendous this temptation was to him and what a very brave struggle it cost him to come out on top of it.[182]

That Denys would risk setting up a potential antagonism among the se-nior brethren revealed how overwhelming was his need to push ahead with solemn professions, even if it meant surrendering to Victor's condi-tions. This would prove a decision that would backfire on the abbot in time, but in 1922 he could only act in accordance with his anxiety that the community should grow.

However regulated a community, personal relationships between the members have a deep impact on its atmosphere and energy. The new influx of monks created a mix of strong characters with great gifts and of a range of ages; yet conflicts and differences were inevitable, especially as Denys's skills were strongest in one-to-one situations, and weakest when leading a group or chairing a meeting. The daily conference minutes of these years on several occasions register his admonition to his monks that remarks should be addressed to him in the chair, and not between themselves across the meeting.[183] These men were not quiet and docile. On one occasion, he spoke 'strongly at length of the necessity of precise obedience in the carrying out of orders given by him'.[184] Denys insisted two brothers were not to discuss a third brother 'or pass remarks' about him.[185] Letters could only be written on Sundays and only two per week, and he requested their 'tone' was to be 'more restrained'.[186] That these matters were minuted is evidence of persistent – not passing – problems.

Perhaps aimed at the younger lay brothers, there were also admonitions about posture and silence, while recreation – the time each day when the monks were allowed to talk to each other in one group, usually held outside if weather permitted – was equally regulated,

> Any kind of horse-play, or lying full-length on the ground, or leaning against one another is on no account permissible at Recreation.
> Unsuitable conversation, e.g. about food or ceremonial is forbidden at Recreation, also any controversial subject.[187]

Denys created an atypical timetable for the daily routine. A traditional pattern for the seven Offices might have been Matins and Lauds in the morning, Terce mid-morning, Sext and None either side of the midday meal, Vespers late afternoon, followed by Compline prior to going to bed. The horarium for Pershore in the early 1920s began with Terce at 7 a.m., Sext and None were said together after the midday meal, Vespers was at 5 p.m. and then Compline, Matins and Lauds were all said together at 8 p.m. in the evening.[188] The advantage of putting the services together, in effect a fourfold Office, was that it left longer stretches of time for work, especially in the grounds and gardens.[189]

Guests were a regular feature of the life. Many appreciated the atmosphere and spiritual space it afforded them, and were respectful of the monks' life. Others were not so thoughtful. In October 1922, the brethren discussed in daily conference the 'question of the noisy and unbecoming behaviour of certain resident guests during meal times'.[190] Some guests were disappointed, like the future novelist Martin Boyd, who visited in the autumn of 1923.

> ... I went to stay for a week with the Anglican Benedictine monks at Pershore, where, I thought, I should find the true vibration of spiritual power, centred in an aesthetic medievalism. Actually the monastery was in an ugly Victorian house, furnished in frightful taste. ... The services, which were in Latin and followed the Roman rite, were held not in the abbey church as I had imagined, but in a bedroom badly furnished as a chapel....
>
> The food at Pershore was mostly badly-cooked vegetables, and early in the week I had awkward pains in my stomach and had to stay in bed for a few days.[191]

His disappointment sprang mainly from having anticipated a fantasy medieval-style Gothic experience. However, his judgement on the food probably approached the truth. A brother noviced in 1924, who would leave the community in 1930, recalled, over thirty years later,

> I have seldom felt so hungry in my life as I felt during my novitiate, because although the food might have been good for the soul it certainly did not nourish the body. It was meagre, meatless and wretchedly cooked.[192]

Someone whose family lived near the monastery remembered her mother was sent a message by Denys asking for a detailed recipe for rice pudding as his were so inedible,[193] while the author of the 1964 Jubilee book noted that in the kitchen 'the method was trial and error, and the unfortunate Community had to eat the errors'.[194] The Abbot's ignorance of the kitchen meant he did little to rectify this state of affairs. It was said he thought a mysterious action called 'putting the dinner on' was done first thing in the morning. He assumed the cook was then free for several hours for other tasks – until another mysterious operation, known as 'taking the dinner off', was performed just before the meal was served.[195]

After Easter 1922, as an experiment, the community stopped eating meat for three months. It was then extended, and the meat-free diet, strictly applied, continued until 1926. Bernard commented that as a consequence the community consumed 'a lot of scrambled eggs',[196] while Anselm complained, years later, that the glaring exception to this rule was that Abbot Denys (and he alone) still ate bacon for breakfast.[197]

The monks' life did not all take place within the monastery and its twenty-seven and a half acres of grounds. Denys's belief in an open

Benedictinism meant he encouraged his monks to take outside commitments within reason. There was activity locally, including preaching, and also helping at the parish Sunday school. Preaching commitments took brethren further afield too. Chaplaincy work was the commonest, especially in retreat houses and women's communities. The Community of the Holy Cross, Haywards Heath, and the Sisters of the Church, then based at Kilburn, in London, were the two sisterhoods most closely connected with the Pershore monks. There were others too; for example, in 1922, Bernard noted that Victor was conducting a retreat for the Society of the Holy Trinity at Ascot Priory, the same sisters for whom he (Bernard) was translating the Office.[198] It must be remembered that many of these engagements earned important extra income for the monastery.

Although he only very occasionally took a holiday, Abbot Denys was regularly away, in London particularly, for engagements or for meetings. As he wrote to his mother, before he was abbot,

> I am sorry, but I have been away. I have to be away a good deal now this place is growing and they are putting me on so many committees. ...
>   I am away again from January 9th to 12th, January 12th to 21st, January 30th to February 4th.[199]

These absences deprived the community of the uninterrupted presence of their leader at a formative time and yet also taught the monks to live the life without him. This was not a group who had a dependency on their abbot. What all the novices and newly professed thought of him specifically in this period is hard to establish. Most of the comments we have are from years later, looking back, and with Denys's later years of decline colouring the memories. What can be said is that there was some ambivalence towards him.

Anselm was clear in his reminiscences of Denys that he had respected the abbot without particularly liking him. He found it irritating that a man of nearly sixty should expect to be 'indulged as an octogenarian', and such 'indulgence' meant the abbot was 'not leading the same life as the community'.[200] But the memories of others were less harsh. Augustine Morris, who joined the community in 1923, remembered Denys's kindness and saw his eccentricities and dependencies as an intrinsic part of a complex character. The abbot was learned and at times profound, but diffidence made him vulnerable to criticism.[201] To Augustine, it was this diffidence that led to hypersensitivity and 'disabled him from forming genuine and fruitful relationships with the difficult characters of those who had joined him.'[202]

Bernard was one of the most powerful characters in the monastery, as well as being physically tall and imposing. Up to the mid-1920s, he was the only one of the professed priests (Denys, Martin, Victor, Peter, Anselm and himself) who had been a vicar: the others had been curates or chaplains, but none bar Bernard had had the responsibility of a parish. Before he went to Pershore, it had even been hinted that he might be put forward for a colonial bishopric.[203] He was generous, outgoing and warm in his manner, and capable in preaching and teaching. It is clear from his surviving letters that he was also self-aware and appreciated his own faults and failings. He had attained a level of emotional maturity not reached by all his brothers. Denys quickly came to rely on him for counsel and advice. Only three months after his solemn profession, and fifteen months after his entry into the community, he was made Novice Master early in April 1923. A month later, he was appointed by Denys as Prior, a position that meant he was the abbot's deputy and would chair Chapter if the abbot were absent.[204]

Victor was another strong character in the community, but in a more subtle way. He was talented and quick thinking, charming and engaging when he wished, but he needed to be the centre of attention. He curried the abbot's favour, but it was not clear whether it was he or Denys who misunderstood or misreported their conversations. They certainly could not both have been right. In later years, after his great rift with the abbot had occurred, he wrote in self-defence,

> Then I found, as I had feared, that he was not always loyal to me, and confusion grew, so that among other members of the Community, I gained a reputation for duplicity which I could not dispel entirely, since all my dealings with the Abbot were without a witness.[205]

His opinion could shift somewhat on significant issues, for example, arguing in 1924 that the Chapter and the community had 'to share responsibility' with the abbot for its own future,[206] yet a year later he objected to an 'over-democratic spirit' and the contravening of the abbot's authority.[207] Augustine remembered him as 'more Papal than the Pope'. He was more consistent in opposing the rush to profession so advocated by Denys and he suggested vigorously that all monks should have a period in temporary vows. However, there is a sense of something unresolved about Victor's attitude as glimpsed in the pieces of surviving evidence, and he had an acerbic tongue at times. He was not an easy presence for the others and perhaps this is why he was used quite heavily for duties away from the monastery. As early as 1922–23, Victor was allowed to go to help the sisters at Haywards Heath for three days a week.[208] Augustine

remembered Victor as influential in the community, although more interested in Jesuit than Benedictine spirituality.[209] Perhaps this was another
example of Victor's approach: he was drawn towards positions a little
contrary to his brothers. He relished an argument in preference to seeking consensus. Martin Boyd's visit to Pershore in the autumn of 1923
provided one further comment on Victor in these years,

> The guestmaster was a pleasant-mannered, but cynical young man,
> who spoke of the unredeemed outside world with more contempt than
> compassion.[210]

Peter was a small, energetic man, hard-working and earnest in his commitment, and was attracted to the Religious life as a means of witnessing to the
faith. He was passionate in whatever he did and expressed his views forth-
rightly as a result. We have one warm passage from a letter of Bernard's
about him, which reveals Peter's humour and companionable qualities.

> I don't think you have met our new mirth-maker, Br Peter. He's a great
> lad, brought up in his youth at Eastney Barracks, where his father was
> chaplain, & has done some years as assistant priest in S. London. He
> is one of those people that has the power of making one laugh with a
> single motion of the head or suchlike even without speaking. ... And it
> all goes quite naturally along with a tremendous devotion to our Lord,
> and with a jolly lot of hard work.[211]

Martin and Anselm were attracted to the order and regularity of Religious
life. They understood that precision and detail have a role to play alongside
a sweeping vision and big ideas. So they were concerned about rules and
having a proper constitution, and were frustrated by inconsistency or inde-
cision in the community's deliberations. Anselm was very gifted musically,
a specialist in medieval music in particular, and a published author long
before he joined the Benedictines. In later years, he would co-edit volumes
two and three of the *New Oxford Dictionary of Music*, and write other
books and articles.[212] He was also known for his dry wit, a master of the
droll comment. Martin was less academic in his activities in the monastery
than Anselm, but maintained a rigorous and clear direction in his thinking.
These two monks provided a stable if conservative counterweight to the
more outgoing and less predictable group of Bernard, Victor and Peter.

Cyril was the other priest, although he was more on the periphery. He
had first been in the Society of Divine Compassion, a Franciscan community
based in Plaistow, London, but his eccentricities had so driven his brothers
to despair that, after six years, they had refused him life profession in 1920,

and he had left. At Pershore, once again a Religious novice, he looked after the animals, including at Christmas 1921 being in attendance on and off with a cow that was calving.[213] Despite his contribution on the farm, he was no more successful alas in fitting in at Pershore than he had been at Plaistow. In 1924, the Chapter agreed to offer him the status of oblate for an initial two years, which he accepted, as they did not feel they could allow him to proceed to profession. In 1925, he moved on from living with the community and, after some years, became a Roman Catholic.

The lay brothers are harder to glimpse in the skimpy evidence that survives. Dominic had been in the monastery longer than any of the monks (except Denys) and he was solemnly professed early in February 1923, a month after Bernard and Peter. He must have been somewhat eclipsed by the new intake of priests. The abbot, however, sent him to Chichester Theological College for courses, as he hoped he would find a bishop to ordain him before too long. For him, Michael, Francis and others, it cannot have been easy to maintain a sense of equal belonging alongside the priest monks. According to a letter sent to the brethren by an old neighbour of theirs in Pershore, Denys apparently sent younger members of the community over to see her mother for 'convalescing when monastery life and monastery food had tried them too sorely', and the family would entertain them to tea. The writer referred specifically to Dominic,

> Dom Dominic was called Gertie by his fellow monks because of his sylph-like figure and his skill in dancing. But what fine work he did among the children at the Sunday children's service in the Abbey.[214]

More laymen were coming to test their vocations in 1923. Not all of these aspirants stayed. One man is said to have come only because he heard and liked the piece of music 'In a Monastery Garden'; but he stayed only eight days, four of them in bed with a cold.[215] Others could not stand the hardship of the manual labour or the lack of good food. In the end, eight stayed long enough to be clothed during that year, as well as two more priests. Even if not all these novices persevered, it was evident that space at Pershore Abbey was becoming too small to cope with the expanding numbers. There were three options: send some of the brethren to found another house, build an extension to the present abbey, or move to a new location. The tensions within the community made such a decision hazardous to its unity, but in the event the abbot ventured to do two of these three. However, amidst it all, external pressures were being brought to bear, especially on Denys.

⊕

5

Manoeuvres around the Episcopate

Difficulties began because Denys wanted the monks to publish a regular journal. Caldey had had *Pax*; now Pershore was to have *Laudate*. It was to be a mix of articles on theology and music and history, with book reviews, and a regular notes section on the community's doings. Over a thousand copies were sold of the first issue.[216] All this was uncontroversial. However, on the first page of the very first issue, dated 1 March 1923, Denys could not resist inserting in bold type the community's claim to episcopal recognition. This included mention of the Charter from the Bishop of Worcester and the 'sanction' of the Archbishop of Canterbury. Whether with naivety or mischievousness, the announcement also claimed that the Bishop of Worcester had confirmed the election of the abbot.

Bishop Pearce was incensed, as this was far from accurate from his perspective. He was already trying to limit the monks' activities in the diocese and looking for a way to prevent their officiating at services outside the monastery. Archdeacon Peile was asked to be 'go-between'. The abbot wrote to one of his sisters,

> I am having trouble again with our Bishop – some Protestant fad of his – but I hope all will be well. The Archdeacon is on my side.[217]

It would appear, however, Archdeacon Peile did not manage to calm the situation. The tightrope Denys had walked since 1919 was beginning to sway again. He had staked the legitimacy of the Benedictine community on diocesan approval. Now, by his flamboyant announcement, the abbot had jeopardized it once again.

Why would he wish to do this? Perhaps the answer may be found in the general upsurge of confidence in the Anglo-Catholic wing of the Church of England. The Anglo-Catholic Congress of 1920, followed by a priests' conference in Oxford in 1921, had been successful in sending a message of strength, perhaps even defiance, to other parts of the Church of England. Denys served on the Congress committee and had given a paper at the 1921 conference on Prayer. He was seen as one of its leaders, reflected in a comment from a letter he wrote at the time,

> I have been in London [and] in Oxford. The leadership of the Catholic party has been practically offered to me, but I cannot take it and build up a Community at the same time. It means being away from the Community too much.[218]

His vow of celibacy as a Religious was certainly significant to the Congress leaders. Matrimony was a sacrament but it was incompatible with Roman rules for priests and so therefore frowned upon by Anglo-Papalist clergy. Denys claimed that Father Marcus Atlay,[219] Vicar of St Matthew's, Westminster, was 'made to resign' as chairman of the Anglo-Catholic Congress on account of his marriage.[220] As an abbot, the committee knew Denys was unlikely to commit this particular 'failing' and 'embarrass' them as Father Atlay had. Therefore they may have wanted to push the abbot into a more prominent role.

Denys certainly also gave some intellectual weight to the movement's leadership, an issue that mattered, as the introduction to the report of the 1921 conference made clear,

> Again, nothing is more certain than that Anglo-Catholic Priests, if they are to evangelize contemporary England, must give themselves deliberately and devotedly to intellectual study. ... The Catholic Faith as fully satisfies the mind as it appeals to the heart and the will: it is not only a Way of life but a reasonable philosophy of living ... it is a foolish blindness which does not recognize in a well-furnished and well-trained intelligence a weapon for the Priest in his missionary warfare no more negligible, no less potent, than a healthy body or a kind heart.[221]

Denys must have seen this as a niche that he and his community could help to fill. The Benedictines could provide an intellectual resource to the Anglo-Papalist cause. *Laudate* was one way of expressing this. Yet, the power of this voice was even more significant if his community was legitimate in the eyes of the Church. That is why the new journal had to proclaim the community's relationship to the bishops and defy anyone who would relegate it to an inconsequential periphery. This was an announcement aimed at impressing an Anglo-Papalist audience not at irritating the bishop. Denys therein established the foundations of his community's legitimacy and perhaps hoped the more protestant bishop would not notice.

Bishop Pearce, however, did notice and he was not going to allow the matter to rest. He saw the Archbishop of Canterbury and then sought the latter's approval for a refutation to be put in the Worcester *Diocesan Gazette* of the claim made in *Laudate*.[222] Davidson approved this measure while gently trying to diffuse the bishop's aggressive stance,

> I have to consider whether I ought myself to publish some such comment on the paragraph which states that I sanctioned the issue of a Charter by your predecessor and another Charter by yourself. It is possible that I may find it right to do so, if the matter becomes one of wide notice or controversy, but would prefer to keep silence if I could rightly do so. I am not anxious to advertise the Community.[223]

Davidson's approach was clear beneath the courteous diplomatic language. He did not wish the Bishop of Worcester to stir up public notice of the Benedictines.

Denys tried to retrieve the situation by inserting a qualification in the September issue of *Laudate* to the effect that while the Bishop of Worcester was supportive of the revival of Benedictinism in the Church of England he was not yet ready to give it '*full* official status'. Frustratingly, this was still not satisfactory to the bishop because, as he complained to the Archbishop in a further letter, the paragraph was sandwiched on page 114 between 'good fiction' and 'orders for fruit'. He saw no reason for the word 'full' to be italicized, or for the phrase to have been put into quotation marks, as if it were from an external source instead of the opinion of the community.[224]

The Archbishop decided to take on the matter himself, partly because he did not trust the Bishop of Worcester not to blow the issue out of proportion, and partly because he had noticed that Denys was making public appearances that suggested a position of power and authority that Davidson felt were unwarranted. On 20 July 1923, the Bishop of London encouraged Denys to wear a mitre for the procession in London to St Martin-in-the-Fields in Trafalgar Square, at the close of the Anglo-Catholic Congress. He had allowed him to do this on a previous occasion too, as Denys reported in a letter two months earlier,

> The Bishop of London also gave me permission to pontificate in his Diocese, and last week I wore my cope and mitre and carried my staff for the first time in a London Church – St Augustine's Hackney, where the East Grinstead Sisters, who work in London, were holding their annual Festival.[225]

Four days after the Congress procession, Denys had an interview with the Bishop of Worcester in which he informed the diocesan of an invitation to 'walk as an abbot' in the procession to be held that autumn at Tewkesbury Abbey, marking the eight-hundredth anniversary of its foundation. The bishop then wrote to Denys on 30 July, making clear that for Denys to wear a mitre on that occasion like a medieval abbot would, in his view, 'be ludicrous', advice supported (though in more moderate language) by Archdeacon Peile. Despite these warnings, Denys did wear a mitre at Tewkesbury on 23 October, the difference on this occasion being that Archbishop Davidson was there to witness it in person.

The Archbishop put all the facts down in a memorandum[226] as he decided how to proceed. He was anxious to avoid unnecessary controversy but he was also becoming concerned about the Anglo-Papalists setting the agenda for the Church of England. Lord Halifax had set in motion a set of conversations with the Roman Catholic primate of Belgium, Cardinal Mercier,[227] Archbishop of Malines, beginning in 1921, in an attempt to find a process by which the Church of England could be reunited with the Church of Rome. These essentially private conversations had no official sanction – they were not negotiations – but the Archbishops of Canterbury and York were kept informed and Davidson corresponded directly with the Cardinal during this period. Pope Pius XI's reservations about these conversations did not emerge until after Mercier's death in 1926, soon after which the contacts would end, but the Archbishop of Canterbury's doubts became known at a much earlier stage. It was evident to anyone in Davidson's position that what the Anglo-Papalists would embrace as reasonable grounds on which reunion could take place would not be acceptable to Anglicans of other persuasions in the Church of England.[228] Yet some Anglo-Papalists acted triumphantly oblivious to this fact. Controversially too, at the July 1923 Anglo-Catholic Congress, its President, Bishop Frank Weston of Zanzibar, had led the 16,000 delegates in sending a telegram to the Pope expressing a prayer for peace and reunion. A public conference on reunion had also been proposed, much to the Archbishop's alarm, but he had persuaded Lord Halifax to abandon the idea. In the autumn of 1923, therefore, with the third set of conversations about to take place in Belgium, the Archbishop was perhaps more sensitive than before to gestures of rank by anyone from the Anglo-Catholic Congress leadership.

The Archbishop's other concern was the lack of regulations about Religious communities among Anglicans. There were no official rules by which bishops could be protected from being embroiled in controversy by communities or in turn the communities protected from hostile bishops like Ernest Pearce. Davidson had been appointed to a committee on the subject set up by the 1897 Lambeth Conference. Its report, published in 1902, had been sidelined, and the attempt to reactivate the issue at the 1908 Lambeth Conference had likewise come to nothing because of the onset of the First World War.[229] The bishops in England wished to return to the issue in the 1920s and it may be that Davidson was using the Benedictines as a 'test-case' to come to some conclusions in his own mind. This specific case might allow him to provide recommendations to any episcopal committee looking more generally into the matter of communities.

Whatever the reasons, Davidson decided to put pressure on Abbot Denys. In his memorandum, he had noted that he believed Denys was 'very uncomfortable' about the claims in *Laudate* and the calling in of Bishop Chandler to install him as abbot. He also noted that he believed it was Dom Bernard who was now the 'dominant spirit' in the community's stance, backed by a 'clique' of clergy in London. On 31 December 1923, he wrote to the abbot asking for an explicit statement as to whether the offending paragraphs in *Laudate* had been withdrawn and an explanation of the reference to the Archbishop's 'sanction'. He asked for Denys's view of the community's position *vis-a-vis* the Bishop of Worcester.[230] Denys replied, justifying his position, and adding a guarded sentence,

> I beg to say that since our house is in the Diocese of Worcester we accept ex animo the pastoral authority of the Bishop of that Diocese to the full extent to which it bears upon a religious house.[231]

He wrote to his mother that good might come out of this process,

> This work becomes more and more arduous, and my fight with the Bishop is not yet over. ... Whatever happens I am glad I took the matter straight to Lambeth. The official English Church is now committed to recognize Benedictinism by my taking the matter to the Archbishop and not confining it simply to the Bishop of W[orcester]. So, perhaps whatever happens, good has been done in this respect.[232]

The correspondence with Davidson dragged on through 1924. One of the issues the Archbishop raised was that of a Constitution for the community. Denys had put this to the Chapter long before, announcing at the daily conference on 5 January 1923 that he wanted a preliminary draft drawn up by the end of that February.[233] However, this was an over-ambitious timetable, and at the beginning of March a sub-committee of Bernard and Anselm presented recommendations to the full Chapter based on the statutes of the (Roman Catholic) English Congregation of Benedictines.[234] The three significant areas that emerged 'for ventilation' were: the relation of the monastery to the diocesan bishop in matters of theology and discipline; how far the monastery could take on board Roman Catholic canon law; and the issue of whether there should be lay brothers distinct from choir monks. The answer to the first of the three was that 'a policy of resistance to episcopal interference touching vital and essential matters might be judged advisable' even if this 'imperilled the Charter'.[235] It was such support that upheld the abbot in his correspondence.

Eventually – in March 1925 – the Archbishop suggested a set of guiding principles, which gave the diocesan bishop the decisive role in: any monk being ordained or working in the diocese as a priest; the admission of any man already ordained; the service and Office books used; the nomination or election of the head of the community, or at the very least a right of veto.[236] These were completely unacceptable as terms for full recognition, and were rejected by the community. The Archbishop then appointed a committee of three bishops (Burge[237] of Oxford, Frere[238] of Truro and Pearce of Worcester) to look into the matter. At first their brief was specifically concerned with the Benedictines, but their remit soon expanded to consider all communities. This episcopal committee finally produced more generic draft regulations in 1926, with no decisions expected until after the 1930 Lambeth conference, so the Archbishop dropped the specific matter of the Benedictine monks. In any case, he now no longer needed to worry about Bishop Pearce, because the community had taken a momentous decision. They were to leave Pershore, and Worcester diocese, behind, and settle in the diocese of Oxford.

The story of the community's move to another diocese was one as much of chance as it was of any strategic plan. At first, the response to the space problem at Pershore had seemed to be one of building. Plans were even drawn up for an extension by the same architect employed at Caldey, T Coates Carter, which would have added a new chapel and rooms for the abbot. At first, Denys seemed to believe this option was a foregone conclusion, writing grandly to his sister,

> Building, of course, is expensive. At least it is here. I am about to build a Chapel ...[239]

It was not to happen. The cost was in the region of a minimum of £8,000,[240] a sum beyond anything they might hope to raise from supporters, especially since the Pershore house as a whole was not in good condition. It was in a damp and unhealthy location too. Above all, the harassment from the diocesan bishop made a fresh start elsewhere more appealing. Having lost patience with Denys, the bishop was now costing the community valuable income too by stopping ordained monks working in a district church near Worcester (£200 per annum) and preventing them taking preaching engagements in the diocese as a whole (£50 per annum).[241]

The community had toyed with having an additional priory in London. The abbot had seen the Bishop of London in May 1923 and gained his approval, but he had delayed the implementation until it was 'absolutely necessary' to avoid expense.[242] The Community of the Sisters of the Church had offered the Benedictines an option to buy a house in Randolph Gardens in Kilburn. This could have served as a base for Denys when he was visiting London for meetings and as a place for retreat work, later perhaps becoming a priory in its own right.[243] But other opportunities made it impossible also to take on this commitment, especially as the Reverend Mother quite understandably asked the monks to share the cost of heating the empty house while they made their minds up. In September 1924, the Chapter finally turned the offer down.[244]

Before this, however, an extraordinary turn of events had occurred. A friend of the Pershore community, H B Ewart,[245] had contacted Denys about a large house near Maidenhead. Princess Alexis Dolgorouki,[246] an English-born heiress married to a Russian aristocrat, had had this grand house built between 1906 and 1909 as a showcase for her generous entertaining. Designed by the renowned and fashionable architect Edwin Lutyens, its location was the Buckinghamshire countryside near the villages of Taplow and Burnham, perfect for weekend parties for the London social set.[247] It was named Nashdom, the Russian for 'our home'. The land had cost £10,000 and the whole mansion over £50,000 to build.[248] After the death of Prince Alexis in 1915, the Princess based herself in the Pyrénées on the Spanish-French border during the First World War, where she died in 1919, leaving no children. Nashdom was left jointly to the families of her husband's siblings, who had been exiled from Russia since the 1917 Revolution. There were legal proceedings over the will, and by 1924 the family's circumstances were such that they wanted to sell. Ewart knew about the house because he was the agent for Prince Serge Alexandrovitch Dolgorouki, nephew of the former owners. In the depressed economy of the 1920s, large country houses were a liability and there were few potential buyers. There was no possibility of recouping the original investment and the family were realistically prepared to accept a bargain price.

Ewart alerted Denys to the forthcoming auction, and the abbot came to know definitely about the property on 1 May 1924. The matter was discussed at Chapter on Saturday 3 May, and the abbot and Dom Bernard went to view the house on the Sunday. Its whitewashed brick walls gleaming, and with its strong, simple lines adorned by Doric columns at the entrance, the house had a bold grandeur. A row of porthole windows on the side of the house facing the road made it resemble a huge liner. On the other side, facing the landscaped gardens, a gentle bay window softened the exterior shape and green shutters splashed colour to temper the white. It was in stark contrast to the nostalgia of the neo-Gothic architecture that so depressed Denys. He had no wish to 'build up the waste places' and restore medieval abbeys. Nashdom by contrast had a twentieth-century feel, ideal for a community wishing to proclaim itself contemporary and a blueprint for the future. The visitors were impressed by its potential advantages in the practical sphere too.

> The House is in thorough repair – central heating; electricity with power station; company's water; timber on the estate, which could be realized, etc. There is not as much land as here [Pershore] but enough (about 14 acres) for vegetable gardens, poultry, and, if necessary, the keeping of a few cows.[249]

It also included a large ballroom,[250] which could be converted into a chapel, a billiard room convenient as a sacristy, while the first-floor panelled picture gallery was envisaged as a Chapter room. There was also sufficient accommodation for both monks and guests. Running costs would be greater than for the Pershore monastery but there would be fewer repairs or improvements needed which would compensate. Denys also claimed he had consulted the diocesan Bishop, Hubert Burge of Oxford.

> I saw the Bishop of Oxford personally – on Saturday last, and he has agreed to our continuing our Latin Services, and says he will not put obstacles in our way.[251]

This was an example of how Denys could misrepresent a conversation out of all proportion, and accordingly deceive himself as well as others. The meeting had not been one formally arranged. Instead, Bernard and Denys had pursued the bishop that Saturday and tracked him down to a railway station near Shefford, a village where he was conducting a confirmation. Bishop Burge then described in a letter to the Archbishop of Canterbury what transpired between them.

> On that occasion he asked me whether in the event of the Community coming to the Oxford Diocese I would license the priests of the Community and also whether I would consent to be Visitor. I told him that I could not even entertain the idea until I knew exactly what their Constitution was and until their Constitution had been

submitted to you and approved. Since that [day] I have heard nothing from Pershore ...

I have been told that they have secured a property near Marlow & intend to establish themselves there but the Community has not referred to me in any way about it so far.[252]

It is unlikely that even the most sympathetic bishop would have made significant agreements with a Religious superior about sensitive and controversial matters during an unscheduled meeting on a railway platform. Any firm decisions would have been reached instead at a subsequent meeting, and then put in writing. As there was no subsequent meeting and no documentation, the bishop's version of events can be judged as accurate. In any case, the abbot could not satisfy Bishop Burge regarding a constitution, as the Chapter as a whole were unable to agree on a text for one,[253] so the bishop would not have proceeded. The sentence in Denys's letter above was therefore a distortion and misleading, an attempt to generate support for a rash decision.

The monastic Chapter supported Denys in authorizing the community's solicitor, H Basil Harrison,[254] to forestall the auction of the property due to take place on 5 May 1924,[255] and purchase it privately on the same day for an agreed sum of £8,000. Denys assured the solicitor that there was sufficient money to buy the property in a Fidelity Trust account, held on behalf of the community, in which benefactions had been deposited. The community used the interest from this to service its Pershore mortgage. In any case, the abbot assured Harrison that he would place an appeal in the *Church Times* that he confidently expected to bring in a reasonable sum. He also (quite erroneously) believed that the vacant Pershore house and estate could be rented out, once the monks had removed to Nashdom. Accordingly, won over by all these financial predictions, the solicitor paid the £800 deposit. In a matter of less than a week, the community had rushed into a complex and critical decision about its future and plunged itself into further debt. The prospective move was inserted into the next (June) edition of *Laudate*[256] so the purchase was very quickly public knowledge.

There had been no time to consult the community's usual financial supporters, who had since 1916 been grouped together in the Pershore Helpers Committee, the membership of which included Lord Halifax and the Duke of Argyll. Its secretary was Dr Walter Seton,[257] an historian at University College, London, who proved a faithful and energetic friend to the monks, before his untimely death in 1927 of pneumonia. Whilst initially helpful, providing vital income in the precarious years of the First World War, the committee became less generous as time went by because so many of the members were landowners, and the 1920s saw their estate revenues much reduced. They simply did not have the means to be so generous to communities as they had before the First World War. Denys interpreted this as 'lack of interest' and had complained to Dr Seton earlier in 1924 of how few members attended the meetings,

> It really seems to me that the Committee exists on paper only, and expects you and me to do all the work.[258]

During the discussions about possibly extending the Pershore property, Seton had warned the abbot that £10,000 or even £9,000 was too great a sum to ask the Committee to raise in the current economic climate. The loan from Philip Bartlett to buy the Pershore house, with interest accumulated, was yet to be paid off. Seton was therefore astonished to find that the abbot had purchased a house for £8,000, publicly announcing it, without contacting anyone on the Pershore Helpers Committee. It was true that Seton had been in Italy at the time of the auction and the opportunity for purchase was fleeting, but it was still an enormous financial risk for the community to take so suddenly and without advice from those with financial or property expertise. On his return to Britain, learning of what had occurred, Dr Seton had to write to the abbot an 'exceedingly frank' letter.

> The matters seem to me to be in an extraordinarily difficult position, owing largely to two mistakes which have been made. (1) That you were under the impression, and told Mr. Harrison[,] that there was £8000 of Pershore money in the Fidelity Trust, whereas there is only £4000, and we cannot get at that without the consent of the Fidelity Trust, and (2) That you were under the impression, although this is quite contrary to what I had said in my letters, that the payment of £2500 to Mr Bartlett would clear off his financial interest in the matter of Pershore, whereas really the amount needed to clear off his interest is £4000, after allowing for his donation of £500.[259]

Seton was, however, calm and reasonable in his advice, asking for a delay in issuing any appeal for funds until he could set it up properly, and in the meantime the community should take a mortgage. Other supporters were less charitable. Bickerton Hudson[260] was appalled and worried about the upkeep of two properties,

> Does the Community realize what the possession of real estate means in these days – the burden of taxation, repairs and upkeep?[261]

Dismissing Denys's argument about the dampness of the present monastery, he declared that Pershore was healthier than the Thames Valley. He was dramatically anxious too about the location of the new house for another reason, fearing that some brethren wanted to be too near London,

> ... my great *dread* is, lest the enemy which overthrew Caldey, – *the world* – is laying snares even more subtle, but with the same trend of temptations – to be '*in the swim*' – for the undoing of Pershore.[262]

He refused to sign the Appeal and maintained this position later in the year when the issue was raised again.[263] Dr E Hermitage Day[264] was equally forthright,

> I am not disposed to approve this decision, and my name must therefore not be appended to any appeal for funds to purchase the Taplow estate.[265]

Athelstan Riley threw in a further complication by suggesting the community move instead to Prinknash Park. The owner of this estate in Gloucestershire, Thomas Dyer Edwardes, was offering it,[266]

> ... with all building, office, electric light plant, garden, with pond, large paddock, upper & lower lodges ... to a *Benedictine community* – Anglican or Roman – whichever will give him £12000 or thereabouts. He sees Cardinal Bourne on Thursday.[267]

Riley soon changed his mind and advised against pursuing this option, and there was understandably no enthusiasm among the Pershore community to consider yet another property. Ironically, the Roman Catholic Church did take up the offer of Prinknash, and eventually it was the former Anglican community from Caldey Island that moved there in 1928.[268]

With respect to Nashdom, Denys made things worse by miscommunication with Charles Freeman at the Fidelity Trust, and yet again Walter Seton had to try to remedy the situation,

> I need hardly say that I entirely agree with you, and sympathize very much in the extraordinarily unbusinesslike and, in my opinion, discourteous way in which you have been treated when you are endeavouring to help the Pershore Community in their difficulty – I simply cannot understand it. I can only ask you to believe that so far as I know it is due to the grossest lack of business capacity. ...

I can only hope that you will endeavour to bear with Pershore with that degree of patience which I am trying to cultivate myself in relation to the whole matter.[269]

The deadline of 24 June for the payment of the full amount for Nashdom, as well as the reimbursement of the solicitor for the deposit, loomed. Fortunately for the community, Freeman and Seton worked hard and creatively to rescue the Benedictines from a perilous situation. Freeman found another account of money that could be used to buy the Taplow estate on behalf of the Fidelity Trust. Just as the community would continue to pay off Philip Bartlett for the Pershore property, the same principle was used for the monks to pay the Fidelity Trust for Nashdom. Year by year, excess income for the community was used to cover these debts. The debt to Philip Bartlett was cleared finally in 1937 but Nashdom remained mortgaged. After the Second World War, the local Rural District Council applied to purchase the Pershore estate, with the threat of compulsory purchase if they were met with refusal. The community therefore finally sold the property, some of it being used for housing, some left as open parkland. The sum received from selling Pershore in 1947 then paid off the mortgage outstanding on Nashdom.[270] This unexpected turn of events concluded the consequences of the impulsive Taplow purchase. Back in 1924, the rash Benedictines had been exceptionally fortunate to have such friends as Seton and Freeman.

Denys was contrite about the community's behaviour:

... these blunders are mainly due to the stress of circumstances, and were made, I think, I may say[,] in good faith. However, whatever happens, the onus is mine and the Community's, though I very much regret the anxiety and great trouble we have caused you, as well as the strain and trepass on your goodwill and time.

... I shall always be most grateful for the forbearance, kindness and self-sacrifice you have shown us in this critical matter.[271]

The question still remained as to why Denys and the Chapter made such a decision. Partly it can be explained by the sheer anxiety that had been created by the Bishop of Worcester's animosity. Moving to Nashdom would solve this problem, they believed, and the potential relief from harassment seemed an enormous prize to the community in 1924. Bishop Burge of Oxford had many Religious in his diocese and was sympathetic to the vocation. He was unlikely to object to the monks living in his diocese or prevent them earning income by serving its parishes, although they were perhaps unaware of his particular ambivalence towards the Pershore community. Bishop Burge certainly had no wish to act as the community's episcopal Visitor.[272]

Denys too was ever optimistic about finance. He had private means, which had to be used for the upkeep of his mother and sisters as well as giving him an allowance; so his own funds could not be considered his 'property' alone and consequently these assets were not submerged into those of the community. Denys was used to dealing with such financial affairs, however incompetently, and, despite the family's intense arguments over money, somehow the sums eventually seemed to add up. This meant he was not afraid of taking risks with property. From his point of view, if the worst came to the worst, Nashdom could always have been resold and might have even made a profit, as it had been purchased so cheaply. Indeed 'a lucrative offer' was received from a firm of jam makers, a proposal that was swiftly rejected.[273]

Denys also was convinced he could make money from the Pershore property, but he had failed to understand that the terms of the loan, and the other donations used to secure it, meant that the house could only be used for monastic purposes. In the event, another community, the Sisters of the Poor at Chesterfield, did wish to rent it[274] but in the end could not do so because of the anticipated opposition of the bishop. Under the legal restrictions of the time, the estate could not be sold either, even if Father Bartlett would have agreed to this.[275] All these factors add up to an explanation for the abbot's lack of caution.

As for the rest of the monks, Denys's chief monastic adviser, Bernard, was somewhat unworldly with money – indeed the community had had to pay off his debts when first he joined them – and so by nature he was not careful or astute in such matters. Others on the Chapter may well have not realized the insecure state of the finances and been falsely reassured (like Basil Harrison, the solicitor) by Denys's optimistic assessments.

The rash decision to buy Nashdom, however, would prove not only beneficial to the growth of the community in the longer term, but would also prove seminal in creating the community's identity. For good or ill, the word Nashdom would become as well-known in the Church as such names as Cowley or Mirfield or Wantage,[276] identified with particular values or attitudes in the Religious life. The hasty decision in May 1924 was formative in creating the public face of the community.

An appeal for contributions was eventually launched in the autumn of 1924 to raise £12,500, and, with the passing of months, Seton persuaded some of the exasperated supporters like Hermitage Day to change their initial stance and back it. Lord Halifax was, however, unable to contribute; a small donation, he believed, would give a worse signal than not sending a gift at all.[277] The Earl of Shaftesbury sent £100, Athelstan Riley £10, but the majority of donations came in small amounts from some clergy and a long list of Anglo-Catholic ladies, many responding to an advertisement in the *Church Times*. Other donations came from the notice in *Laudate*, an issue that included a photograph of Nashdom as its frontispiece.[278] The total received from all these sources by mid-January 1925 was disappointingly only about £650.[279] Denys did have other private sources, and certainly had separately raised over £500 for moving expenses long before the appeal.[280] Through the early part of 1925, workmen had been expediting essential repairs and alterations at the new monastery. Martin Travers was employed to furnish the ballroom as a chapel in the baroque style during the spring and summer. All seemed to being going forward despite the anxieties.

Nevertheless, the whole episode took a toll on Denys, both physically and psychologically, and for the first time as a monk, he agreed to take a long holiday. In the late summer of 1924, he wrote to his mother,

> The uncle of a friend of mine (a priest) is a Cardiff ship owner, and I [am] hoping to get a more or less free passage on one of his ships down the Mediterranean, stopping in Spain, Algiers, Sicily etc. ...[281]

To add to the pressures upon him, Jessie Prideaux then died on 1 January 1925. Denys had spent years trying to live up to what he believed his mother wanted and to make up in some way for her sense of social humiliation by becoming successful and of importance in the Church. For someone so diffident about his own abilities, this was a huge pressure. He craved recognition for achievement to bring honour to his family name, yet at the same time shrank away from it in case success was accompanied by criticism or judgement as well as approbation. In Denys's mind, there was an exhausting and endless struggle between the need to achieve versus the fear of failure. This was a conundrum that sapped his nervous energies. His mother's death brought both a certain relief from these pressures and yet also guilt that he had perhaps in his own estimation failed her. His need to get away was intensified. He left in mid-January for six weeks' recuperation in Europe.

A postcard survived, dated 7 February 1925, sent to one of his sisters from Mallorca in the Balearic islands, which told of visiting the place where Chopin had written preludes, and looking forward to further travels to Valencia, Granada, Seville, Cordoba, Madrid and Toledo. Whether he travelled as far as Sicily is not recorded, but he returned home by the end of the month hoping to prepare for the move to Nashdom, yet knowing that matters with the Bishop of Oxford remained unresolved.

Denys had realized that the issues at stake were more than he could deal with alone. Like many other Anglican Religious, he appealed to SSJE for help, in particular its superior, Father H P Bull.[282] Bull accompanied Denys to a meeting with Bishop Burge on 28 April 1925 in London.[283] Some weeks later, the move towards resolution was halted again because Bishop Burge became ill and then died. In a letter to the Archbishop of Canterbury, Bull outlined the deal he had attempted to broker with the late bishop on the Benedictines' behalf, that is that the community might be given leave to

> ... carry on its life & services as it has done so far ... without prejudice to any arrangement that might be come to later, & without assuming on his part any official responsibility in relation to the Community.
> He said he thought it was a reasonable thing to ask ...[284]

However, the Archbishop would allow no decisions to be made until the new bishop was in post. Fortunately the choice came relatively swiftly: Bishop Tommy Strong[285] would be translated from the diocese of Ripon to Oxford. Strong was not as sympathetic to the Religious life as Burge, but equally he had no hostility to it. He became the chair of the episcopal committee on Religious communities in succession to Bishop Burge, only because he was the next Bishop of Oxford, or, as he put it in a letter, 'shoved in, so to speak on the hereditary principle'. He openly admitted in the same letter,

> I am not really instructed in the business, nor much interested in communities, and whenever I take the chair at the meetings I feel that the business suffers from the fact I am not familiar with the kind of questions which arise.[286]

Davidson sent him all the papers about the community and warned him of the matter 'to grapple with',

> I mean these very difficult people the Benedictines of Pershore ...[287]

It was some months before the move from one diocese to the other was expedited, and any subsequent correspondence between Bishop Strong and the abbot has not survived, but the new Bishop of Oxford's reluctance to be embroiled in Religious community issues meant he must have been sympathetic to the compromise suggested by Bull. Strong was concerned about producing overall regulations for Religious and he was drawn to a wider conclusion of the issue than a particular agreement with one community. The Pershore monks could therefore move to his diocese but there would no formal recognition, no Charters, or responsibilities specific to the Benedictines, and he had no wish to be their episcopal Visitor. Denys and his monks, after all the problems in Worcester diocese, settled for no formal diocesan or indeed archepiscopal recognition in exchange for being left relatively free. It was over two years before they would even have another Bishop Visitor. Denys's manoeuvres around the episcopate – Pearce, Davidson, Burge and Strong – had ended in stalemate.

It could even be judged Denys had failed. He had made central to his claim that his community was genuinely Benedictine the fact that it had diocesan recognition. The move to Nashdom represented a retreat from that principle. The abbot now had little defence against the majority of the professed, who wanted to move the community in an ever more Anglo-Papalist direction, a fact that would have profound consequences for its subsequent development. Ironically, Denys wished to move to Nashdom to free the community for growth. In doing so, however, he inadvertently wrested it from some of the Anglican moorings that he had cherished for so long.

The move finally took place in September 1926. The monastery was transported in sections, over a fortnight, with the library alone accounting for four lorry loads, the books packed in fruit and vegetable hampers. One lorry skidded on a hill near Henley and overturned, but fortunately no one was hurt nor was there much damage to the contents. A caretaker was left to look after the empty house at Pershore. The last part of the move saw the Conventual Divine Office suspended for three days.[288] The abbot had to stay in a hotel for this period while his younger brethren sorted out the boxes.[289] However, not all the brethren of the community were there that September, when the Office was first prayed in the new chapel. Indeed, throughout many of the events detailed above, some monks had been thousands of miles away, for in 1923, Denys had sent several to work in another continent.

6

Propagating by Cloisters

During the spring of 1922, probably during a visit to London, the abbot had met Mowbray O'Rorke,[290] Bishop of Accra (the city that is now the capital of Ghana). The bishop was back in Britain to recruit priests for his diocese. A man described as 'widely-read and independent-minded', he had proved an autocratic leader who had difficulties getting on with his staff.[291] He had pressured the handful of expatriate priests by insisting they administer communion by intinction. Refusing to diverge from the rubrics of the *Book of Common Prayer,* they had resigned. The diocese had encouraged indigenous vocations to ministry, but so far only a few had reached ordination.[292] Hence, there was still a significant need for support from priests from England, and the missionary society known as the Society for the Propagation of the Gospel (SPG) was trying to help find them. A convinced Anglo-Catholic, O'Rorke saw the possibility of a monastic foundation as a further step in building up diocesan life. Denys invited him to visit Pershore so that he could speak to the senior monks, from among whom any possible foundation would necessarily be drawn. Bernard noted that the bishop was expected to stay for a few days in the second week of May 1922.[293] The Jubilee book implied he visited in June.[294] Whatever the timing of his visit, O'Rorke assured the community when with them that it was the establishment of the Religious life that he sought from Pershore, not extra missionary priests. He expected the monks to minister in the mission and around the monastery, yet be continuously resident there, not moving to other locations throughout the country. His suggestion was a Benedictine house at St Cyprian's, Kumasi, in the rural Ashante region.

Denys followed up these conversations with others at the headquarters of the SPG in London and also with Archbishop Davidson at Lambeth Palace.

Yesterday I was in London for an interview with the Archbishop of Canterbury at Lambeth and also with the Secretary of S.P.G. about undertaking work in the Diocese of Accra. I have practically decided to form a branch-house there next year, and am writing to the Bishop of Accra to accept. ... You will be glad to hear that the Archbishop was most kind and sympathetic about our undertaking this work and also about our Community. He fully accepted the status of our Community and the status of its head, myself, and said if we went out to Accra, we should go out with his approval and Blessing. It is, however, a rather big undertaking for us at present, though we continue to grow in numbers.[295]

Caution must be exercised over the claim that Davidson 'accepted' the abbot's 'status', for this could be another example of Denys's creative listening in his conversations with bishops. However, the encouragement over the branch house would be consistent with Davidson's long-standing concern for this particular diocese. Denys waited to implement the decision until three more monks had been solemnly professed early in 1923. On Wednesday 7 March 1923, Dom Peter and Dom Dominic left for Ghana, then known as the Gold Coast, to found a monastery at Kumasi (then sometimes spelled Coomassie). During the week before, the Chapter met several times and made authority lines clear. Peter was to be in charge of the new foundation, and all matters concerning it were to be decided by him in consultation with the abbot and the bishop. The Chapter as a whole would not be involved in these decisions.[296] In due course, if any novices were received at Kumasi, they would have to spend the last six months of their novitiate at Pershore.[297]

This was a brave and in some ways curious decision by such a young and small community. One of the main reasons was that it would gain respect for the Benedictines in the Church of England. Bishop Pearce had made it clear when he refused to install Denys as abbot that one of his main concerns was that he could not defend young active priests 'being secluded' when the need for all the ordained to help spread the Gospel was so pressing.[298] The venture to Africa was a response, as was evident from the notice in *Laudate*, when the foundation was announced.

> The importance of this experiment can hardly be exaggerated, for a thousand years ago to propagate the faith by cloisters (rather than by missionary societies) was the usual custom.[299]

The pressure to justify their existence was a familiar one to Anglican Religious communities, which was why contemplative communities were more likely to emerge from foundations originally for 'active' work than be started with the immediate intention of being cloistered. From the beginning, Denys had not wished Pershore to be an enclosed community:

responding to the call of the Church outside the monastery was part of the charism he had laid down. The Gold Coast venture would be part of the abbot's defence against attacks on the community in the following years, so its existence was partly a protection for the abbey in England. The Benedictines *were* now labouring openly to spread the Gospel: Bishop Pearce's criticism was rebuffed.

Of all the possibilities for a branch-house, the abbot may have believed that it was safer to found one in an unequivocally Anglo-Catholic diocese like Accra than risk an English diocese where the presence of more protestant sensitivities might hamper any new work. Bishop O'Rorke did not hesitate to issue a Charter (dated 21 March 1923) for the establishment of the monastery, giving unconditional permission for the fulfilment of the *Rule of St Benedict* 'in its entirety' and to render 'the Liturgical Offices of the Benedictine Order at any place within our Diocese and Jurisdiction'. This was exactly the kind of diocesan recognition that Denys had craved. He now had a precedent for the future.

A second attraction of the foundation was that the Bishop of Accra was only too willing to ordain any lay monks Denys sent there. This solved another difficulty therefore for Pershore: the priesting of choir monks after they had entered the Religious life. Prior to the First World War, Abbot Aelred on Caldey Island had solved this problem before his secession by sending George Chambers and David Tugwell to serve curacies in London and Scotland respectively. This had not proved a helpful precedent to Denys, as the brethren in question had moved away from the community spiritually as well as geographically as a consequence. Both ended up leaving the Religious life. So Denys needed an alternative. Bishop O'Rorke had no qualms on the matter and within weeks of Dominic's arrival in the Gold Coast on 21 March 1923, he ordained the young monk a priest at Sekondi on 8 April.

Another advantage of the foundation was that it allowed the abbot to divide his strong-minded community between locations. Pershore was a crowded house full of clashing personalities. Sending monks elsewhere gave him leeway to provide an alternative for those (especially the young) who had proved less suited to the contemplative life. As a consequence, there could in future be a wider spread of vocations and temperaments in those accepted for the novitiate.

The diocese to which Peter and Dominic went was relatively young in the Anglican fold. There had been missionaries on Cape Coast in the eighteenth century, but in 1900, there were perhaps only two or three Anglican congregations in the coastal towns of Ghana, and the evangelical-leaning Church Missionary Society had not sent any missionaries there because they regarded it as an area reserved for the Methodists.[300]

The climatic conditions were also very tough for a European and so there were few recruits for this mission work. In 1909, the diocese was carved out of the original jurisdiction of Western Equatorial Africa, but it gained its distinctly Anglo-Catholic direction after the appointment of O'Rorke as its second bishop in 1913. Much of the expansion among Anglican congregations was through indigenous evangelism, not missionary activity, and some of the laity were consequently involved and organized in church life. They had to be, given the shortage of priests. St Cyprian's, in Kumasi, had been without a resident priest since 1920.

The local royal family was associated with Anglicanism.[301] They had encouraged the growth of Christian congregations, as for them missionaries meant teachers. They founded the Anglican school at Kumasi, and also funded other congregations at Jachie and Nkawie. One of Peter's early tasks on reaching the Ashante region was to visit the paramount chief at Nkawie, noting that while the chief was happy for his people to be Christian, he could not convert himself because he had far too many wives.[302] The two monks arrived at their new home on the Wednesday of Holy Week. The church of St Cyprian held six hundred people, and for Easter Day it was packed, with even more people standing outside. Peter reported that there were 131 penitents and 156 communicants, ninety per cent of whom were men, and that members of the congregation gave prior notice if they wished to receive the sacrament.

The Monastery of St Gregory was a large, well-built bungalow, adjoining the church, its exterior steps leading first to a broad verandah. The brothers made one of its rooms into a chapel and, from mid-April, the sacrament was reserved there and the recitation of the Divine Office begun. A few parishioners attended too, especially Sunday vespers. Most of the buildings in the 'mission' had been built in 1914 and so, once the June–July rainy season was over, one of the first goals was to expedite repairs in September 1923, especially to the church and school. Another more long-term aim was to learn the local language. There were four main ones in the Gold Coast: Ga was spoken in the south-east and in Accra; Hausa by the Muslims in the northern territories; Twi in Ashante; and in southern districts, Fante, a dialect of Twi. Peter and Dominic 'wrestled' first with Twi, and found that their Office was of help as the vowels were pronounced in a similar way to ecclesiastical Latin.

The monks were aware of the Muslim quarter in the town. If the wind were in the right direction, they would hear the Islamic call to prayer at 5 a.m. each morning at the same time as they were saying Matins. Relations were cordial between the faith communities. At High Mass on one occasion, around the time the Gospel was recited, some 'reverent and courteous' Muslims arrived 'just to see'![303]

The school was very important to the brothers' pastoral work, and, as many of the pupils (some as old as twenty-one) came from surrounding villages, Peter began to visit the outlying locations where they lived. This was especially so during 'vacation' periods, when the students would return home and try to earn some money to pay for their pencils and books.

In July 1924, Dom Peter attended the very first Boy Scouts camp in the Ashante region, held at a place twelve miles from Kumasi. For the forty people involved, the chief had instructed that an area of bush be cleared, and here they erected bamboo and palm leaf huts for their ten-day sojourn. The flag was saluted at sundown while the Angelus was said in a merger of political and ecclesiastical symbolism.

But not all happenings were so familiar or so comfortable. A visit during the camp, to Sacred Lake, seven miles away, brought contact with the thirty-three villages around its shores, many of the inhabitants of which were affected by leprosy. Back in Kumasi, plague was rife, with fifty to sixty deaths in a fortnight, some people dying within hours of showing symptoms. It particularly affected the Muslim quarter. Eventually schools had to be closed and the quarantine was only lifted in October.[304] Dominic had gone home to England on furlough at this time; but, although on his own, Peter still refused to move to the European part of Kumasi.

A major change happened within a year of the foundation of St Gregory's: Bishop O'Rorke resigned his see. From their arrival, the monks had realised that the bishop was not popular, his high-handed and dictatorial style not being well-received by the St Cyprian's churchwardens and others, some of whom had written formal letters of complaint. In view of the continued bad feeling in the diocese, Archbishop Davidson persuaded O'Rorke to step down.[305] A replacement was quickly found: John Aglionby.[306] Ordained in 1911, he had earned an MC during his time as a chaplain during the First World War, and since 1918 had been Vicar of Monkwearmouth. Before he left England following his consecration in February 1924, the new bishop included a visit to Pershore in his preparations for his new work. Once he had arrived in Ghana – and Peter was one of those who met his ship at the port[307] – the monks believed they had a bishop equally as sympathetic as O'Rorke: on 5 November 1924, he would counter-sign his predecessor's Charter to the community. He sanctioned all their services, including benediction.[308] Peter wrote,

We have had our bishop here for 3 days & like him very much. He has heaps to learn but seems very willing to learn it.[309]

One of his ideas was to offer the Benedictines the Principalship of the new St Augustine's College, a venture to train local men for priesthood. It was to be opened in Kumasi in October 1924 with around twelve students: Denys chose Martin to take on the assignment. He had been a lecturer, so was experienced in teaching, and he possessed the organizational skills required in creating a college from scratch. The only other possibility among the professed was Bernard, who had recently been appointed Prior and Novice Master, and so was already committed. Dominic had been back on furlough since May 1924, and when he returned in October, Martin travelled with him. It was a significant venture, for as Peter described it,

> It is a big thing because it ensures the catholic training of Ordinands in this Diocese.[310]

This assignment was accepted during the period that Denys was dealing with issues concerning Nashdom, with all the pressures that involved. It might seem odd that he would take the risk of sending yet another senior monk to Ghana at a time when he would need all the support he could muster to arrange the community's move. Yet in the context of his overall strategy, the decision made sense. Two monks did not make a *conventus*, or community, the minimum being three. When one monk was on furlough, as Dominic was at the time of the decision, the other was essentially a solitary Religious, which was hardly fair to anyone who had joined a community. At some juncture therefore, more monks would have to be sent out to build a community, both for the sake of the professed assigned there and also as an example to any potential local vocations in the future.

The other reason was that theological education was an area Denys had long imagined as a suitable ministry for his monks. An intriguing passage in the Chapter minutes back in 1916 had been 'struck out at the Warden's desire' but the words are still legible,

> The Warden announced that in time he had hopes of making the house a seminary ...[311]

This idea was therefore long in the mind of the abbot, but was hard for him to make a reality amidst suspicious bishops in England. However, just as the Bishop of Accra had issued a Charter precisely to Denys's liking, so now the work offered was precisely the kind of task with which he hoped the community would be entrusted. Accra again was proving a model diocese for his vision of the Benedictine life and Denys could not resist seizing the opportunity.

The College premises were situated next to the monastery, in buildings that had previously been a dilapidated infant school, and with great skill Martin oversaw their transformation. They were constructed of sundried mud with corrugated iron roofs, with two of the three buildings ceiled with wood. Along with the monastery, they formed a quadrangle. He hoped to improve facilities in due course by installing concrete floors and having furniture made with local odum wood, which white ants refrained from attacking. On the academic side, Martin established a similar curriculum to an English theological college, and by early 1926 he was writing that some of the students could be ready for ordination within eighteen months to two years.[312] The bishop was pleased with the progress,

> As far as I would judge he was doing excellent work at the College & I have every confidence in him & showed it by giving him a free hand & never interfering with his plans.[313]

The bishop certainly kept to his word in allowing Martin freedom at St Augustine's. However, he did not maintain his predecessor's promise to keep all the monks resident at St Gregory's, so that the Religious life could be properly established. Quite unexpectedly, he appointed Dominic to look after a congregation at Christ Church, Cape Coast, news that reached the monk only on the journey back to Ghana after his furlough, so that he was diverted from re-settling in Kumasi. Meanwhile Peter was expected to look after a large number of out stations (nine of which had churches of their own, and schools too which he had to administer financially) and spent much time travelling as the two furthest were respectively seventy and ninety miles away. These were huge distances to travel in the difficult local conditions. He did obtain the use of a car, but roads were rudimentary in many places, and one outstation in particular could only be reached by a sixteen-mile trek through the bush on foot.

Peter went on furlough early in 1925, so that after two and a half months Martin was left alone at the monastery. On Peter's return at the end of June, he was directed to look after Holy Trinity Church in Accra and administer the diocese while the bishop had a time of leave. However, back in England, the bishop went down with malaria and in the end was unable to return until January 1926. Full powers in writing were given to Peter by Bishop Aglionby to take decisions on his behalf, so it was an official commitment with episcopal powers, and the responsibility was enormous, lasting more than six months. All this meant that the three Pershore monks were living in different parts of the country and therefore unable to live a common life. Denys tried to alleviate this un-satisfactory development by sending out Francis to join the group, after his solemn profession in March 1925. However, he was only twenty-one and to be assigned to a situation where monastic life was not being lived was not conducive to the flourishing of his vocation. It may be that Denys wanted him to be ordained and this was the simplest way of achieving the aim. In March 1926, the bishop did indeed ordain Francis a priest in the chapel of St Gregory's. Living individually was now a reality for the monks in Ghana. Even links with the abbey were poor. Peter had been left with little information about even something as important as the possible move to Nashdom, 'I know very little so far, they are not good writers!'[314] It was 1929 before the Chapter officially minuted that 'all reports and remarks' were to be sent to the members of the community working in Africa.[315]

The chances of the monastic life surviving, let alone flourishing, with this pattern of work and life were minimal, and by early 1926 very se-rious problems had already arisen. Peter and Martin had been unable to avoid the emergence of a strong personal antagonism. A few weeks before the monks in England moved to Nashdom, Bernard was sent out as an impartial assessor, arriving on 26 August 1926, and his subsequent report detailed the sad chain of events. He spoke to everyone involved and then wrote a long letter to the abbot.[316] He pinpointed the beginning of the troubles as a decision by Abbot Denys.

I should trace right back to the day at Pershore in the autumn of 1924 when you informed Fr Dom Martin that though he would be the senior member of the Community in West Africa[,] you intended nevertheless to make Fr Dom Peter Prior.

He went on to note that on the way out to Africa when news came through that Dominic was to proceed to Cape Coast instead of Kumasi,

... immediately Fr Dom Martin began to consider and to discuss whether, on the grounds that there would not after all be a conventus of three at Kumasi, he might withhold from Fr Dom Peter the letter which he was bearing from you to him appointing him Prior.

Dominic opposed such a course of action and so Martin presented the letter. Denys's choice of Peter as prior for the monastery was an obvious and sensible one. He had been in Ghana for eighteen months and had already built up much knowledge and begun to learn the local language. Martin was a newcomer to the situation and would have been at an immediate disadvantage if he had been put in charge. The abbot's choice was, however, the beginning of a deep resentment.

Martin was left alone in Kumasi during almost all of 1925 as Peter was first back in England and then based in Accra, running the diocese. This meant Martin had responsibility for building up St Augustine's College from scratch and at the same time running the mission at Kumasi, with its congregation of hundreds. Martin dealt with these administrative responsibilities with confidence: he enjoyed being in charge. Therefore he was excellent with his students, who by the very nature of their position took their lead from him, but he found it difficult in the mission where in contrast he could not exercise the same unchallenged control. The congregation were used to having some independence, after the years of no resident priest, and they had rebelled against Bishop O'Rorke's autocratic ways, so helping force his resignation. They had no intention of now submitting to what they regarded as Martin's high-handedness.

Some of the congregation wrote to Peter (who was now the quasi-bishop) making, 'serious complaints about Fr Dom Martin's treatment of those Africans who were wearing European dress.' They claimed he would not speak to them until they changed their clothes, yet some of them had never worn any dress other than European. After his arrival, Francis witnessed Martin treating local people this way and corroborated the claims made in the letters. Peter believed it better for members of the congregation to wear their own national dress, because otherwise there was a sense that European ways would be seen as 'superior' and African 'inferior', but he did not believe in being harsh or trying to compel. He wished to encourage people to take pride in their own customs. In contrast, Martin was attempting to make an absolute rule out of something that was an aspiration.

Bernard noted that he had rarely seen 'a more extraordinary love of a priest shown by his people' than that shown to Peter. Personal sacrifice and patience even in extreme weariness were his hallmarks, and Bernard said he had never seen Peter be discourteous even under pressure. He gave himself completely to the Ghanaian people he met. With Peter inspiring this kind of popularity, and having established such a strong rapport with local people, it was hard for someone as reserved and precise as Martin to follow him in post. Added to his sense of demotion by the abbot, he must now have felt second best in the eyes of the mission's people too, and perhaps this was why he wanted to make his (very different) mark on how things were run.

In addition, the two monks clashed over money. When Peter sent cheques from Accra to Martin, these were the equivalent of those sent by the bishop. Peter was clear in the allocations in his accompanying letters, instructing how much was to be for the college and how much for the mission church. Martin, however, had other ideas. He claimed Abbot Denys had sanctioned him borrowing money from the other accounts to use for the college when it was 'in need'. But these funds were from diocesan not community accounts. The authority came through Peter from the bishop not the abbot.

When Peter discovered the 'unsanctioned diversion of monies', he was understandably annoyed and wrote curtly that cheques should be used 'as I instructed', adding,

> You will forgive me for saying that I think you owe something to my official position, such as it is, & that directions from me should not be altered ...[317]

Martin wrote back in equally stern terms, claiming that his borrowing money from the mission for the college was 'not immediately your concern' and that Peter should pay the college sufficient funds, and leave Martin to adjust the accounts at his own discretion. His resentment at Peter's dual authority, both as Prior and as proxy for the bishop, then boiled over in his adding that letters such as Peter had sent him,

> ... do not make easier the working of a very difficult diocese and if I receive any more of a similar character I shall feel obliged to lay them before both the Bishop and Fr Abbot.[318]

This was an impertinent letter from one who owed Peter obedience on two counts. Unfortunately, Peter's legendary patience gave way and he replied with exasperated sarcasm,

> It is interesting because it [your letter] enfolds to me for the first time an entirely novel system of finance. Delightfully haphazard too & a great scheme for getting the Diocesan A/C in a jolly old chaos. e.g. You feel at liberty to take whatever you like out of a cheque made payable to St Cyp[rian]'s. I, of course[,] the B[isho]p, don't in the least know in turn that you are doing this or to what extent ...[319]

Peter then took steps to re-establish tighter control over finance while Martin remained defiant. Bernard's report summed it up as Martin being in the wrong but that Peter's reply,

> ... does seem to have been couched in terms which, in view of Fr Dom Martin's temptation to resent his authority, made submission on Dom Martin's part ... very difficult if not impossible.

When Bishop Aglionby finally came back to Ghana, Peter could at last return to Kumasi at the end of January 1926. A few days before his arrival, Martin sacked a teacher at St Cyprian's School called Antony after some misdemeanour was committed. He had put to the erring member of staff two unpalatable alternatives. Everyone else thought both of these were very severe given the fault they were meant to punish and that they demanded a huge humility from Antony. The teacher preferred dismissal to compliance with either. Martin was away at an outstation when Peter returned and, having heard the story, Peter reinstated the teacher without waiting to hear Martin's side of the story. When he commented on this incident, Bernard concurred with the re-instatement but felt Peter should have waited until he had had chance to assess both parties' views.

The incident was a humiliation for the proud Martin and his response was to refuse to set foot in St Cyprian's church. On 19 and 20 February, with Peter away at an outstation, and with Francis still a fortnight away from his priesting, Martin persisted in his refusal to say mass in the church, the only time during the whole of the community's ministry in Kumasi that the tradition of daily mass at St Cyprian's was not maintained. Martin also, citing illness, failed to attend the choir recitation of the Divine Office.

The bishop, still recovering from his severe bout of malaria, was dismayed at the conflict. He tried to find a resolution as he wanted to lose neither of these very able monks. He thought of putting Dominic at Kumasi and sending Peter to Cape Coast, but he felt that Dominic would not get on any better with Martin. Reluctantly he wrote to Denys in May 1926,

You will have realized from the letters of Fr Martin and Fr Peter how wide is the breach between the two men. It is not mainly a question of the relationship between the Rector of the College & the priest in charge of S. Cyprian's but it is the personal antagonism between them. I am convinced that it would be hopeless for the two men to go on living together in the same house especially in this country where it is notoriously difficult for two white men to live together. ... Now while making full allowance for what Fr Martin says in his letter there is no doubt that he has antagonized a large section of our people at S. Cyprian's. At their Easter vestry meeting[,] which was attended by all the representative Africans[,] they passed a unanimous resolution requesting the Bishop that Fr Martin should not again be in charge of S. Cyprian's Church & School. ... Fr Francis ... writes that the vestry meeting represented the point of view of the majority of the congregation. He considers that Fr Martin completely antagonized the litterate

[sic] Natives but got on well with some of the Cholt people & school boys. ... The only solution is that Fr Martin should be replaced ... The whole dispute has been very distressing to me & I have given to it much anxious thought in the hope of finding some other way out of the difficulty.[320]

Martin by this time had gone home on furlough: this was not because of the dispute but as it was his turn for a rest period, having been in Ghana eighteen months. It was the bishop's conclusion that prompted Denys to send Bernard to Kumasi and make a report before considering if Martin could return. Bernard noted sadly that the bishop was more upset than perhaps his letter had conveyed to the abbot, not understanding how such a good college rector as Martin could persist in a *non possumus* attitude towards the situation, acting upon it for weeks on end. Bernard was convinced that

> ... the prestige of the Community as a whole has been to some extent lowered by it [the dispute], at least for some time to come in the eyes of the Bishop.

There would be occasions in the years to come when Martin's tenacity and refusal to give in would be a great asset to the community. His pride and rigour made him strong in a crisis and someone on whom others would lean for support. But in Ghana, his strengths became weaknesses. In a situation that required a patient and subtle approach, his need for clear-cut rules made him seem harsh and rigid. In a culture of which he knew little, his pride made him unable to admit there was much of which he was still ignorant, and so, for example, he made an immediate disciplinary decision when listening for longer might have brought resolution. He could teach the local people much but he failed to be open to learning from them in return. He strove to remain in control so as to hide his insecurity. Above all, his personal pride erected obstacles in the way of his being obedient to his legitimate superiors, who had more knowledge and experience in this situation than he did. Martin was a man who, it appeared, could be truly a team player only if he were the captain; and if another person was captain and made a mistake, he might well refuse to participate at all. As Bernard put it in his report,

> He appears to think that a fault towards him on the part of a superior is ground for refusing obedience, and he does not see that such an action puts him more or less 'out of court'. To me this would seem to cut at the whole root of Religious Obedience.

85

Denys did not allow Martin to return to Kumasi after his leave. Francis had meanwhile taken over as acting Rector at St Augustine's College. Bernard reported that the young monk had done a considerable amount of reading to fit him for this role and was doing a competent job. He had dealt well with discipline problems but was as yet not sufficiently confident to exercise what Bernard termed 'the human touch', but he was sure this would develop with time. However, he did think, after all the upheavals, Francis needed a furlough.

But under the cool intellectual exterior he had developed, Francis was breaking down under so much responsibility at the young age of twenty-two. When he went on his leave back to England late in 1926, he suffered a significant vocational wobble. For a rest, he went to stay with Father Richard Langford-James[321] and his wife Dorothy at St James's Vicarage, Edgbaston. The vicar wrote a sombre assessment of the state of mind of the young monk,

When Dom F[rancis]. first came here, I was really alarmed at his cynicism. He seemed to have no good word to say about anybody or anything. He seemed to have a special 'down' on the Abbot ...

I have never – to be quite frank – felt that the Abbot treated Francis wisely when he went out to Africa, after all into a strange country as a very young man, and much more into the world than he had ever been before. He left him too much alone – in my opinion – very seldom writing to him ...[322]

However, both Langford-James and his wife concluded that the abbot was not the significant problem. Francis was 'blowing off steam' at the authority figure. The deeper cause was that he had mistaken a vocation to priesthood with a vocation to the Religious life. Now both a solemnly professed monk and a priest, Francis had realized that he only wished to be the latter. This was the beginning of a long struggle for him. *Laudate* proclaimed Francis was not going back to Africa yet because of 'malarial trouble' and then in the next issue claimed he was going away on the advice of a doctor as he was 'still suffering from the effects of the West African climate'.[323] But this was a smoke screen: Francis wished to leave the Religious life. From November 1927, he petitioned for release from his vows, a necessary formal step if he were to find a parish position in the Church of England. Denys released him in 1928 without reference to Chapter, which caused long-standing problems, especially when Francis married in 1931 and became for a short while a Roman Catholic.[324] He quickly returned to the Church of England and parish ministry. It was June 1936 before the Chapter finally nullified his solemn vows formally,

86

on the grounds of invalidity because he had been professed before the age of twenty-one.[325]

With Martin and Francis not returning, the branch house in Africa was fragile. Another priest was sent out, Gregory Dix, who had only recently been noviced, but who had taught at the University of Oxford and therefore could be of immediate help in the academic life of the college. His year in Ashante was, however, dogged by ill-health. He went down with appendicitis and had to have an operation in Accra, before returning to England with complications, which put him in the Ross Institute for Tropical Diseases for some time.[326] He too was not sent back to Ghana.

It was Bernard who became the mainstay of St Augustine's College and its Rector for five years. His achievements were remarkable. He oversaw the erection of new buildings for the College 'after the style of a native village', built on the highest part of the terrain in Kumasi. At the back of the buildings there was a farm growing yams, cassava, pineapples, mangoes, and vegetables. He tried to include the whole community in some of the college's activities and build relationships with the web of faith communities in the area. He encouraged contact with Methodists, Presbyterians and Roman Catholics. Even the Chief of Zongo, a 'staunch Mohammedan' came twice or three times to a Eucharist, and once to a feast day procession around the grounds.[327]

Yet more influentially, he became a model for others on how to impart knowledge as an equal, in an atmosphere of sharing rather than commanding. Bengt Sundkler, who wrote much on Christianity in the African continent, judged him 'one of the greatest theological teachers in Africa.'[328] His style was to live alongside his students, even though he was the Rector, giving them an example of holiness and commitment. Every Saturday, he would clean the lecture room himself, asking the senior student to inspect his work, in the same way that he checked their domestic chores in other parts of the college. Every afternoon, he wore 'native kente cloth, and sandals', and at other times went barefoot. He thanked all those who gave him gifts with the local words: 'Mida sio ah oyefe'. In an imperialist context, when some believed patronising attitudes were acceptable, even necessary, Bernard in contrast was deeply committed to the equality of all races. He was passionate in opposing all condescension or superiority by Europeans towards Africans. He tried to encourage Europeans to attend the college Eucharist with the Ghanaian students, and, quite atypically for an Englishman of his time, he was at ease staying as a guest in African houses when going out of Kumasi.

He shared his enthusiasms with the students: playing the piano and making music; growing flowers; playing (and teaching) tennis and football. He used 'the tonic of laughter' to ease anxieties, and at times helped poor students with money towards their vacations, and on one occasion arranged for a student's mother to be released from a debtor's prison.

As for his teaching, one of his former students in Kumasi, Canon George Laing, wrote,

> Father Rector came to us as our teacher. At lectures we drank deep from his knowledge. He made all subjects interesting and easily understandable. He would make us laugh one minute and not very long afterwards carry us to another world; and when he brought us back into this one you could hear every student sigh. ... His favourite subject was Ascetical Theology. This subject was as easy for him as it was delightful to us, because we saw in the life of the teacher the practical expression of that branch of theology. After each lecture he would go out, not failing to say 'thank you'.[329]

The ability to connect with the local people in a classroom situation mirrored Peter's work in the mission, pastoral work in which Bernard also participated whenever possible.

In 1927, the two of them went on a trip together through the Northern Territories. It lasted a fortnight (6–20 January), covered 1,400 miles, and they were fortunate that their 'Dodge' car did not have a single puncture throughout the tour. The monks sat in the front and their cook in the back with the provisions. They were impressed with the work of the Roman Catholic White Fathers and White Sisters they met, Religious who had worked in the area for nearly two decades. The sisters ran a famous carpet factory that gave employment to women and girls. They found the Roman Catholic Bishop of Wagadugu sympathetic to the Malines conversations. They saw the annual manoeuvres of the Gold Coast Regiment, and dined with a French commissioner at the colonial frontier, a border that was quaintly acknowledged by a tree stump with E marked on the British side and F on the French side. In the north-west, they also met Muslims, as Islam was the predominant faith around Wa. Some adventures were hair-raising, not least when they ferried their car over the River Volta on a raft of canoes, with their cook insisting on swimming over despite the presence of crocodiles. Once back at Kumasi, they reported to the Bishop of Accra which areas they judged to be the best for future Anglican missions, although they were sure the work would be slow and require patience.

Two years later the bishop asked the Benedictines to found a new mission in the Northern Territories.[330] To plan for this, Peter and Dominic (now running a church at Sekondi rather than Cape Coast) went on another tour in the north in January 1930. However, Peter, after years of immensely absorbing yet draining and strenuous work was becoming overtired. He asked that when the new mission was founded, he could be relieved of being Prior and priest-in-charge, posts that the bishop believed had to be held by the same monk to avoid any clashes of authority.[331] This was an understandable request as there had been no further help from Nashdom, no other monks being sent out to back up the hard-pressed group of three. However, it was the first sign of unsettlement in Peter's mind.

Peter returned to England on furlough, arriving at Nashdom on 21 February 1930. We do not know what discussions he had with the abbot during this rest period, but on his return to Ghana, he suddenly and unexpectedly announced that he had decided to become a Roman Catholic. It was a bombshell to his brothers and to the diocese. Bishop Aglionby, attending the Lambeth Conference in London, wrote to Denys in July 1930,

> ... Fr Peter's secession is a great blow to us as it must be to you. These past 7 years he has been so much to our Ashanti Christians that they will be bewildered at his leaving them in this way, & the R[oman]. C[atholic]s. who are strong in Ashanti will make the most of his going over ... So far I have not been able to make any definite plans about the future for the defection has come so suddenly ...[332]

It may be that it was simply the claims of the Roman Catholic Church or its attractions for him that finally overcame his Anglican roots and allegiance. Yet, it was more likely to have been a combination of factors that led to such a step. Peter was tired, and had been given less support than he required. The monks in Africa were getting remoter from Nashdom, and perhaps Peter found it less and less of a home when he went back on furlough. Certainly, the focus of the community seemed to be further away from the priorities of missions in Africa. There were no young monks at Nashdom eager to join the three in Ghana.

Peter had lived his vows faithfully in Africa but had not had a monastic life-style. Perhaps, like Francis before him, he now saw his future in parish ministry once he left Ghana. Yet would he be able to do that as a monk of Nashdom? From his perspective at that time, it seemed unlikely. Yet to leave the community when in solemn vows would put him in a delicate relationship with any Anglican bishop. He knew how opposed the Chapter was towards other priest monks seeking dispensation.

Finally, in his visit back to England, he would have observed how elderly the abbot was becoming, psychologically fretful as well as physically infirm. Whenever the day came that Denys retired or died, who would be his successor? Bernard was one obvious candidate but he had been in Ghana since before the move to Nashdom and so was unfamiliar with developments at home. During his furlough, Peter must have realized that it was Martin on whom the community had come to rely for the smooth running of the abbey. Given their previous antagonism, the thought of Martin as abbot must have created a certain discomfort if not fear in him.

To Peter, becoming a Roman Catholic must have seemed an 'honourable' way out of his solemn vows – it was the 'back door' that was always open, as Abbot Denys was fond of saying, a matter of conscience rather than desertion. As a Roman Catholic, Peter could avoid the conundrums of his relationship with Nashdom, start all over again and, he must have hoped, serve as a parish priest. That was exactly what would happen, after he became a Roman priest.

Sadly, this secession had an unsettling effect on Dominic. He too, since 1924, had been leading a non-community life as a mission priest in the south of the country. He was tired of Sekondi and wanted to move. The Northern Territories scheme would have given him another challenge and brought him back into regular work with Peter, but the latter's loss meant the new foundation was impossible. Bernard insisted he came to Kumasi for a few days' break but found him 'restless and tired', 'jumpy and nervy'.

> He only seemed to continually want [sic] to talk to people all day – I daresay he is a bit lonely at Sekondi.[333]

Dominic was due back in England for his rest period in January 1931, but before his planned departure date, he too became a Roman Catholic, and eventually, like Peter, ended up a parish priest back in England. This second secession was a fatal blow to the community's work in Africa, as Bernard could not stay in Ghana alone and there was no one else able or willing to join him. Much to his sorrow, and that of the people in Kumasi to whom he ministered, Bernard was recalled to England and resigned as Rector of St Augustine's in the spring of 1931.[334] His farewell letter, sent after the dinner given in his honour on 17 April 1931, revealed both his love of the Ghanaian people and the reason they responded so warmly to him.

> ... I think God sent me to Africa five years ago so that I might learn from you some lessons in humility and love and service[,] which my hard and rough heart didn't learn in Europe. And you Africans whom God has used as tutors to teach me these things[,] I thank you very

much, because even when I have been very foolish and said sometimes hateful and stupid things to you, you have still gone on in great patience, giving me your love and friendship and letting me share in your joys and sorrows in a way that no merits of mine could possibly have entitled me to do.[335]

With no one to replace him, the College did not survive Bernard's departure for long, and Bishop Aglionby decided to concentrate ordination training at Accra.

The Anglican Benedictine monks had been out in Ghana for eight years. Sisters from the Order of the Holy Paraclete at Whitby had arrived in 1926 and have maintained (to the time of writing) a presence for Anglican Religious in the country. But there have been no more monks. Yet those who did minister there helped strengthen the foundations of the diocese, and their example in running the mission and teaching in the College set a standard for others who followed in other locations. Had the monks been able to stay together and create a stable community, it might have been possible for a Benedictine monastery to survive. Yet we cannot know this for certain. Even living apart did not stop the clash of strong personalities.

Perhaps the greatest weakness was the lack of connection with Nashdom, a relationship hard to maintain at such a distance, long before the development of modern communication networks. Records reveal no great interest in the Ghana work within the community in England. Denys's decision to keep the matter out of the hands of Chapter and make it a matter for himself and the Bishop of Accra must have stilted involvement. In any case, it was not overseas mission work that attracted those applying to Nashdom to try their vocations. They were looking for a rich liturgical life and an Anglo-Papalist witness.

7

Settling at Nashdom

The community at Nashdom still remained quite poor, saddled with mortgages and living precariously. The days of large-scale appeals were gone, especially with Walter Seton's death in 1927, and the lack of replacements for the great pre-war benefactors of Religious communities (although there were many who were generous to the monks on a smaller scale among the increasing number of guests). The estate, smaller and more wooded than Pershore, was not suitable for farming and there was insufficient grass for poultry. Experiments such as breeding chinchilla rabbits did not last long.[336] Much of the heavy manual labour of Pershore days was replaced by the gradual evolution of handicrafts, eventually to be sold in the Nashdom Abbey shop, opened in the early 1930s.[337] The main income for the community remained the preaching, Lent courses and Holy Weeks and retreat work of the senior brethren, and fees from articles and royalties from books. Anselm went on several lecture tours in the United States from 1932 onwards.

However, even if the community was not wealthier than before, it now had a grander context. It certainly *looked* richer and felt more confident. The liturgy had been performed previously in a cramped bedroom at Pershore, with barely any room for guests. At Nashdom, the chapel was a spacious ballroom, which adapted well to its new use, with space and lightness. A gallery meant guests and visitors could view the sacred mysteries and Divine Office and be present as the community fulfilled its main purpose, the worship of God. Brother Bruno, member of the community from 1924 to 1930, recalled in his memoirs (written long after he had become a Roman Catholic) that the performance of the Divine Office at Pershore/Nashdom was

> ... well[,] even meticulously[,] performed. The chant, under the direction of Dom Anselm Hughes, the well-known authority on Plainchant, would have compared favourably with that of almost any great Catholic monastery.[338]

The improvement in the quantity and quality of voices increased the number of Offices sung rather than said, and by the early 1930s, High Mass was offered each day instead of only on Sundays and feasts. This richness of worship and its setting attracted a number of novices, although some found their pre-entry fantasy of chanting and spiritual asceticism wore thin once they had attained the black habit, and when the hard questions that Religious life asked began to challenge them.

There was perhaps more freedom in the late 1920s as Denys began to age and had less energy to attend to the newcomers. This made Nashdom somewhat different to other communities. In long-established communities, for example, the sheer weight of a tradition formed novices in the mind and practice of a particular expression of Religious life. It could be harsh, and the novices were left with the stark choice of leaving or sublimating their individuality to the group identity. In a large community, this identity could be overwhelming. Just as a young soldier would be regimented into the discipline and teamwork of an army, so the monk was inculcated into a regular way of life, spiritually as well as practically. In contrast, in new communities, this powerful sense of a particular tradition could not be so present and was usually substituted by a charismatic and forceful founder, who by personal strength of vision had a similar effect. He held the centre firm while the community assembled and grew, moulded by the sense of purpose he imposed. However, Denys was not such a leader and so there was neither depth of tradition nor force of personality to produce conformity. The *Rule of St Benedict* was normative at Nashdom, but who would interpret it?

Despite as able a man as Bernard being the novice master from 1923 to 1926, Augustine Morris, who was a novice from 1923 to 24, could not remember there being any lectures during his novitiate.[339] There were a few classes, but all by those not formally trained in the Religious life themselves. He relied instead on reading books on monasticism, as well as the texts from Roman Catholic Benedictines, such as Butler's *Benedictine Monachism* and Delatte's commentary on the *Rule of St Benedict*, or for spirituality the works of Dom Columba Marmion.[340] Butler's book was considered the text that the community followed wherever there was doubt over the interpretation of the *Rule*.[341] Yet, as Augustine put it, in his experience the education at Pershore was a 'kind of osmosis' through a novice's own reading, with very little questioning of whether it was right or wrong.

Bernard was relieved of the novice mastership before he went to Ghana in 1926, and in his place the abbot appointed Victor. But Victor had been given permission also to accept the wardenship of a women's community and was absent for longer and longer periods, so that his guidance of novices was not always as close as it might have been. Bruno recalled the strengths and weaknesses of this regime, comparing it to the Roman Catholic orders he came to know later,

> The main differences on the credit side were that there seemed to be more mutual kindness and understanding between the superiors and their young subjects. There was great firmness, but less desire to break down the personality by humiliation. More was left to God's grace. … On the deficit side, I should say there was too little discretion. Individual mortifications of the more spectacular sort were encouraged among the fervent young, but they were not sufficiently controlled. This had bad consequences for the physical health of the individuals. Perhaps there was too much liberty allowed to the individual young monk before he was mature enough to profit by it, with consequences that were not always happy.[342]

The influence of some strands of continental Catholicism, which emphasized fasting and penances, may have been evident here.[343] However, Denys had consistently taught moderation and he was suspicious of all 'excesses' as being the product of emotion untempered by thought and spirit. Religious life was simply a life for him, an expression of the personality and wisdom of Christ, a harmonizing of the personality to be as Christlike as each person could attain. It was therefore not about monks pushing themselves to physical or psychological limits and using deprivation or harshness to induce spiritual sensations. If Bruno's comments were accurate, therefore, it would be evidence of Denys losing some control over the novices. Certainly Victor was not moderate and he enjoyed the possible eruption of dramatic and intense spiritual experience. As novice master, he may well have encouraged more ascetic personal practice, which Denys was not observant enough to counter.

However, some things did become more moderate. Nashdom saw an easing of the spartan diet, with meat allowed on the menu once more, although the relative poverty of the community (that is building rich, cash poor) meant the quantity and variety of food remained limited. There were times when the brethren ate endless meals of rice and vegetables because little else was available. Mother Elizabeth SC[344] of the nearby House of Prayer in Burnham took pity on them in the very early Nashdom days and gave the monks a 'weekly dinner'.[345]

One area where the abbot remained both vigilant and strict was in the matter of 'particular friendships', for he reacted with distaste to anything sentimental. Bruno remembered that if Denys noticed such relationships, he 'often sent both of the monks away on the spot, if they were novices'.[346] This attitude was sometimes seen as harsh by observers,[347] but perhaps Denys was sensitive because he remembered the whiff of particularity that – rightly or wrongly – clung to some of Aelred's attachments, years before on Caldey Island. Denys was more concerned the novices concentrated on their spiritual development and were not distracted by emotional entanglements.

In 1928, Denys took over again the direct responsibility for novices, with Martin looking after those in temporary or junior vows.[348] Six months later he gave the official title of 'assistant novice master' to Dom Michael Warner, an acknowledgment that perhaps he could not do as much as he hoped. The abbot was running out of energy and he left much of the teaching to others. Classes on the *Rule of St Benedict* were handed over to Benedict Ley, a priest who was in temporary vows at the time, and other lectures to Bede Frost,[349] a resident oblate.[350] However, the abbot still insisted on being 'in charge' of all the jobs he asked others to do. Some were frustrated at having responsibility without any real opportunity to make decisions. This was indicative of Denys's general approach at the time. Although his physical frailties and psychological anxieties were beginning to restrict him, he would delegate tasks but not any authority. There was no Prior, for example, once Bernard had gone to Ghana. However, in practice, some control was slipping from the abbatial grasp: those appointed to 'assist' him were frequently required to expedite a job alone.

There were some strides forward for the community in the late 1920s and none more significant than the appointment of a Bishop Visitor. Walter Frere, Bishop of Truro, and a Religious himself, being a member of the Community of the Resurrection, agreed to act in this capacity. Chapter formally elected Frere on 31 October 1928. However, Archbishop Davidson's suspicions of Denys had remained. In 1927, a Benedictine monk who had left Nashdom to become a Roman Catholic had asked to return to the Church of England and Denys had been very sympathetic. The Archbishop heard of this and wrote to the Bishop of Oxford,

> ... I heard from the Bishop of Chichester that the Abbot so-called who is now in your Diocese has been receiving back Roman Catholics and expecting them to be accredited to ministerial work without any episcopal sanction for these proceedings. I am also greatly afraid that at the coming Anglo-Catholic Congress (a most mischievous thing in any case) the Abbot is likely to be in his glory, bearing a part with full recognition of his supposed official status.[351]

The business of status and mitres still rankled with Davidson. But in 1928, he retired and was succeeded by Cosmo Gordon Lang,[352] an archbishop more sympathetic to both Anglo-Catholicism and Religious life than his predecessor. Almost immediately, there was a change of attitude and Denys was invited to the enthronement in Canterbury Cathedral. Even though he was unable to attend, the invitation marked a lessening of hostility.

Nashdom was also becoming more influential among other Religious communities, particularly those of women. The new location was very near both Burnham Abbey, home of the Society of the Precious Blood since 1915, and the House of Prayer, home of the Cistercian-inspired Servants of Christ since 1921. For both these communities, the Benedictine monks provided priests. Indeed, the chaplaincy of SPB was made a 'cell' of Nashdom, so that Benedict Ley, then still a novice, could both canonically continue his novitiate while acting as chaplain.[353] Denys took on the chaplain-generalcy of the Community of the Sisters of the Church,[354] a sisterhood committed to social work in London and other parts of the UK and outside.

One of the closest relationships was with the community at Edgware, which had been founded in 1866 in Shoreditch, developing a special ministry to care for disabled and sick children. In the 1870s, they began building a new convent and hospital at Edgware, which then became the community's principal location. From their foundation, the sisters had used the *Breviarium Monasticum* for their Offices. Mass was also celebrated in Latin. However, at the behest of the Bishop of London, a new chaplain in 1905 led them to use English for all services. Under the leadership of Mother Raphael,[355] elected superior in 1926, the sisters strove to reclaim their full Benedictine traditions, beginning with the re-introduction of the Divine Office in Latin that year. The Nashdom monks became significant in helping them in these developments and the sisters were generous in return. The organ installed in the chapel at Nashdom Abbey was a present from them.[356] Fearful of episcopal influence, the sisters were wary of electing an Episcopal Visitor, and, in 1929, Abbot Denys became their 'major superior'. This meant that the Abbot of Nashdom assumed the authority of a Visitor to the community.[357] Eventually in 1935, the Edgware sisters formally adopted the whole of the *Rule of St Benedict* and Mother Raphael became an Abbess. This was a step towards the revival of the 'congregational' idea, abandoned in 1915.[358]

These relationships with women's communities were significant in giving the Nashdom monks a wider influence. Another way was the return to the idea of running a seminary at the Abbey to train for the Church of England priests who would be imbued with the Anglo-Papalist viewpoint that the Nashdom monks so strongly advocated. The successful examples from other men's communities who ran theological colleges –

CR at Mirfield and SSM at Kelham – were an encouragement. As mentioned earlier, Abbot Denys had toyed with this idea in 1916, but now the success of theological training at the College in Kumasi made such an educational charism appropriate for the community back in England. In addition, some ordinands (and aspiring ordinands) were asking the community to teach them during their sojourns at the monastery. So the demand was there. With Martin Collett and Gregory Dix having returned from the college in Ghana, and with several other academically minded men having joined the community, the resources to teach at Nashdom were also in place. The Chapter instructed Martin, Gregory, and Father Edward Cryer (a resident oblate) 'to go carefully into the details and to submit their recommendations to Fr Abbot.'[359] The scheme was publicly announced in *Laudate* at the end of 1928.

> The long-desired Theological College and Alumnate in connection with the Monastery seems to be in a fair way to becoming an accomplished fact.[360]

The next issue of the magazine noted that the seminary was growing. The students were not only studying but also 'sawing firewood' for physical exercise. They were also practising polyphonic music and singing as a choir. In subsequent issues, the seminary was reported as 'flourishing' and then 'taking up all available accommodation'.[361]

Gregory Dix was appointed the Director of Studies, but found the position frustrating as he had little power to plan and develop the seminary. The 'directive power' was divorced from the 'executive power'. Decisions he wished to implement were held up by lack of action from the abbot, such as repairing walls so damp that students' clothes were becoming afflicted with mildew even in the summer. Conversely, the abbot would act in matters of which he did not have first-hand knowledge, such as the appointment of staff and the admission of students. The seminary had no separate bank account, and charges were arbitrary, based on a subjective judgement of the abbot's as to how much a particular student could pay. This varied from £50 per annum to more than £132. For these sums, the students did not have a library, a common room or a playing field, which Gregory thought unjust and which he claimed was being commented upon outside the community. In a long memorandum to the Chapter in November 1930, he detailed all these matters and made it clear that the seminary needed a Rector who was free of the control of the community with respect to the seminary's life and finances.[362] Monks who were heads of schools attached to Roman Catholic monasteries had such discretion and power, and he felt this situation was parallel to those examples. Only such a reformed administrative structure could sort out, as he saw it, the significant problems and shortfalls of the seminary.

It should be noted that Gregory's own position was also somewhat tenuous with respect to the community. On his return from Ghana, Gregory had completed his novitiate and in October 1929 had been elected to take temporary vows in choir.[363] However, the ceremony scheduled for 21 November did not take place and instead Gregory became an intern oblate – meaning he lived alongside the community but was not fully of it, and was free to withdraw at any time. It was as an oblate therefore that he was running the seminary and this may have made both abbot and some members of Chapter reluctant to give him executive power. Gregory was also having doubts about the Church of England and it is certainly during this period that he at one stage left Nashdom intending to convert to Roman Catholicism. But after praying for four hours in the (Roman Catholic) Adoration Reparatrice Chapel in London, he found himself unable to take the final step.[364] Consequently, he stayed an intern oblate until resuming a path back into formal membership of the Nashdom community in 1936, being professed in 1937. However, the crucial period for the seminary coincided with the unpredictable years of doubt as to his future. This meant the project was fragile for he was its mainstay, devising the lecturing and teaching programme. Gregory's ambivalence about Anglicanism must have filtered through to others outside the community and made them question the wisdom too of having him in charge. He was undoubtedly a distinguished scholar with a first-class mind, but should one who was so unsure of the Church of England be in charge of training others for its priesthood?

To be sustainable in the long-term, the seminary required the formal backing of the Church and this was refused in 1931. The official reason given had nothing to do with the facilities or personnel – or indeed theological slant – of the project. It was instead the presence at Nashdom of priests taken in for periods of time while they dealt with severe problems in their lives, whether addiction, sexual problems or psychological instability.

> The Bishops did not feel able to accede to the request, on the ground that Nashdom was doing useful service in helping men, already ordained, who had failed in their ministry, to regain their character, and it did not seem to the Bishops that this particular activity was consonant with the further activity of training young men for the Sacred Ministry.[365]

In other words, the bishops did not want ordinands to live alongside priests who were 'under discipline' or who had had breakdowns. In response to this judgement, there seemed little point putting resources into a seminary that had no prospect of backing from the Church. Therefore, the Chapter decided to abandon it, as the majority agreed with Bernard's opinion that the community, in any case, was not large enough to run it. (Martin, it is minuted, did however speak in favour of the experiment.)[366] Although it was specifically stated that it was not a factor in this refusal, the community's Romeward leanings might well have been the reason for the bishops not seeking a way around their officially-stated concern. However, even if the decision had gone another way, it is hard to see how Gregory's frustrations could have been alleviated so long as Denys was abbot.

The difficulties concerning management and authority over the seminary were symptomatic of a general problem in the young community. This stemmed in part from the lack of a constitution and a set of unequivocal rules being laid down for its governance. The inconclusive results of the 1923 discussions about a constitution alluded to in an earlier chapter were followed by a further attempt in 1924–25. Just as the first had been prompted by pressure from the Bishop of Worcester, so this later effort was probably begun because of the Bishop of Oxford. As the community intended to move into his diocese, he would not entertain giving full recognition without a constitution.

The discussions included whether monks should have a specified period in temporary promises before proceeding to either simple life vows or (indissoluble) solemn vows.[367] Then there was the matter of what to do about the lay brotherhood,[368] men professed in the community but not able to participate fully, perhaps because educationally they were not able to handle Latin. They could not therefore 'be in choir'. These men were crucial to the domestic maintenance of the monastery and its grounds, and some were skilled in crafts. But the question was whether they should take vows or remain like oblates such as Brother Charles Hutson. Should they be allowed to vote in abbatial elections?

Another issue was whether choir monks had to be ordained (or be proceeding to ordination) or whether they could retain their lay status. One lay monk, Mark Milner, requested profession in choir rather than membership of the lay brotherhood, yet did not wish to be a priest as was normative in Roman Catholic Benedictine communities. Eventually, the Chapter agreed a compromise, whereby he would be a lay choir monk, but would then have charge of the lay brothers. However, it was minuted that one member of Chapter suggested that this should be 'exceptional' and the abbot noted that in the Roman obedience,

> ... all choir monks were normally ordained, and he himself thought it desirable as furthering a certain esprit de corps.[369]

This discussion was an example of how matters were being decided on a case-by-case basis rather than through adherence to a constitutional procedure or guideline. At the June Chapter meeting, a sub-committee of Bernard, Anselm and Peter (on furlough from the African house at the time) was formed to look into the details of a constitution, especially for the teaching of the novices. This in itself was controversial. Peter commented that

> ... ambiguity was a cause of friction and disquiet which would be dissipated and dispelled when constitutions had been finally drawn up and settled.

The minutes record that Anselm and Michael agreed with him, and it can be reliably assumed that Bernard did too. But Victor was against anything that appeared to undermine the abbot's current personal authority and deplored what he saw as a 'commercial and over-democratic spirit', threatening to vote against a constitution as a protest against this, even though he might feel the document itself had merit. This disagreement allowed Denys to insist the community was 'not ready' for the step, especially given that the solemnly professed had not had a true novitiate (of a year's enclosure) and had little training in the Religious life.[370]

The surviving evidence points to this fissure in the community – the abbot and Victor versus Bernard, Anselm and Michael – causing considerable personal antagonism in the monastery. (Martin and Dominic were away in Africa and so played no direct part in this controversy.) The next meeting of Chapter a week later was substantially documented. Bernard, the Prior, deplored the fact that the question of a constitution had been made a 'personal matter'. The abbot believed this made the argument for delay more compelling, because the 'spirit' in a community was as significant as the 'machinery' if a set of regulations were to work. This spirit was not evident at present, he felt, as feelings had

> ... run so high among members from time to time, and there being many distorting elements, internal and external.

Bernard asked for assurance that if the matter were dropped,

> ... there would be a cessation of the personal feeling and tension in the house which we all so much deplored.

Denys could naturally give no such assurance and asked in turn for a promise to be made by

... Dom Victor and others that differences arising between two brethren be talked out between themselves and not brought to the Abbot.

The sub-committee's main recommendation was that the community
should follow the Roman Catholic *Codex of Canon Law*, published
in 1917. Whilst Denys thought this acceptable, there was the problem
of what to do where the *Codex* stipulated hierarchical procedures that
could not easily transfer to Anglicans, such as appeals to the Pope or the
Abbot President of the (Roman Catholic) Confederation of Benedictines.
He suggested the community might create an appeal body for themselves
for such cases, with members such as Bishop Walter Frere CR and Dr
Darwell Stone. However, Denys worried that too precipitate a settling of
regulations, without detailed reflection on potential scenarios and outcomes, might give rise to difficulties in future.

> Fr Abbot said a time may come when such ideals as we once had might
> be swamped entirely by a new spirit using its majority through machin-
> ery we create now. Plaistow and Mirfield had Constitutions without
> any very brilliant results. He said that the opinion has to some extent
> been disseminated that the Abbot rules arbitrarily, that he is not fair,
> and so forth. He said that what he had done as a matter of fact was to
> try to see some sort of ideal which might save this place from the atro-
> phy and individualism so evident in the Anglican Communion.[371]

It is possible to judge this as Denys not wishing to give up his own far-
ranging power and to perpetuate his personal rule. However, he must
also have been aware from his experience of Caldey of the dangers of
taking on a constitution from a Roman Catholic source without tem-
pering the regulations to an Anglican context. The wrong constitution
could easily take the community into a position where remaining Anglican was impossible. For the Pershore/Nashdom community to convert to Rome as Caldey had done would be a negation of everything he
had tried to do since 1913. He must have been anxious lest his younger
brethren could not see the dangers that he did. With individual conversions to Rome from the community unavoidable from time to time,
Denys was adamant in doing all he could to safeguard the community
from leaving the Church of England. The 'new spirit' he feared might
'swamp' the community might well be the unrestrained Anglo-Papalism
that would create momentum towards conversion to Rome. Whilst he
was abbot without any constitutional limitations on his authority, Denys could prevent any such drift. With little episcopal oversight to back
him, he may have believed he alone now safeguarded the foundation

from moving towards Anglo-Papalist excess and a repeat of the Caldey experience.

It is a measure of the abbot's success that at the end of the century, Dom Augustine Morris could reflect after seventy years in profession that he had not once heard a private conversation in community, let alone a Chapter discussion, about a possible corporate submission to Rome.[372] Certain monks considered their individual conversion, and some did leave, but the community as a whole remained much more rooted in Anglicanism than perhaps even its members appreciated. Disparaging various bishops of the Church of England may have developed into a community 'sport', but the community identity had been firmly established as Anglican despite the Roman Catholic liturgy and the protestations of devotion to the Pope. For that, Denys was responsible. His attitude to a constitution in the mid-1920s can therefore be seen as part of his building of this identity.

This was no mean feat. Bernard insisted that he would only drop the matter of a constitution if acceptance of the postponement were made a 'matter of obedience', a stance backed by Peter, as the only way of 'allaying the atmosphere of uncertainty'. Anselm threatened to write to the Archbishop of Canterbury 'praying for a Visitation' if no progress was made in monks transferring all property to the community (a threat particularly aimed at the abbot himself who, as has previously been noted, still had possession of Prideaux family investments on behalf of his family as well as himself). Denys parried these threats with a promise to consult the superior of SSJE that same week and report back before Peter left for the Gold Coast in mid-June. In the event, the community did not formally adopt any constitution at this juncture, but decided to use Roman models informally for the next two years.[373]

It would be the legal and financial necessities of incorporating the community[374] that would eventually give impetus to re-open the matter. Full Chapter discussions took place in early 1933 and a constitution was adopted in 1935, by which time many of the needs and policies of such a document had been established through the ongoing decisions made in the intervening years. Through living together for a longer period, the community then found a consensus that had proved elusive in the mid-1920s.

For the abbot, the growth of a stable community was far more significant at this time than formal regulations. The instability would be pointed out in the charge delivered by Bishop Frere after his 1932 Visitation, when he stated that, reflecting on the previous few years,

... the number of these [novices and juniors] who have come and not persevered seems to be above the normal figure ...; and it seems to suggest that some real vocations have been lost for lack of care while others may have been too hurriedly professed after insufficient training in the Religious Life.[375]

Denys was aware of the problem long before this charge was delivered and it worried him deeply. Some of the younger monks had even contemplated forming a new community, separate from Nashdom; part of the property of the sisters at Malling Abbey was considered as a possible location. In the end the break-away did not happen as its main participants decided instead to become Roman Catholics or leave Religious life altogether.[376] The instability evident among the professed[377] worried Denys the most, as he was particularly agitated about gaining and maintaining the Church's respect. A lack of stability in membership did not give the community a sense of permanence and reliability in the eyes of those outside. These anxieties were brought together in one specific problem the abbot faced through the second half of the 1920s: what to do about Dom Victor Roberts.

As has been discussed earlier, Victor had made an uneasy monk, regularly taking a contrary view to his brothers and, despite his talents, being a disruptive presence. Abbot Denys had permitted him considerable freedom in order to maintain harmony. He had allowed Victor to become a chaplain to the Community of the Holy Cross at Haywards Heath in Sussex during his novitiate, and his relationship with these sisters grew over the years following his profession. The Reverend Mother CHC requested that Victor be allowed to stand for the position of Warden of their community, a role that fell vacant in the autumn of 1924. This was a significant position, as it involved being both the senior chaplain for the sisters and also chairing the Chapter meetings. Denys agreed to this and in January 1925, Victor was duly elected by the sisters to be their Warden. It was a role that would use Victor's talents but also be a temptation to his weaknesses. He enjoyed the power that the wardenship gave him, and the sisters' appreciated his ideas and suggestions in a way that his brethren never had.

He still attended the brothers' Chapter, first at Pershore and then for the first few months at Nashdom. Denys had made him novice master at the same time as his CHC appointment, perhaps to keep him anchored in the heart of the community's deliberations, but it did not have that effect. His absences meant he delegated much of the job to another brother. In March 1927, Victor was relieved of the position and given permission to live permanently at Haywards Heath. Denys was keen to keep Victor in the community and therefore gave in to the latter's demands, despite the separation it entailed from his community obligations. With brothers in Ghana leading independent lives for the sake of ministries, it was difficult for the abbot to refuse Victor's request, given what appeared to be the excellent pastoral work he was doing at Haywards Heath. However, this decision led to Victor rarely visiting Nashdom and becoming estranged from his community. He still wore a habit and put the letters OSB after his name, but to all intents and purposes he had removed himself from his brothers and his vow of obedience to the abbot.[378]

Victor's view of these events was different to that of his fellow monks. He claimed in later years that he had never wished to be a professed monk. As an extern oblate of the Benedictines from 1919, he had asked Denys if he could live at the Pershore monastery as an intern oblate. He had found parish work uncongenial and wished to have some time to consider his options. Once at the monastery, he claimed Denys pressured him into becoming a novice and then being solemnly professed in 1922. He further claimed that he had only agreed if his vow of obedience was 'conditional', and that it would not be operative if he lived away from the monastery. He believed this made his vows invalid. In his mind, the move to Haywards Heath was to separate himself from a community that he no longer believed had been canonically established.[379]

However, the problem with this point of view was that if Victor had believed sincerely in this argument, he would surely have asked for formal separation from the community at a much earlier stage than he did. If he moved to Haywards Heath in 1927 because he no longer had confidence in the abbot, the community or the validity of his vows, it was odd that he made no attempt to clarify his position at that juncture. Instead, he did so only when the abbot asked for his return to Nashdom. The difficulty in relating to Victor's narrative of events was summed up some years later by one of those who served as a chaplain at CHC,

> I never thought of him as a liar, but as a person who could not help seeing things as he wanted them to be. I no longer believe what I at first accepted in his statements about the Nashdom trouble. He has had a good deal against him, is very sensitive and was the adored only child. His parents[, who] were at C.H.C. when I came there, submitted with this same adoration to being terribly kept in their place. In his childhood, his father had given up a living in order to move to a Town, so that they need not send him to a boarding school.[380]

Abbot Denys was not such an indulgent father. The recall of Victor came about as the abbot had become alarmed at certain reports that were coming to him from visitors to Haywards Heath and its retreat house at

Limpsfield. One of the sisters of the Holy Cross community, before becoming a nun, had been in the Wolverhampton parish in which Victor had been a curate from 1919 to 21. He had acted as her confessor and when she had expressed a desire to enter Religious life, Victor had consulted Denys as to which community she should approach, and they had agreed she should try her vocation at Haywards Heath. She had been professed in May 1923 as Sister Scholastica. As early as her novitiate, this sister claimed to have experienced 'visions'. Victor, as community chaplain and then Warden, was her spiritual director once again and decided that these experiences were genuine. In 1926, Scholastica apparently received stigmata – wounds in her hands that resembled Christ's at his crucifixion – during an 'ecstasy'. These occurrences appealed to Victor's sense of spiritual dramatics and he wrote several letters to Denys concerning these 'supernatural' phenomena.[381] A flavour of his involvement can be grasped from the following extract,

> ... ten of the happenings involved were miraculous, and in three of them, I have had the honour to have my hands used by our Lord as His own, in ways as striking as the events of the New Testament.

Denys had a life-long distrust of anyone claiming to have psychic, supernatural or other 'mystical' experiences. He suspected hysteria and worried that Victor was encouraging a young sister to interpret, quite erroneously, unbalanced emotional sensations as being of spiritual origin. He noted that a member of the Sisters of the Church had had similar experiences when Victor had been deputy chaplain to that community, and these 'visions' had ceased once Victor no longer served there. Scholastica's 'visions' also oddly contained explicit references to Abbot Denys, saying he was not a true abbot, and disparaging remarks about the validity of the Church of England.

Denys might have left the matter alone, despite his misgivings, had it not been for the fact that clergy visiting the community's retreat houses also heard the 'bad-mouthing' comments. Prominent London clergy contacted Denys insisting that he disciplined this wayward member of his community, as Nashdom was being brought into disrepute. Bad publicity for the Benedictines hit a raw nerve with the abbot: 'we are shamed in front of the whole Church of England', he apparently bemoaned frequently.[382] With the unanimous backing of the Chapter, he wrote in July 1928 to the Reverend Mother CHC and to Victor insisting that the latter resign as Warden and return to Nashdom. Mother Mabel objected strongly to such a precipitate decision, without any warning, while Victor flatly refused to comply.

It was only at this point that Victor decided to apply for release from the community on the grounds that his vows were invalid. With Walter Frere having been recently elected the community's Episcopal Visitor, it was agreed that the bishop would chair a special Chapter meeting to consider the matter, at which Victor was allowed to make a statement. Release, however, was refused. One member of Chapter wanted immediate dismissal; the rest decided to give their brother three weeks either to return to Nashdom or else he would be dismissed.[383] The day the grace period expired, 1 December 1928, Victor called at Nashdom in the afternoon. He left his habit and said he would be returning to Haywards Heath. From that day, he considered himself no longer a Religious. The community subsequently formally expelled him.[384]

However, this could not be the end of the matter for Denys or the Chapter. Victor was considered as one who had betrayed his lifelong solemn vows made to God and the Church, and was regarded in the same light as someone who had abandoned his marriage vows. A divorced priest would not be given an episcopal licence. Denys considered therefore that equally Victor, an apostate Religious, should have his licence in the diocese of Chichester withdrawn. He wrote a formal complaint to the Bishop of Chichester, Winfrid Burrows,[385] requesting this be done. Dr Darwell Stone, who resigned as Visitor of the Community of the Holy Cross because he too believed the sisters should have forced Victor's resignation as Warden after the latter had 'broken' his vows, supported this complaint.

Bishop Burrows died before dealing with the matter and it was left to his successor, George Bell,[386] to attempt a settlement. The new diocesan formally visited the community twice in April and May 1930, and cleared the sisters of any 'aspersions or imputations', commending their 'high standard of religious observance' and the 'spirit of charity' and good relations within the convent.[387] It seemed many were not aware of the full extent of the 'visions' being experienced by one of their number: it had been a matter between the Warden and the sister concerned. Some would have strongly disapproved if this type of experience had been revealed and pronounced as normative by the Warden or anyone else. Reassured, Bishop Bell agreed to become their new Visitor. Despite the incidents related above, he also saw the value of Victor Roberts' work among the sisters. He consequently negotiated a form of words of release to satisfy both the Benedictines and the Warden of CHC. This proved a long process, but finally it was accomplished and the bishop's report was published on 29 December 1930.[388]

The matter may have been over in a juridical sense,[389] but emotionally Abbot Denys found it hard to move on. He felt the humiliation and embarrassment of a monk abandoning solemn vows. Francis, Peter and

Dominic all did the same, but the anguish seemed for Denys to concentrate on the mercurial figure of Victor. Augustine later wrote that Victor's perceived 'disloyalty'

> ... overclouded and embittered the last years of Abbot Denys's life: indeed the matter became a positive obsession, and he could think and talk of nothing else. His monks wearied of perpetual conversations on the subject, which went round and round without reaching conclusion: such conversations were appropriately referred to as being 'on the wheel'.[390]

This was one of the indications of mental decline in the abbot. To lessen the strain on him, the brethren insisted he took holidays and, under protest, he gave in. After the 1925 trip in the Western Mediterranean, he went on pilgrimage to the Holy Land in 1926, visiting Orthodox monasteries and some of other eastern churches.[391] In subsequent years, he visited Italy and France.[392] He still regularly attended meetings in London and elsewhere, preached and took part in conferences. In 1931, he was elected the first president and priest-director of the Society of Mary (an amalgamation of two smaller organizations).[393] He still wrote for *Laudate* and other publications, especially book reviews.

However, Abbot Denys began to do less and less in the monastery itself, especially after he damaged his leg in a fall from a ladder when fetching a book from a high shelf in the library. The daily community meeting had been abandoned when the monks moved to Nashdom. Denys still presided at the silent meals but rarely went to recreation where talking was permitted. Bruno James, before he left the community in 1930, acted as the abbot's secretary, and he noted that already Denys, although at times 'witty and enchanting', had 'fits of black melancholy disturbing and rather frightening'.[394] The abbot still attended the Divine Office in chapel but required more and more support. His eccentricities[395] and mild paranoid symptoms grew. An exact diagnosis of his mental condition is hard to give, as there is no surviving evidence that any specifically psychiatric examination was made at the time. He did not appear to suffer memory loss and he did not have consistent dementia; his state of mind resembled more that of anxiety and depression, the intensity of which fluctuated, and which could leave him confused or fearful.

Whatever an accurate diagnosis might have been, his behavioural symptoms made it difficult for his monks. According to Augustine, some hoped that when Bishop Frere made his formal Visitation in 1932 he would recommend a change of leadership when he addressed his charge to the community.

I well remember Abbot Denys's demeanour at that moment, sitting with head bowed, as one about to be arraigned and condemned for heinous crimes! But no condemnation followed.[396]

This apparent vindication of his continuation in office, however, did not disguise his growing dependence on Martin. Bernard on his return from Africa in 1931 had begun a busy outside apostolate, preaching and teaching, and engendering much goodwill (as well as earning income) for Nashdom Abbey. It was Martin, within the monastery, who became the mainstay of its administration. So, for example, it was he who, as the 'assistant' novice master under the abbot, was in practice shouldering most of the burden. It was Martin who sorted out the scheme for priest oblates.[397] When Brother Mark, a qualified accountant before entry, left the community in 1933, it was Martin who was given responsibility for the accounts.[398] As Denys's physical and mental decline accelerated, he was persuaded to sign a document on 7 June 1934, giving Martin powers as acting superior, an instrument renewed on 6 September. Augustine and Gregory then took the abbot away for a rest on the south coast. At times, he would be confused and believed he was back in Leipzig or somewhere dear to him from the past. He had long suffered from bronchial problems and neuritis,[399] but now he also had phlebitis.[400] His frailties were becoming a frustration for him.

On 16 September, Denys reached his seventieth birthday. By the end of October, he was back at Nashdom reading Aristotle in Greek. On 29 November, he was left alone for a while in his room, as he had been on countless previous occasions, while the monk whose turn it was to look after him went to Vespers. By some sudden burst of strength, Denys somehow went to the window and opened it. Had he mistaken the window for a door? Was he merely trying to get air into the room? Or was he trying to escape, frightened by a wave of paranoia or a dream? We shall never know the answer to those questions. All that is known is that he must have fallen over the sill, and, some time later, he was discovered lying on the terrace outside. The accident had taken his life.

The death was not unexpected, but its manner was. It was an embarrassing shock too. There was an inquest, which produced a verdict of 'accidental death'. It was a concern that, from the now public circumstances of the death, it might appear to some outsiders that the brethren had not looked after their frail senior, but this was far from the case. No one could have imagined that Denys would have had the ability in his state of health to open a large sash window. The abbot had in the end been no more conventional in his dying than he had been in his life. He was buried on 4 December, the first to be laid in the community's new cemetery, in an area once an orchard and only recently cleared of its trees.

The gratitude for Denys's contribution to the revival of Benedictinism was considerable in the community. The monks knew that without him there would have been no community to join. They had been irritated by his eccentricities, and some even found it impossible to warm to him as a result, but they nevertheless blessed his memory and valued his contribution.

Assessing that contribution is not easy as so much of it was hidden. Denys was essentially a one-to-one person. His greatest work was in the confessional and spiritual direction, which by its very nature is beyond the detailed account of any historian. However, the effects of his spiritual and psychological advice are evident. He steered the fledgling community away from the distraction of 'spiritual sensations' and the temptations of inward-looking asceticism. He wanted a community that was able to look outwards and serve the world in addition to being at heart a community of prayer and worship. He achieved this by his one-to-one influence on his monks rather than by his chairing Chapter discussions or giving lectures. He could explain himself through advising on a personal difficulty much better than in a formal statement in a larger gathering.

This sense of being better one-to-one than in a group was something he understood about himself. In Religious life, he saw himself as ideal oblate material, in the role of a chaplain perhaps. He did not wish to be a Religious, let alone an abbot, because of the group responsibilities this carried. But when he realized that he could not revive Benedictinism among Anglicans as an oblate (after nearly a decade of trying), he accepted that he had to take on the greater burden himself and become an abbot. He made mistakes and exposed at times regrettable flaws in his character. Yet, his vision for Religious life was of fallible people living an ordinary life. Monasticism was not about escaping into a medieval pastiche or 'leaving the world' or being perfect. It was about embracing the world in all its imperfections. The monastic round of prayer and work was a way of living an ordinary life closer to God and to Christ, not an end in itself. Religious could best be channels of God's grace not by being something esoteric and apart, but by being of, and in, the society around them. That is why he did not favour strict enclosure and allowed the monks to take outside engagements. Monasticism should seek simply to inspire others to follow Christ.

Under pressure, other 'founders' of Anglican Benedictinism for men had faltered: Ignatius Lyne had fallen back into surreal egoism and eccentricity, Aelred Carlyle had converted to the security of Rome, while Anselm Mardon had also walked away by returning to the comfort of

Caldey. In contrast, Denys not only took it on but also stubbornly remained in the Church of England that he loved deeply (despite his continual complaints). The role of 'founder' did not fit him well, and at times
he was diffident and awkward in it. He was not by any means the best
person for the job, yet he avoided being the wrong one. It was a great
achievement for one so socially diffident and psychologically complex,
and should not be underrated.

Like any true reviver, he built the community around the principles
and the life and not around himself. At his death, he had proved it was
possible to be an Anglican Benedictine monk, both completely loyal to
Benedictine tradition and also to the Anglican Communion. It is the clear
vision to maintain those two loyalties together that he bequeathed to his
community.

8

Ecumenism and Expansion

The election of an abbot to succeed Denys took place on 6 December 1934. Those eligible to vote were the seven solemnly professed choir monks, ordained and lay. The one life professed member of the lay brotherhood within the monastery was not allowed to participate, as at that time such professions were not solemn. Anselm Hughes was on a lecture tour in the USA and voted by proxy; the other six[401] assembled under the eye of Father Horner CR[402] who was the Bishop Visitor's 'referee'.[403] The first ballot produced three votes for Martin, two for Bernard and two for Anselm. The second ballot was as inconclusive, with Anselm's total dropping to one, and a single vote cast for Benedict, the totals for Martin and Bernard remaining the same. The choice was in effect between Martin and Bernard. Martin represented financial and administrative competence, a priority for liturgy and observance, and he was a monk rooted in the abbey's day-to-day life. Bernard, however, was the man with charisma, who was well known outside the monastery as preacher, retreat-giver and (later) broadcaster, but less noted for meticulous financial management. The voters were clearly divided as to the best man to take them forward.

At this juncture, after two inconclusive ballots, Bernard 'declared himself unwilling to stand for election'. This broke the impasse and on the next ballot Martin was elected the second abbot. Bernard's action can be explained by two factors. First, it is unlikely he wished to be abbot. He would have accepted the role if it had been the clear wish of his brethren. However, as there was no such clarity, he probably preferred not to be hemmed in by the burdens the abbacy imposed on its incumbent. Second, he had already an alternative position: before Denys's death, the Bishop of London had asked Bernard to be the next Vicar of All Saints', Margaret Street, in London's West End. Being a monk, he had passed on the request to his superior to make the decision; Denys had decided Bernard should accept. The induction had been fixed for the 18 December, but this was now subject to him not being elected abbot. When he escaped the abbacy, the Chapter ratified Denys's earlier decision and freed

Bernard of the control of the community with respect to his new parish, for a period of at least five years, but retained the right to veto any engagements external to it.[404] The 'loan' of Dom Bernard was not without cost to the community, as he was no longer available to earn income for them from outside engagements, something Abbot Martin was characteristically direct in pointing out to the congregation when he visited the church to preach (and ask for donations) on 14 July 1935.[405] Bernard tried to spend most of August each year at Nashdom, but he was destined never to return full-time to the abbey, as he was still Vicar of All Saints when he died unexpectedly in 1942.[406]

If Bernard was freed to take a new direction in 1934 because he was not elected abbot, for Martin the same event provided the relief of confirming him in the job that he had been doing as a proxy for some time. He had effectively run the abbey in Denys's last years, yet without being given the necessary authority (until June 1934), and now at last he was properly the 'captain' of the team. As his obituarist in the abbey *Notes* would wryly comment years later,

> Abbot Martin, though not inclined to stand on ceremony, had a great sense of the dignity of his office. Indeed, it might be said that though he often suffered under the burdens he carried, he had a natural fondness for being Abbot.[407]

It is possible that the office of abbot was a role behind which his reserved personality could rest. The dignity of his office allowed him to conceal his emotions more readily. He was no longer under obedience to anyone else. He was perhaps not as confident as he seemed outwardly. Martin was helped by Mother Elizabeth, Foundress of the Congregation of the Servants of Christ, whose convent was very near to Nashdom. He had been chaplain to her community since 1929.[408] Elizabeth was a noted spiritual director and was consulted regularly by others considered themselves spiritual adepts, such as Father William Sirr of Glasshampton. She was austere and meticulous in her Cistercian-influenced Religious life, and quite autocratic in wielding power in her own community, so some found her intimidating. Yet, she was also an able woman, incisive and wise in her observations, and not without humour to lighten her counsel. Augustine Morris judged the new abbot owed her much in both practice and ideas. He also remembered Martin saying that he had learned about the depths of Religious life from hearing nuns' confessions.[409]

However, it is not easy to gain more direct access to Martin's thoughts and motivations. Unlike Denys, he did not have family to whom he wrote regularly and who preserved his letters for the archives. He was a systematic destroyer of correspondence and left little evidence therefore of the motives and hopes behind his decisions. Some surviving letters that others preserved show a writer who communicated information in precise points with little emotional content beyond general remarks. This reflected his public style, which had bearing and dignity especially in liturgy, but otherwise remained undemonstrative. The Jubilee book records that the new abbot could rarely be persuaded to give talks, theological or spiritual, to his community.[410] He was a scientist by training, not a theologian, so he did not consider doctrinal exposition a gift he possessed. With respect to spirituality, he concentrated on encouraging the outward observance of the monks to be as perfect as possible with little exhortation concerning the inward life of prayer, which he left to the individual to cultivate.[411] Gregory Dix called him 'humble, paternal, zealous, efficient'.[412] The community had had the choice between an administrator or a charismatic communicator; they had chosen the former. If in the years to come they sometimes missed the benefits of the latter, they certainly reaped the rewards of the choice they did make.

Martin was not slow in taking up the reins of administrative power. Foremost was the restoration of financial stability to the community. The tenure on a cottage at Walsingham, taken at Easter 1930 to allow brethren to help in caring for pilgrims to the shrine there, was given up in December 1934 to save money.[413] The drain of the upkeep of the old abbey house at Pershore – virtually unlettable because of the terms of the original purchase and consequently empty for most of the years since the monks left in 1926 – was now tackled. Upkeep of the defective roof alone had been a source of large bills. Father Bartlett's loan from 1922 was paid off except for £500 due in two instalments in 1936 and 1937 respectively, and with the deeds finally in the community's hands, Abbot Martin arranged for the building's demolition.[414] Now free of encumbrance, the land was let and thereafter provided a modest income. An appeal was launched to raise money to replenish the community's 'well-nigh exhausted' reserves.[415]

Also in the first few years of his leadership, the constitution was finalized and signed by all the solemnly professed.[416] The issue of incorporation was pursued with more vigour until brought to a conclusion. The community gained official recognition as a charitable institution.[417] The community cemetery was completed. A new chapel was planned (although destined never to be built). Repairs to the house were expedited, as many matters were in need of attention, it being a decade since its purchase. On the outside, ivy was removed and donations were explicitly requested to restore the whitewash of the exterior. By late 1935, the roof, for the first time since the monks had arrived at Nashdom, was able to withstand the onslaught of heavy rain without springing leaks.[418]

The oblature too was organized. Abbot Denys had accepted external oblates as personal to him rather than to the community: all the decisions as to their acceptance and their rule were a matter for him alone. As a consequence, it was difficult to find even an authoritative list of those who had been accepted for this status and some were unclear about their obligations. Denys and Martin considered regulations for a separate intern oblature for priests in 1932 and the rules for them were accepted in principle later the same year.[419] But now the new abbot took hold of the issue as a whole – oblates internal and external – and made the process for receiving them clear and consistent. It would be Chapter that would make the decisions, as oblates would now be members of the community not associates of the abbot alone. They would have clear written obligations and personal rules. In time, there would be an oblate master who would bring forward names of those to be noviced to Chapter and then again when ready for profession. Denys's lay extern oblates, all of whom had made life commitments, were accepted *en bloc*. There were ten women, including the mother of Dom Augustine. Mrs Lilian Bond was the senior in profession,[420] although no one could establish exactly when she had been admitted, as Denys had kept no written records, but it was definitely at Pershore and hence before 1926.[421]

Another substantial matter was of great significance to the new abbot: the matter of ecumenical contacts. At the beginning of his abbacy, Martin expressed the wish that ecumenism should be a priority for the community. He wished to devote his abbacy to the object of the Reunion of Christendom.[422] This was also an Anglican project as the worldwide communion had been bidden to explore unity by the 1920 Lambeth Conference, resolutions 9–31 of that gathering being concerned with the subject and they included *The Appeal to All Christian People*.[423] There had been some response from the Orthodox churches and, initially, some interest from Roman Catholics, which led to the Malines Conversations already discussed.

But Roman Catholic–Anglican contacts in particular had suffered setbacks in recent years with the apparent petering out of those Malines Conversations with few tangible results. Then Pius XI's encyclical *Mortalium Animos* in January 1928, that forbade Roman Catholics from participating in Reunion movements, seemed to rule out any further discussions, at least for a generation. Added to this, the fiasco among Anglicans over parliament rejecting the new Prayer Book in 1927, and then again in 1928, had shown how captive the Church of England was to a House of Commons full of those who were not even Anglicans let alone

Catholic-minded Anglicans. This crisis reminded Anglo-Papalists how very far they had to go before they could achieve the goal of a Church of England able to reunite with Rome. The fact that they had disliked the new Prayer Book, for reasons such as its (to them inadequate) rubrics about reservation of the Blessed Sacrament was only small consolation.

Yet Reunion was the *raison d'être* of Anglo-Papalism and therefore the Nashdom community, despite the disappointments, was bound to pursue this goal. This did not only mean finding partners for dialogue. In perfecting their performance of the Catholic liturgy, the monks were in a real sense united with their Roman Catholic brethren in other Benedictine communities, which is why Martin laid so much stress on outward forms and the need never to deviate from the Roman way of doing things. This was a profound sharing – not, as his critics would have it, a slavish mimicry. It was an ecumenical deed more powerful than pages of words.

In the field of ecumenism, Martin was able to build on the wide foundations laid by Denys. With his command of many languages, Denys had been able to facilitate contacts throughout Europe, East as well as West. Among Anglo-Papalists in general, there existed a network of rumour and intrigue concerning ecumenical contacts with Rome, Constantinople and elsewhere, and Denys was informed from time to time of 'negotiations' supposedly taking place. During the First World War, amidst the division and horror of the conflict, there had appeared to be a desire for closer relations between churches so as to tip the European political balance towards reconciliation. Denys expressed this explicitly in a letter of 1917, along with his own doubts as to its eventual success. It sums up his attitude, both interested and involved yet ultimately sceptical about the long-term prospects for unity, so it is worth quoting at some length.

> ... it is only after the war that anything can be done for Re-union, if even then. To hurry things now would be fatal. The Bishop of Arras says that Benedict XV is preparing a scheme for our Conditional Re-ordination after the war; and much the same thing is said by Palmieri, one of the Pope's Officials in America, and a great authority on the Eastern Church. We are also in touch with some of the Dominicans in England, who are discussing matters with us (I mean by 'us' not ourselves here, but certain priests of the Catholic Party), and who are anxious to facilitate a Uniate Church in England, or some form of Inter-communion between the R.C.'s [sic]and us. I have just recently drawn up the lines of an interview with Benedict XV, touching on Reunion, which a friend of mine is having. He leaves for Italy tonight; ...
>
> I tell you this *in confidence*. Personally, I don't think anything will come of all these schemes. The time is not ripe. It is, however, possible

that, since we shall be closely bound up with France after the war, and the Holy See will have to keep on good terms with France after the war, B. XV may clear the air as to Anglican ordinations more than any of his predecessors have done. It is on record that Pius X [ie, the previous Pope who had died in 1914] told Prof. Briggs of the American Episcopal Church, who worked so hard for Reumion [sic], that the Papal condemnation of Anglican Orders was not an a [sic] Infallible Bull, but merely a disciplinary measure. On the other hand, we must reckon with the fact that our closer contact with the Eastern Church after the war will at first be adverse to any recognized intercommunion with Rome; and that the popular animus in England against the Pope in consequence of his supposed Germanizing tendencies, while as a matter of fact his policy has been one of the soundest during the war, is being exploited by the Archbishop of C. and many of the bishops in favour of an independent National Church.

... But all of this is conjecture. I doubt if anything can really be done in our life-time.[424]

This letter illustrates how Denys parted from the position of many Anglo-Papalists, many of whom fervently believed that their ecumenical goals could be reached in the foreseeable future. For Denys, Benedictinism and its establishment in the Church of England was of far greater importance than chasing dreams of corporate reunion. However, despite his scepticism, he was generally kept abreast of all the latest schemes and propositions.

Father Hrauda, who had stayed at Pershore in 1917–18, wrote to Denys in August 1921.[425] He claimed that a plan had again been put to Pope Benedict himself and involved a response to the Lambeth Appeal. He claimed that the Pope, Cardinal Bourne (head of Roman Catholics in England and Wales) and other Roman Catholic bishops had all approved. The Anglican bishops would be presented with this process for reunion and if they rejected it a group of Anglo-Catholic clergy would go ahead irrespective. This group would prepare by reading a prescribed set of theology texts and would then be 'examined' on them. Those who passed would be 're-ordained' as Roman priests at once. However, Hrauda ended by claiming that the 'negotiators' on returning to Britain 'found the opposition up in arms, & ready with plenty of cold water.' Other leaders of the Anglo-Papalist party believed more Anglicans needed to be brought into their fold before corporate reunion could be realistically attempted: premature action would see only a handful of essentially individual conversions, which would undermine the very concept of corporate reunion. (Little perhaps did Hrauda realize that this was essentially

Denys's view as well.) Unsurprisingly, the latest scheme (or attempt at one) came to nothing. In any case, the death of Pope Benedict XV in January 1922 and the election of Pius XI led to a lessening of Papal involvement in such proposals, although individual Roman Catholics remained committed to exploring ecumenism.

For Denys the problem was not the papacy so much (even though he criticized Rome's tendency to over systematize about inessentials) as the lack of unity among Anglo-Catholics.

> ... what proof is there in history that any religious movement has held its own for long without more coherence than the Anglo-Catholics have ever had? It is useless to quote the Eastern Church. The Eastern mind is not the Western, and the Eastern Church has been kept together largely through its attachment to the State. Where there has been no such link, it has gone to pieces, or has become fossilized and unmoral, its religion being largely spectacular liturgics. I am not sanguine about the Anglo-Catholic party, but this does not mean I am Romanizing.[426]

This is proof of Denys's desire to concentrate on strengthening Anglo-Catholicism and therefore the Church of England, so that Anglicanism was neither stifled by the state nor propped up by it, as some of the Orthodox churches were. Yet he is clear that this is not meant to be simply about reunion with Rome. Ecumenism was a long-term project and should involve all the Catholic-minded.

In the 1920s, therefore, Denys turned more frequently to contacts with the Orthodox churches and he became a Vice-President of the Anglican and Eastern Churches Association (whose chairman was Athelstan Riley, one of the community's most loyal supporters). Denys had an especial concern for the Russian Orthodox, particularly given the persecution of Christians in Russia since the 1917 Bolshevik Revolution. In 1928–29, a Russian émigré called Serge Bolshakoff[427] stayed at Nashdom Abbey for some time. He had originally studied to be a civil engineer, but, following the Russian Revolution in 1917, he had moved to Estonia, where he studied economics, sociology and theology. In 1924, at university, Bolshakoff had founded a lay religious society called the 'Logos Circle'. Three years later, its members had asked him to devise a new rule and constitution, as the old one was no longer practical now they were scattered throughout Europe. This request prompted a tour of European monasteries and, staying with French communities, he learned of Nashdom. To his delight, he discovered that its abbot spoke Russian. His dialogue with Denys could therefore reach an even greater depth of understanding than with other Religious superiors he had met.

During his long stay at Nashdom, Bolshakoff came to the view that the members of his society should become an independent confraternity of Benedictine oblates. Although the Benedictine Order was not present among the Religious communities of the Orthodox churches, nevertheless they still revered Benedict as a saint. This new confraternity had social action as its main objective[428] but now, as a result of Bolshakoff's link with Nashdom, it also dedicated itself to improve relations between Russian Orthodoxy and the Church of England.

The leader of the Russian Church abroad was (the exiled) Metropolitan Anthony of Kiev[429] and he gave his approval for this new oblate confraternity. Bolshakoff was formally clothed as a Benedictine oblate on 27 December 1928 in the chapel at Nashdom by the Russian Orthodox bishop in Berlin, Tikhon.[430] The Nashdom monks had received the bishop solemnly and, after the recitation of the Te Deum, he addressed them in Russian about the need for unity among Christians. (An attendant translated his words into French and then Gregory Dix translated the French into English.) Vespers followed and then the clothing. He left the next afternoon.[431] Later the following year, Metropolitan Anthony too visited Nashdom, as he was in Britain to consecrate Archimandrite Nicholas[432] as a bishop for the Russian Orthodox in England.[433]

These visitors to Nashdom became the first of a steady stream of contacts with the Orthodox churches. Many of them would happily say the Office with the Anglican monks and, until the 1960s, there was more 'warmth' in these relations than those with Roman Catholics.[434] For the Orthodox, who had a long-standing and intense rivalry with Rome, Nashdom presented them with a version of Catholicism with which they were able to feel more comfortable as it was not under direct Papal jurisdiction.

In contrast, contacts with Roman Catholic Religious and clergy in Britain tended to be by letter and for the purpose of scholarly communications, such as Augustine Morris's correspondence with Dom Bede Winslow,[435] a monk at Ramsgate Abbey, or Gregory Dix's with the Jesuit Maurice Bévenot.[436] A Nashdom monk would be regarded as 'pseudo-Benedictine' by many Roman Catholics and accorded no recognition by their hierarchy in Britain, not even to share a time of prayer.[437]

Roman Catholics in Belgium and France seemed to have less prejudice against Anglicans and some therefore saw the Nashdom monks in a different light. To them, Nashdom represented a part of Anglicanism with which dialogue was possible. The Anglican monks were using the same liturgy as they did and held almost the same doctrinal positions. Whereas many British Roman Catholics could not at this time overcome the view of Anglicans as bitter rivals for the leadership of the country's religion, continental Roman Catholics, being at a remove from the historic *political* animosities, were more likely to see the possibilities of partnership.

The Church Unity Octave, celebrated between 18 and 25 January,[438] was a significant catalyst here. This had been established in 1908 by a small Anglican Franciscan community in the USA, called the Society of the Atonement, and its leader, Father Paul Wattson,[439] after his correspondence with a priest in Britain, Father Spencer Jones.[440] Its purpose was to intercede for Christians to be united under the Pope. This Franciscan community was received into the Roman Catholic fold soon after, but Father Paul continued to observe the unity octave and made it part of the charism of his community. Commended by Pope Pius X on 27 December 1909, indulgences were granted to participants by Pope Benedict XV when he extended its observance to the whole of the Roman Catholic Church in 1916.[441] Decades before, the Anglican bishops at the 1878 Lambeth conference had called for a 'season of prayer' for unity near Ascension Day each year,[442] but only in 1894 was this implemented. Rome established its similar annual novena of prayer for unity in 1896 from the Feast of the Ascension to Pentecost. However, it was the January dates that gained momentum as an inter-denominational time of prayer, principally through the efforts of a French priest called the Abbé Paul Couturier.[443]

As well as being ordained, Couturier was a lecturer in science at a college in Lyon. In the years after the end of the First World War, he had come into contact with Russian émigrés, who widened his ecumenical outlook from the narrower views of his pre-war priestly formation. He then visited the Benedictine Abbey of Amay-sur-Meuse in Belgium, founded in 1925 by a friend of Cardinal Mercier called Dom Lambert Beauduin.[444] This new community was established in response to the 1924 initiative of Pope Pius XI when he asked Benedictines to devote one monastery in each congregation to the cause of Christian unity. The proposal in general saw no widespread response until the end of the 1950s, but the founding of the abbey at Amay – the 'Monks of Unity' as they became known – was its initial fruit. Beauduin coined the phrase 'The Church of England united not absorbed' to describe any future union. This phrase brought him such heavy criticism in the years after Cardinal Mercier's death that the Vatican exiled him from his community from 1928 until 1950. Only then was he allowed to rejoin them in their new home at Chevetogne. Hence, when Couturier visited Amay in 1932, its founder was not present, but his spirit still imbued the attitudes of the monks in residence.

Couturier met Serge Bolshakoff too. As Denys had told the Russian about the unity octave in the late 1920s, the latter had adopted it as an instrument of his own confraternity, and he spoke to Couturier about it. The French priest then pushed the idea of the octave in Lyon and broadened it to be a Week of Universal Prayer for Christian Unity in 1934, thus stripping it of its original more Papalist intention. Despite criticism from some in the Roman fold, the 'Week of Prayer' became a great success there in the mid-1930s, with substantial Orthodox participation.

As a result of conversation with Bolshakoff, the Abbé had made contact with Nashdom even before Abbot Denys's death. He wrote to ask the monks to participate in the observance alongside the Archdiocese of Lyon; each approached other Religious houses known to them to share in this intention.[445] At Ascensiontide 1936, Benedict Ley went on pilgrimage to Lyon[446] and met Couturier, from which a lifelong personal friendship began. Four months later, after Couturier had written to Martin requesting an Anglican speaker, Gregory Dix accompanied Father Fynes-Clinton,[447] an Anglo-Papalist incumbent in London and President of the Church Unity Octave Council, on a similar journey to Lyon, but this one had a more academic purpose. Once there, they gave papers (in French) on the relations between Rome and Canterbury and then later repeated them in Paris, where they lectured to Dominicans and Sulplicians. Gregory disarmed his audience by saying he too would have 'played safe' in 1896 and condemned Anglican orders as Pope Leo XIII had done that year in the encyclical *Apostolicae Curae*.[448]

Couturier came to England for the first time in September 1937. It was a personal trip with no official sanction. Dom Benedict Ley from Nashdom was one of those who met him on his arrival in London. The Abbé came again in 1938, this time with the backing of the new Archbishop of Lyon.[449] On both trips he stayed for some time at Nashdom and also visited other communities. The consequence of his two sojourns was the beginning of the official backing of the Church of England for the Week of Universal Prayer for Christian Unity. In such developments, the atmosphere of trust that the Nashdom monks engendered in their Roman Catholic friends was a significant part in ecumenical advance. Despite their apparent position on the margins of mainstream Anglicanism, their presence was of ecumenical significance. This was precisely the influence that Martin strove to win right from the beginning of his term of office.

One of the main instruments of ecumenism in the view of the Nashdom community was personal holiness. By striving for holiness of life, and thereby enacting a greater articulation of the truth of the Christian Gospel, churches would grow together spiritually, and therefore more effectively than through 'negotiations'. It was therefore understandable that Martin and his monks were very moved by the witness of nuns at the Trappistine monastery of Grottaferrata, located among the Albano Hills a half an hour out of Rome. Inspired by Couturier, the community there had made prayer for unity a priority. After the Week of Prayer in January 1937, one of their elderly sisters, Mother Immaculata Scalvini, had asked their Abbess, Mother Maria Pia Gullini,[450] if she could dedicate what remained of her life as an 'offering' for the cause. The Abbess agreed and unexpectedly within a month Immaculata had died (25 February 1937).[451] The nuns believed this was a sign of supernatural significance.

Couturier related this turn of events to Dom Benedict at Nashdom and the latter then began a spiritual correspondence with Mother Maria Pia in 1938.

> ... Among the principal commitments of the [Nashdom] community is that of working for the reunion of the Anglicans with the Roman Catholic Church. Therefore you can understand how the immense charity of Mother Immaculata struck me to the very depths of my heart.
>
> The visible acceptance of her offering on the part of the good God is for your separated brethren of England a most valid encouragement to persevere in their labour, often misunderstood and ridiculed, in order to return their Anglican brothers to the fold of Peter.[452]

The letter reveals how significant the response of a Roman Catholic community was for the aspirations of Nashdom. In a cool ecumenical climate, it was understandable that Benedict would be deeply touched that there was such spiritual support coming from someone far away. It was this sense of a spiritual link to which the Nashdom monks clung when official action from both sides was so weak for the goal of reunion. An ecumenical link of prayer had been established – and it was to become even more intense.

Each year in the Week of Prayer for Unity, the Abbess read Couturier's invitation to participate. After the 1938 week, another sister, this time one in her twenties and professed only a few months before, had responded by asking to make a parallel offering to Immaculata's. She appeared a fit and healthy young woman, yet, within weeks of making this suggestion, she became ill with tuberculosis. Sister Maria Gabriella[453] underwent much suffering during the next year and died on 12 April 1939. Throughout her ordeal, Benedict maintained contact with her community. His letters form part of the documentary evidence used to illustrate the power of the young nun's sacrificial offering. In the years following, her story inspired many and in 1983 she was beatified and made Patroness of Unity by Pope John Paul II. For Nashdom, she remained a special inspiration, and the link with Grottaferrata was treasured. Benedict and others from Nashdom prayed at her tomb in later years and attributed to her many 'favours'. The community sent its abbot to Rome in the 1980s to attend ceremonies leading to Maria Gabriella's beatification.

This type of spirituality may be less attractive to modern minds than it was in the 1930s. Embracing suffering and 'offering' it for particular causes may be analysed now and dismissed as unhealthy psychologically. That Maria Gabriella said she felt her life was worth very little, and that this offering therefore gave it meaning, could be interpreted as a case of low self-esteem being manipulated into self-destruction. Yet this would be to misunderstand the motivation. When soldiers fight for their country, they risk, and have sometimes to surrender, their lives for the protection of the people, and way of life, that they love. This 'ultimate sacrifice' had not been something rare for this generation. Such a witness hung heavily in many European societies in the first half of the twentieth century. In 1938, the appalling loss of life of one world war had ceased barely twenty years previous, and another equally devastating and seemingly inevitable conflict already threatened, owing to the seizure of power by dictators in several countries, including Italy. The poverty of many European societies from economic depression had also meant suffering and hardship were close at hand for the poorer classes. In such an environment, to give one's life for a cause was not so unimaginable as it is to those inhabiting a rich and more individualistic society in the twenty-first century.

For Martin and his community in the late 1930s, the fact that a young Roman Catholic nun would ask to give her life for the cause they held most dear was a precious reaching out. It revealed that others felt, as they did, that reunion was the greatest prize of all and to which it was worth dedicating one's life. It was therefore a justification of the vocation of the Nashdom monks. In a time when many Roman Catholics rarely took Anglican Religious seriously, the sense of creating a bridge across the denominational divide was powerful. It was spiritual comradeship of the most dramatic force.

All the looking outward to Christians of other communities did not mean that Martin neglected relationships within the Church of England. Here, one of the main channels of influence was through working with other Religious communities. He was keen to recruit others into the Nashdom orbit. The sisters of Edgware Abbey had embraced the Benedictine Rule formally in 1935, and in turn they gave refuge to some smaller communities: The Canonesses Regular of Our Lady of Victory and later the Sisters of the Transfiguration. The Sisters of St Peter at Laleham Abbey, under the forceful Mother Sarah,[454] also looked to Nashdom for a paternal oversight and Martin became their 'regular superior'. The new abbot encouraged the Society of the Good Shepherd on Canvey Island to move towards Benedictinism too. Originally under the Franciscan Society of the Divine Compassion, the sisters appointed Martin their Warden in 1936 and they soon adopted the *Rule of St Benedict* in modified form. When their Foundress[455] died in 1938, the sisters elected an SSP sister from Laleham to be their new mother, and then they moved to Twyford in Berkshire to live a more contemplative Benedictine life nearer to Nashdom. Martin was also involved in the last years of the small Benedictine Community of St Mary and St Scholastica[456] and later with the Community of St Katharine of Egypt. However, he did not realize the long-term goal of a 'congregation' of Benedictines in any substantial or long-lasting form, an aspiration that was destined to remain elusive.[457]

Perhaps the main reason it remained so was that any congregation created in the 1930s, while it would have been led by Martin and the Nashdom monks, would nevertheless have been dominated by nuns and sisters, as the only possible partners in the congregation were the women's communities already mentioned.[458] It is clear too that the Abbess of Edgware and the Mother Superior of Laleham, while anxious to have the guidance of Nashdom with respect to liturgy and worship, and as a counterweight to support them if they experienced episcopal pressure, nevertheless were far too strong-minded to submit to a new structure that would limit their own power. Both exponents of 'personal rule', they were women operating in a male-dominated world and, to safeguard the well-being of their communities, they had to be robust in ecclesiastical dealings. Abbot Martin therefore may well have concluded on reflection that he too might be best advised to keep some distance from their autocratic impulses. Finally, the other potential partner in any 'congregation' would have been the community at Malling Abbey. Yet after Denys had broken the connection with them in 1915–16 (see chapter 3), the nuns' spiritual adviser, Father Vasey, remained wary of any involvement with Pershore/Nashdom. After his death, Abbess Magdalen Mary[459] retained a similar caution. So, despite Martin mentioning them to the Chapter when he raised the congregational idea, it is unlikely they would have been tempted to participate in any formal alliance.

Another important goal was realized however, with significant input from the Benedictines of Nashdom – the creation of an advisory council to consider the issues of concern between bishops and Religious communities.[460] As discussed in chapter 5, in 1925–26 the then Archbishop of Canterbury, Randall Davidson, had used the Pershore community as a 'test case' for his own suggested regulations for this delicate relationship. When the Benedictines moved to Nashdom, he referred the matter of such rules to a committee of bishops. They considered several drafts and they intended to put their refined proposals to the 1930 Lambeth

Conference. Rumours of what was afoot reached various communities and they began to fear their exclusion from the process. A meeting was called in Oxford in January 1930 attended by about one hundred Anglican Religious. Abbot Denys was unable to attend and so Martin represented the Nashdom monks, with Anselm attending to represent the Edgware sisters. The bishops' proposals were deemed utterly unacceptable by the gathering, as they would have given bishops a wide range of powers to interfere in the internal affairs of a community. An advisory committee was formed of bishops and Religious to review the matter in more detail and Denys was asked to be a member, as a consequence of his immense knowledge of the history of Religious life. He was assiduous in attending its deliberations, but no agreements were ever reached either before or after the Lambeth Conference. At further open meetings of community representatives Anselm and Benedict accompanied him.[461] One major sticking point was whether communities could choose their own Bishops Visitor or whether the diocesan bishops would have that power.

The only decision eventually reached was to continue the advisory committee, but make it official (The Advisory Council on the Relations of Bishops and Religious Communities), and it came into formal existence in 1935. Originally it was expected in time to produce regulations and those communities that 'signed up' to them would have the right to vote for representatives for the next Advisory Council. In the end, there was no 'registration' procedure as the council decided its 'directory' of regulations would be voluntary. Through the decades since, this has worked well and both communities and bishops have kept to the suggested guidelines without controversy.

The reason for this outcome had much to do with Abbot Martin. Whilst most communities were exercised about the issue of Visitors, for Nashdom and the communities close to it, there was a second issue: liturgy. The whole spirit of Nashdom was tied to the use of the Roman Catholic missal and the Office books of Roman Catholic Benedictines. All were in Latin. The fear was that any body given power to create regulations for Religious might at some point decide to insist on the use of Anglican liturgical forms and the *Book of Common Prayer*, which would be unacceptable to Nashdom. Martin therefore was determined to hold firm against any legislation or any rules whatsoever if they were deemed binding on all communities. Once the principle had been surrendered even on matters that were uncontroversial, opposition on matters that were more significant would be weakened. When Martin presented the proposal concerning the setting up of the Advisory Council to the Nashdom Chapter, it was minuted that they did not believe that the abbot accepting a seat on the new body committed them to 'any agreement'.[462]

The superiors not concerned about the issue of Roman Catholic liturgies were, nevertheless, afraid of the communities as a whole being split into factions. They were still suspicious of episcopal involvement in their affairs and attempts to control them, and so it was essential that all of them spoke with one voice. In this they took their lead from Father O'Brien,[463] Superior-General of SSJE, who formed an alliance with Martin to ensure that nothing was agreed without unanimous support. It was a successful collaboration and led to others in future years, most notably on the opposition to the Church of South India Scheme. It marked the acceptance by the other (then) major men's communities – Society of St John the Evangelist, Society of the Sacred Mission and the Community of the Resurrection – of the Benedictines as a crucial element in Religious life in the Church of England. This is shown by the fact that in the first edition of the Council's 'Directory' of voluntary regulations, published in 1943, he was able to have inserted a separate excursus on Benedictinism.[464] Denys had been intellectually impressive, but was a muddled communicator in public situations, and somewhat over-sensitive and unpredictable. Martin was much more a man with whom they could establish relations. He was reliable, thorough and consistent. They may not have always agreed with all his views but they knew where they stood.

Martin's contributions at the regular meetings of the Advisory Council helped establish a reputation for both himself and Nashdom, and with the bishops as well as the other Religious superiors. Bishop Walter Frere, the Bishop Visitor at Nashdom, and himself a member of the Community of Resurrection, wrote to the Archbishop of Canterbury in 1936,

> I am much better pleased (or less displeased) with the whole Abbey than I was. It has got out of several bad ruts, I think: & is now at least respectable, however popish.[465]

This change of perception must be credited in significant part to Abbot Martin.

The other noteworthy achievement of Martin's abbacy was the foundation of a priory in the United States.[466] Most Benedictine foundations arise from a community deciding to send a group of its members to establish a new priory elsewhere, just as the Pershore monks had gone to Kumasi. Then if local vocations arise, the priory may well grow and eventually become independent of the 'mother' house. In the case of Nashdom's American priory, the initiative came from outside. It was American aspirants wishing to begin Benedictine life in the Episcopal Church of the USA who asked Nashdom to train them. Foremost among these was Father F Rolland Severance, Professor of Apologetics at the Anglo-Catholic Nashotah Seminary in Wisconsin. Some of the ordinands at the college were also interested in Religious life. To support these men, Father Vivan Peterson[467] of St James's, Cleveland, in Ohio, became the leader of a group calling itself the American Benedictine Foundation, which aimed to raise funds to make a new venture possible. In time, it began a publication called *Benedicite* to provide information for members and potential supporters. Father Peterson had known of the community since its Pershore days and saw the value of aspirants being trained by an established monastery.

Anselm Hughes crossed the Atlantic several times to earn money for Nashdom by giving lectures on medieval music. He was on such a tour in the autumn of 1934, including a visit in November to Nashotah. In the United States, as he later reported informally to Chapter, he had meetings with no fewer than twenty aspirants, and had been informed that 'a fine estate, with premises' had been offered as a location for a monastery. However, it was not possible for Martin to send monks to train the aspirants in the USA. The Nashdom community still had only seven in solemn profession.[468] Bernard had only recently moved to London, and Michael and Augustine were studying for ordination. The only solution was for the Americans to train in Britain.

Matters moved quite speedily, and on Christmas Eve 1935, Father Severance arrived at Nashdom to begin a postulancy. The following Epiphany, Father Theodore Black joined him. They were clothed together as novices on 25 May 1936, then simply professed for three years on 29 June 1937, taking the names Paul and Meinrad respectively. Five more priests arrived between August 1936 and September 1937. One managed to stay only six weeks, another three months, while two others, Leo and Francis Hilary, were professed during 1937–38. By mid-1938, there were therefore four American monks in junior profession and one novice.

The political situation in Europe was worsening, with Nazi Germany's annexation of Austria in March 1938, and the prospect of further threats from the same source against other countries in central Europe. By the end of the summer, three of the professed Americans had been at Nashdom for two years, judged to be the required minimum, and Martin decided they should look to make the foundation sooner rather than later. A most suitable property at Rye Beach had been offered the brethren, fully furnished and ready for occupancy. Martin wrote to the Bishop of New Hampshire, John T Dallas, asking for his permission for the priory to be founded, as it was to be located in that diocese. When Paul arrived back in the USA in October 1938, he found to his dismay that the bishop would not discuss the matter, saying he was 'utterly opposed' to the idea, and refused even to answer any questions.[469] Certainly one of the people who had influenced the bishop was the Archbishop of Canterbury. Bishop Dallas had written to him in September, asking confidentially of the 'advisability of encouraging them, a group which apparently look toward Rome'.[470] Archbishop Lang's reply was unequivocal,

> ... I write quite privately as otherwise I could not give you the advice which I ought to give in answer to your request.
>
> I am bound to say frankly that I regard this Community with considerable suspicion and I have not a great deal of confidence in the Abbot. It has indeed some members of a different kind such as Dom Bernard Clements who is now Vicar of All Saints, Margaret Street, and in much demand throughout the country as a preacher and religious influence. But the Community as a whole seems to me to be definitely on the Romeward side and I think you would be running considerable risks if you welcomed a branch of it in your Diocese.[471]

The American bishop may have received other advice too but this letter must surely have influenced his negative decision. There is little further evidence to suggest why Lang had taken such a dislike to Abbot Martin. Perhaps it was because he saw the growing influence of Nashdom on other parts of the Church of England and was uneasy. Perhaps he feared the monks would become Roman Catholics and cause a sensation as Caldey had done a generation earlier. Martin was 'one of the most active members' of the Advisory Council, according to Bishop Kirk[472] of Oxford,[473] so the Archbishop would have been made aware of the abbot's staunch views on church matters. He certainly did not like Martin wearing a mitre, any more than his predecessor had Denys. He let Nashdom's Bishop Visitor know that Martin had worn a white mitre at the requiem in London for Metropolitan Anthony of Kiev, and the Archbishop regarded it as 'rather absurd that the Abbot should dress up in this way at public functions.'[474] By 1938, Archbishop Lang had clearly found his negative image re-enforced a sufficient number of times for him to contribute to the blocking of the well-made plans for an American priory.

However, the American brethren had done novitiates at Nashdom in order to found a house in their own country. Paul could not give up and go back to England. He began to search for an alternative home. Negotiations with the Bishop of Northern Indiana resulted in the offer of a house in his diocese at Valparaiso, where the brethren were expected to run three missions. The bishop proved understanding about their liturgical needs. The internal affairs of the house were subject to the authority of Martin and the bishop allowed them to use the Latin Missal and

Breviary in their chapel. The new foundation, St Gregory's, opened in March 1939 and gradually took shape. Father Francis was an artist and his talents were used in carving for the oratory and in arranging the furnishings they had. The monks made their own choir-stalls and prayer-desks. The four simply-professed eventually settled there: Paul, Meinrad, Leo and Francis: the novice, Clement, decided to withdraw soon after his return to the USA. Paul was made head of house and was incumbent of the parish, and the others worked in different parts of the mission districts. They were poor and their life was frugal, but in this they shared the hardship of many whom they served.

Back at Nashdom, the Chapter worked out the guidelines for the relationship between the abbey and its new foundation, made complex because of the outbreak of the Second World War in September 1939.[475] For example, the abbot's proposed visit across the Atlantic in 1940[476] had to be cancelled. The American brothers alone were to vote on professions to their own community, although their decisions were subject to ratification by the abbot and Chapter in Britain.

The difficulty with the new foundation was that, while the Divine Office was observed from 6 May 1939, the house was still in many ways a clergy house more than a monastery. The rhythms and focus of Religious life in which they had been trained at Nashdom were by necessity blurred by the exigencies of the demanding mission work. Whether this was the reason or some other factor was paramount, nevertheless two of the four vocations became insecure. In May 1940, Paul and Meinrad were elected to solemn vows,[477] but the profession never went ahead. Meinrad had concluded that he could not proceed and then left the community when his three years in temporary vows expired.[478] Leo also decided to leave some months later.

Paul felt it best not to take solemn profession alone and so renewed his simple vows in June 1940. When Francis was elected to solemn vows early in 1941,[479] the two remaining monks took solemn life vows together on 21 March 1941. The claustral prior of Nashdom, Anselm Hughes, received the professions in the presence of the diocesan bishop,[480] who became the Episcopal Visitor. The house could now formally be designated a priory with Dom Paul its first conventual prior.

Six months later the USA entered the Second World War after its naval base at Pearl Harbour was attacked by Japan. Back in Europe, the conflict had already been raging for two years and the life of Nashdom had long been interrupted. The abbey was now full of nuns and children under their care. As for the monks, they had been on the move.

⊕

9

Rising to Challenges

The outbreak of another war in Europe in September 1939 was not a surprise given the political tension of the previous few years. The territorial demands of Nazi Germany against its neighbours meant that the advent of war appeared only a matter of 'when' and not 'if'. So preparations for a European conflict were evident long before the eventual declaration of hostilities. The monks were not immune to this political climate and made contingency plans.

> In the event of war our National Service would continue to be what it is now – the Opus Dei. But, foreseeing that it would almost certainly be impossible to continue the solemn public recitation in choir, we have been through a course of instruction for the St. John Ambulance Association, and eighteen of the brethren have already passed the qualifying examination. We shall thus, in an emergency, be able to give help as a single unit.[481]

Abbess Raphael at Edgware realized war would necessitate the removal of her community and the disabled children in its care to a safer location than the outskirts of London: Nashdom was her choice, the 'nearest and most convenient refuge', as the Abbey notes put it.[482] Martin therefore agreed the monks would move. The SSP sisters at Laleham, near Staines, ran a school and they too felt they must evacuate their children's work from the expected air attack on the capital. Mother Sarah offered their vacated school to Martin as a temporary home for his monks. A few stayed on in the guest house at Nashdom to help the Edgware nuns run the monastery and act as local ARP wardens. Gregory Dix went to run his ordained brother's parish in Beaconsfield when the latter went off to be a forces chaplain, and Maurus Benson[483] accompanied him as his assistant. The rest of the monks moved to Laleham.[484] It was a short sojourn however. By January 1940, the SSP sisters concluded that the mass evacuation of children from London had been an unnecessarily cautious move and wished to reopen their school at Laleham. To facilitate this, the Nashdom monks moved to the guest house of Malling Abbey in Kent, which had its own large chapel created from a medieval tithe barn.[485] When the Malling nuns left their main abbey for the greater safety of a house in Herefordshire in May 1940, the monks then moved into the more spacious accommodation of the abbey itself. This was their third move in nine months.

However, the community's numbers were reducing. The circumstances of the war meant only five new postulants entered during the next six years of the conflict, although four of these eventually proceeded to vows. At the same time, others, who had been professed before the war, withdrew. Martin had known from the onset that his younger non-ordained brethren were liable for 'call-up' to the forces, and many in any case felt it their duty to volunteer. His hopes that they would be taken as a unit into the RAMC[486] proved unfulfilled. Several left without permission and the Chapter minutes over the next few years note three occasions where monks were 'dismissed'. This was the usual response to a monk leaving of his own volition instead of with the abbot's agreement. Others waited for their simple vows to expire before leaving for the forces, or they were formally granted 'leave'. Brother Anthony (Hyde Phillips) joined the Tank Corps and was sent to the North African front. He was killed on active service in the Libyan desert in July 1942. Although his simple vows had by that time lapsed and he was no longer formally a member of the community, the brethren still felt his loss.

In October, a more significant loss had to be borne: Bernard, still a vicar in London, died unexpectedly aged sixty-two, of complications following an operation on his appendix. As a broadcaster and preacher, he was one of the public faces of Nashdom, and, as noted in the letter from Archbishop Lang already quoted, he was an 'acceptable' monk to the leaders of the Church. The reputation that led to this judgement was based much on his preaching. Bernard was concerned in sermons with how to be a Christian and live a good life, and not in any consideration of complicated theological controversy, so his words had an immediate relevance, something to say even to a non-churchgoer. The BBC broadcast a service from All Saints', Margaret Street: Bernard as Vicar was the preacher. One of those involved in it noted in the relevant BBC file: 'The Church should be used again; the singing was lovely and the address simple, direct and telling.'[487] It was Bernard's conversational style that appealed to a radio audience. Instead of preaching grandly to a gathering, Bernard's voice and words had an intimacy that seemed to speak to each listener personally.

The first successful broadcast sermon led to Bernard being asked to do a series of short lectures on prayer on five successive Sunday afternoons in the autumn of 1935.[488] Further invitations followed and Bernard's fame reached its zenith during the first years of the Second World War, the years immediately prior to his death. This meant a huge audience for his ministry, which led to him receiving hundreds of letters each week; he had to hire a secretary to deal just with this correspondence. The radio audience responded to his combination of honesty and realism with a sense of encouragement and solidarity the Gospel message brought, especially amidst the pain and anxiety of wartime.

He did 'thoughts for the day' before the morning 8 a.m. news bulletin, as well as Sunday slots, with further addresses being broadcast at special times such as Holy Week. His short, pithy homilies during the weekly broadcasts to the troops in Malta during 1941–42, a series that lasted over a year, were also well-received. His first book of sermons came out in 1930, when he was still resident overseas, but a series of around a dozen books, putting his broadcasts into printed form, began in 1936, and some went into reprint several times within the first year after publication. How could the Archbishop not judge this monk 'acceptable'? Bernard was preaching the Gospel movingly to a far wider audience than any one church pulpit could ever reach.

Bernard's influence and public profile were incalculable and were significant in giving his community a 'name' both in the church and among the more diffuse and diverse audience of the BBC. His death was therefore a great blow to the community and he was much missed in its deliberations in subsequent years.

In November 1942 came another loss: Brother Thomas More. Adrian Bishop,[489] as he was known before his monastic life, had joined the community in 1937, after a flamboyant and unusual life. He had seen service in the First World War before studying classics at King's College, Cambridge. He had a gifted mind and a great facility for learning languages quickly, was famous for his charm, and entertained with his witty, intelligent conversation. He went to Austria after graduation to continue his studies (and so for the rest of his life would speak German with a Viennese accent). Sadly, he frittered away his time there. Consequently, he lost his chance of an academic career.[490] He took a job with an oil company, lived in Persia (now Iran), where again he became quickly fluent in the local language. But discovery of his risky homosexual private life eventually lost him his job and he spent the first half of the 1930s earning a living by translating and language teaching in various European countries. Many thought of him as brilliant but too hedonistic and lacking in self-discipline to put his talents to creative use. One writer remembered him as 'a handsome ill-fated dandy', another as a 'wonderfully gifted and charming man'.[491]

According to one of his close friends, the Oxford academic Maurice Bowra, Adrian 'regarded most orthodox opinion as a conspiracy against enjoyment' and expressed a 'belligerent rejection of religion'.[492] However, when in the USA in the winter of 1936–37, Bowra received a letter from Adrian saying that he had become a Christian, after recovering from a serious bout of sleepy sickness.

> His hostility to religion and his derisive jokes about it indicated that it played a larger part in his mind than if he had been merely indifferent. His letter was in his usual comic vein and did not state anything clearly, but there was no doubt that something transcendent had happened. He had had a vision, and it had changed his life.[493]

The result was that he entered the Nashdom community in 1937, and was elected to simple vows in November 1938. With respect to Religious life, Bowra related that his friend 'accepted with delight all its obligations' and 'treated it with utmost seriousness'.

In 1940, Brother Thomas More was recalled for intelligence work in the army, first with the prospect of going to Europe; but in the event, with the fall of France in mid-1940, he was instead first sent to Baghdad (Iraq) and then Tehran (Iran). He remained a monk, but one 'on leave', and renewed his vows in 1942 while serving in the Middle East. He died in Tehran in October 1942 when he fell several storeys through a stairwell after a banister gave way.[494] This was another significant loss for the community as he,

> ... had won great esteem and affection during the short time he had been with us; and there were those who looked forward to seeing him play an important part in the development of the Community, for he possessed great gifts not only in scholarship and devotion, but also in personality ...[495]

These losses from among the brethren added to the air of uncertainty about the future that was now a part of their lives. Settled at Malling, monastic life was daily disrupted by air-raids and sirens, necessitating the monks, even if in the middle of the Divine Office, evacuating to the safety of the abbey's cellars. Kent was an area where many dog-fights between German and British aircraft took place, and crashing planes and descending parachutists were not uncommon sights. Surprisingly the only close encounters with bombs that the abbey suffered were when one dropped in the driveway (though causing only minimal damage) and another, more tragically, destroyed some cottages outside the grounds, causing the deaths of eight people (six of whom were children).[496] Once the Battle of Britain was over, however, the dangers were less threatening, as Martin noted in a letter in 1942,

> Here except for the noise of planes and all too frequent funerals of RAF men, there might not be war at all; I can't say how long this will last, but it has been thus for a long time now.[497]

By the end of 1942, the tide of the war began to turn against Germany and its allies and by the end of 1944 the eventual defeat of Nazism seemed inevitable, even if the final victory would take some time to accomplish. By the autumn of 1944, the Malling nuns were keen to return home and the monks were 'house-hunting'.[498] The Sisters of the Church lent the monks 73 Christchurch Avenue in Brondesbury, north London, and the move there took place the next spring. It needed to be only a short-term refuge, as, with peace in Europe, the Edgware nuns managed to organize returning to their own premises sooner than anticipated. At last, the community could reassemble back at Nashdom on 16 August 1945.[499]

Absence from Nashdom during the war years did not mean the community halted its confident presence in the Church. Much of that presence was achieved around the quixotic personality of Gregory Dix. It is not the aim of this book to give a biography or historical judgement on Dix, as he has been the subject of work elsewhere.[500] Yet, his influence both in scholarship and ecclesiastical politics was the spearhead of that gained for Nashdom Abbey itself, so that he needs to be considered at this juncture in his work on behalf of the community.

In academic writing, his most famous contribution was *The Shape of the Liturgy*,[501] a massive book of over seven hundred pages published in 1945, which brought together many of the scholarly insights of the liturgical movement to present a case for revision of the eucharistic rites. Written with style and lucidity, it captured not only the attention of the academic community, but also many clergy and laity in the Church. Subsequent critiques of aspects of the book's thesis cannot detract from the observation that for more than a generation this book came to dominate liturgical debate and reform. It was part of a scholarly contribution of books, articles and reviews that spanned the period from the late 1920s to the 1950s. Certainly Gregory was the person whose contributions gave *Laudate* (the community's regular periodical) its academic edge once more, after the decline of Denys's literary powers.

Yet if it was his academic output that made him respected, it was Gregory's sharp personality that made him notorious. His fellow monk and friend, Augustine Morris, recalled that there were three stages to 'getting to know' Gregory: initially, one would be charmed and impressed; then came the shock of discovering his acerbic critical side, which could 'sting' people; and finally in time came the engagement with the 'genuine' man underneath the acid tongue. Many people walked away at stage two and remained wary or hostile.[502] Gregory had a quick mind that could turn to wit or withering sarcasm: he was the master in debate of the clinical 'put-down' that could appear to demolish his opponents, (even if in retrospect it might be judged he was the one in error). Thus he was a formidable participant in meetings and conferences, to which his scholarly reputation won him invitations. But his style, while devastatingly effective on an immediate level, did not necessarily win him further support. A participant would recall of one meeting that

> The discussions were dominated by Dix whom I found charming, brilliant and totally unconvincing.[503]

There was a sense in which Gregory's sharpness limited his (and therefore Nashdom's) influence. A thoughtful engagement with another's point of view can win that person to your cause whereas a scathing dismissal usually alters nothing. Gregory for all his fluent interventions could be guilty of this misjudgement. What redeemed him in these situations was that there was nothing personal in his attacks. He found it as easy to be friendly to his opponents after a debate as he did to attack them during it.

Gregory's fight for the Anglo-Papalist cause reached a certain climax during the years of the Second World War, owing to the issue of the Church of South India. In this he was pivotal not only in putting his community at the forefront of a fierce ecclesiastical controversy, but also in seeing that Nashdom led the Religious communities as a whole even into defiance of the Archbishop of Canterbury.

Christians in the Indian sub-continent had long found it difficult to evangelize among the non-Christian majority of that vast country because of the competing claims of different denominations. To the religious sensibilities of many Indians, these clashing beliefs and practices made no sense. The more tolerant outlook of the majority religion, Hinduism, compared favourably with the rivalry of the different churches, and, throughout much of the nineteenth century, Christian missionaries were holding meetings to find some way of mitigating the negative effect of their denominational quarrels. Early in the twentieth century, the Presbyterians, Congregationalists and some others in south India united into one ecclesiastical body: the South India United Church. This was despite the fact that their denominations remained separated elsewhere in the world. In 1919, negotiations began to bring the Methodists and the Anglicans of the same region into this union, and thereby create a new and episcopal Church of South India. The process gained the encouragement of the 1930 Lambeth Conference of Anglican bishops.

This possible union was an anathema to the Anglo-Papalists. Firstly, in principle, they opposed anything that suggested ecumenism was a matter of pan-Protestantism. Protestants, they believed, were happy to join together by loose associations in which there was still no definitive doctrinal agreement, content to remain 'congregationalist' at heart with no Church in the Catholic understanding of the word. The Anglo-Papalists advocated reunion around the leadership of Rome, and with the goal of a universal Catholic Church built upon the historic episcopate handed down from bishop to bishop since the time of the first Apostles. Pan-Protestantism would in their view impede this goal because the larger the Protestant 'association' was, the less doctrinally defined it would be, and therefore the more resistant to union with dogmatic Roman Catholicism.

Secondly, they were opposed to Anglicans in particular taking part in such unions because they believed that Anglicanism was a legitimate, though separated part, of the Catholic Church, as it had upheld the sacraments and the historic episcopate. It was therefore Catholic not Protestant. Methodism, Congregationalism and the other denominations had not done so and were therefore unquestionably Protestant. If Anglicans united with Protestants, they would not lead Protestants to become Catholic, but rather lose their own Catholic legitimacy, which would impair immeasurably the possibility of reunion with Rome. This is why the issue of the Church of South India was such an enormous problem for Anglo-Papalists. They felt that everything they stood for was at stake.

In addition, as the process of union in south India seemed to be heading to a conclusion in the 1940s, the precise terms themselves of the agreement began to make the matter even more contentious. One example will suffice: the ministers of the non-Anglican churches in the union would not be required to be 're-ordained' by a bishop in the Apostolic Succession. All those in the Church of South India to be ordained in the future would be episcopally ordained, but there would be no retrospective action. This meant that the Catholic validity of the sacraments in the new united church could not be guaranteed for at least a generation. For all Anglo-Catholics in the widest sense, the new church could therefore not remain part of the Anglican Communion. For any Archbishop of Canterbury to contemplate acceding to this agreement would be to acquiesce in a schism from the Anglican fold. It was painful for a part of the Communion to break away, but for it to separate by the agreement of the Archbishop of Canterbury was for Anglo-Papalists an utter scandal.

William Temple,[504] translated from York to Canterbury in 1942, became the target of their wrath.

For Gregory, this was a perfect vehicle for his polemical political talents. He believed this was an opportunity for the male Religious communities as a group. Whilst sympathetic bishops were in a complicated position because of their place in the Establishment, and would have to be judicious in their interventions, however passionately they felt about the matter, the communities were in contrast far freer. For Gregory, the Nashdom monks must spearhead a lucid public denunciation of the scheme. If the male communities of the Church of England had come into alliance through the creation of the Advisory Council, the opposition to the Church of South India scheme became the first occasion on which they could work together effectively on a particular campaign outside the issues that were of concern only to themselves.

Opponents of the south India scheme had had a meeting with Archbishop Temple in January 1943, as the proposals were to be debated in the Church's Convocations of clergy during that year and consideration given to the Church of England's relations with the proposed new body. The delegation included the former superior of the Community of the Resurrection, Keble Talbot,[505] as well as three academics and the poet T S Eliot. Temple, however, was clear that the union scheme was the responsibility of the participants themselves and that he could not directly interfere. His view was that the new church would grow into Catholicity. This was worth the short-term ecclesiastical ambiguity that the union presented. A partial communion would remain in place with the new Church of South India until such time as it had grown into full Catholic order.

This was unacceptable to the Anglo-Papalists. There was either full communion or none. There could be no fudging of the matter. Gregory was determined the communities should take a stand and he pressed for a meeting of the leaders. Later in 1943, representatives of five men's communities[506] met at the CR retreat house at St Leonard's-on-Sea. Nashdom was represented by Abbot Martin, Gregory and Anselm (at last back from the USA), with the abbot choosing Augustine as the fourth member of their group. Father O'Brien, the superior of SSJE, attended and CR's group was led by their newly-elected superior, Raymond Raynes,[507] a contemporary of Gregory's in Oxford in the early 1920s. There were no minutes kept of the meeting and so only the participants could later attest to what happened. Years later, Augustine could still remember clearly some of the events of the meeting.[508]

Raynes, zealous and dominant in his own community, seemed determined to take charge and assumed the chair. But Martin quickly took the initiative and suggested that another of the CR delegation, Rupert Mounsey,[509] should act as chair. Mounsey had been a bishop in Borneo, but had retired back to England through ill-health during the First World War. After a few years as a vicar in London, he had joined CR at the age of fifty-seven. By this meeting, he was in his mid-seventies and the senior in age present. By pushing him to be chair, Martin had neutralized the eager Raynes from any chance of dominating the gathering.[510] Augustine remembered that it was Raynes and Gregory Dix who were the principal debaters, and that the lively discussion was of high intellectual content. It was by no means a foregone conclusion as to what action the participants would agree.

The final product, dated 4 November 1943, was the 'The Unity of the Faith: an Open Letter to His Grace the Lord Archbishop of Canterbury from the Superiors of certain Religious Communities' – soon published as a pamphlet by Dacre Press. The Archbishop was alarmed at the final section that threatened schism by 'hundreds, we might say thousands, of loyal clergy, with strong lay support'. It was a threat to create a separate 'Church of England' made up of those who held an Anglo-Papalist view, a kind of 'Non-Juring church'. Ironically, it was an attempt to prevent a schism in India by threatening another in Britain; the serious difficulties of such an action were pointed out to Gregory by his friend Bishop Kirk of Oxford.[511]

To Temple, the tone of the offending sentences in the open letter was not merely forceful but blackmailing – and this was the likely reason that Stephen Bedale,[512] superior of SSM, refused to join the others and sign the document, even though he was against the South India scheme itself. Despite a private meeting with the group of Religious, the Archbishop could not persuade them to omit the threat. Gregory was clear that they should not give way,

> I feel very reluctant to omit the passage. ... because I do not believe that anything but a clear threat will stop the slide now. But a clear threat very well *might* stop it at this stage. And I do want to stop it, because the alternative is disintegration.[513]

One of the formulations in the document was certainly drafted by Richard Roseveare[514] of SSM and Augustine during a morning coffee break.[515] That Gregory was instrumental in writing much of the letter, however, is probable. The Archbishop certainly believed it was Gregory who was behind the text as a whole.[516] Including a threat of the consequences of ignoring the missive was typical of Gregory's polemic style. Backed by Martin, he was here showing the freedom of action possible by Religious.

Parish priests were dependent on their bishops, even when they did not like them, and it was far more difficult for them to speak out. Nashdom was showing that Religious communities could speak out on their behalf and be leaders of the Anglo-Papalist movement not just prayerful adherents of it. However, it should be added that he was in his own mind seriously exaggerating his possible support,

> I feel utterly miserable about the whole affair, but much more determined than before that I won't accept, come what may. I think you may take it as probable that the day after the Archb[isho]p's present proposals take effect the only Religious Communities left in the Provinces of Cant[erbur]y and Y[or]k will be Kelham & the Prioress of Whitby (with perhaps a sprinkling of odd members of other C[ommuni]ties.)[517]

There is no evidence to indicate such an exodus would in practice have taken place. In the long run, the threat neither achieved its end nor was it implemented. The Church of South India came into being in 1947, and in 1950 compromise proposals, from among others Bishop Kirk of Oxford, took much of the heat out of the issue.[518] The resulting negotiations are outside the scope of this study, but what needs to be noted here is that Gregory's tactics in 1943 had made Lambeth take notice of Nashdom, but their argument had not prevailed. It was the principled but undramatic approach of Kirk that brought a solution. For all the fireworks, Gregory and Martin had won only a hardening of suspicion about their community.

One unforeseen consequence of the South India controversy was the issue of Nashdom's Bishop Visitor. To appreciate this fully, we have to go back a little to just before the Second World War. After the death of Bishop Frere CR in 1938, the monks had hoped that the Bishop of Oxford, Kenneth Kirk, would agree to be his successor. Although he did not sympathize with Nashdom's Papalism, Kirk was much respected as unshakeably Anglo-Catholic and would, like Frere, not be interfering. He was also the monks' diocesan bishop, having succeeded Tommy Strong in 1937, and Denys's ideal of Benedictinism being 'diocesan' still held some influence in the community. But as Kirk made clear in a letter to Archbishop Lang of Canterbury, he was not inclined to disturb the *status quo* with regard to Nashdom's place in the diocese.

> My own view at the moment is that if such an invitation [i.e. to be Visitor] is made to me, I ought to refuse it, or better still that I ought to prevent it being made.

So far as I can discover Nashdom has no official status or recognition in this Diocese. This is, of course, highly unsatisfactory but perhaps inevitable for the time being, and in view of all the problems involved, it might be the wisest course not to disturb the existing situation.

But if the Diocesan became the Visitor, the whole question of the relation of Nashdom to him and to the Diocese would have to be attacked immediately; and I cannot avoid the belief that this would bring in the province, for the Community has or may have at any time branch houses in other Dioceses.

Nor would it be easy to bring the matter before the Communities Council as the Abbot himself is one of the most active members of that Council.[519]

However, alternative suggestions were not pursued, as Kirk succumbed to a lengthy bout of illness[520] and the monks decided to postpone any decision, even though it meant being without a Bishop Visitor for more than a year. They presumably hoped they could still persuade him in due course to take on the Visitorship. By 1940, they had succeeded. Kirk wrote again to Archbishop Lang.

In July 1938 you were kind enough to advise me on the subject of the Visitorship of Nashdom Abbey. Since then, I have seen a good deal more of the Abbey, and the Abbot, and have also obtained more experience of these matters through the Chairmanship of the Advisory Council on Religious Communities.

The result is that I have rather changed my mind on the matter ...

He stressed that he wished to be Visitor in a 'personal' not a diocesan capacity. He and the abbot had drawn up a 'semi-official memorandum' giving details of the present position of the abbey. He continued,

If they asked for any kind of recognition, either Provincial or Diocesan, as a Community, this would bring up problems which the Advisory Council on Communities would have to consider, but which in my mind are not yet ripe for discussion – notably, of course, the problem of the use of the Latin rite in Anglican Communities.

In fact, however, they neither have, nor are likely to put forward any of these requests; and indeed if I became Visitor I should be more able to prevent such approaches. This being so I cannot see that any canonical difficulties stand in the way of my accepting the Visitorship; while if I accepted it, it might perhaps do something to keep the Community loyally within the general framework of the Church of England.[521]

Lang, however, was not disposed to agree, despite Kirk's persuasive argument, as he had 'long been concerned' about the position of Nashdom, being both 'within' and 'apart' from the Church of England, at least 'apart from its corporate life'. He could not see how Kirk could be both the Diocesan and yet also the Visitor only in a 'private' capacity. The roles would be confused and might give the impression that the diocese approved of Nashdom's Roman Catholic practices.[522] Kirk agreed to act according to the Archbishop's wishes.[523] The new Visitor was chosen from among retired bishops and the one selected was F J Western.[524]

The controversy over the Church of South India, however, caused tension between Western and the community, for he had been a bishop in India and was in sympathy with the scheme. In 1944, he resigned. Kirk consulted Archbishop Temple, suggesting another retired bishop as replacement,[525] Vibert Jackson.[526] Clearly, all Kirk's ideas of being the Visitor himself had now disappeared, despite a new archbishop who might have proved more sympathetic. This must have partly been influenced by the vigour of Nashdom's campaign over South India. Temple would surely have been disturbed by any gesture that suggested the Bishop of Oxford endorsed the Nashdom hard line and Kirk too would have been uncomfortable with such a link, so there was now no question (unlike in 1940) of Kirk volunteering himself for the Visitorship.

Despite the pressure tactics of the *Open Letter* to which he had been subjected by Martin and Gregory among others, Temple still wrote with kindness about the monks.

> I am not surprised that in the present circumstances there should be a little tension between the Community and the Visitor! And I fully agree that it would be difficult at present for an English Diocesan to become Visitor of Nashdom. I know some of its members and have a great regard for them, and yet it is the one Community about whose standing within the Church of England I cannot avoid some anxiety.[527]

The campaign on the South India issue, therefore, had given Nashdom a leadership role in the Anglo-Papalist wing of the Church of England, but the suspicion of the bishops remained a block to the community's wider recognition. Archbishops like Lang and Temple had no difficulty respecting and encouraging the Religious life among Anglicans, but Nashdom was still too extreme for their comfort. The *Open Letter* had helped prevent the official diocesan recognition that for a short while had seemed possible with Bishop Kirk.

We can assume that for Abbot Martin diocesan recognition was far less significant than upholding Anglo-Papalist principles. We know he remained very committed on the South India issue.[528] When Archbishop Temple died unexpectedly in October 1944, he seemed unmoved by the tragically early death. He saw only the ecclesiastical and political fallout of the event.

> God has not informed me why he has removed William Tample [sic] so suddenly and unexpectedly, but I must confess to a feeling of great relief that a very real danger to the Church of England was at any rate lessened. There can be no doubt that Archbishop Temple's policy would, if continued, have finished the work of destroying the Church of England that Cranmer started ...[529]

The extra strain of the war years had not been easy for the abbot. Throughout them, Martin had struggled with his health. The first winter of the war, he had severe influenza and spent weeks in bed.[530] Recovery was slow and he regularly suffered a sense of 'devastating fatigue', which only started to leave him in 1942.[531] His heart and lungs were weak and he was prone to bronchitis. Attendance at the earliest office of the morning was beyond him for many years. By the end of the war, his pulse and blood pressure improved, but even in the middle of 1945, he could not preside at his daily Mass and was even forced some mornings to stay in bed.[532] Only on the return to Nashdom that August did he seem to find again his energy levels of the pre-war period.

But it was not to be for long. Early in 1947, his health began to fail once more. He continued valiantly, including through several operations and stays in hospital, but by the autumn it became apparent he was unlikely to make a full recovery. Martin dreaded turning into what he considered Denys had been in his last years: an invalid abbot clinging to power. So, under obedience, he had laid on Gregory the task of telling him when the time had arrived for him to resign. Although reluctant, Gregory had no choice but to fulfil this order and gave his opinion to the abbot. Consequently, Martin resigned his office effective on 10 January 1948.[533] Under the expert nursing of the Edgware sisters, he lived another two months and died on 12 March.

There is no question that Martin left the Nashdom community much stronger than it had been in 1934. At Denys's death there had been eight monks in life profession (solemn or otherwise), with several more in simple profession. By Martin's death – without counting the American brethren – there were more than double that number. This was in spite of his abbacy having included the downward trend of the war years. Financially, helped by several large legacies, but also by Martin's astute management, the community was solvent and, as the Jubilee Book put it, 'were no longer vexed with headaches about how to pay the monthly bills'.[534] The community had a much higher profile and, even though controversial, commanded respect as speaking for the Anglo-Papalist point of view in the Church of England.

Martin's influence, however, was at a deeper level too than administration and extending outside influence. He had moved the community to a more definitive identity. Denys had been concerned with reviving the Benedictine life. Martin was concerned with identifying Benedictinism with an Anglo-Papalist agenda: Catholicising the Church of England (and as a consequence pushing this transformation out to the whole Anglican Communion) and then reunion with Rome. For Denys, the Anglican Benedictine life was independent of Rome and an end in itself, and its justification and future could, if necessary, be separate from the reunion agenda; for Martin, the Benedictine life was a path to Rome and reunion, and therefore a means to an end.

This proved an advantage, both in attracting vocations from men trained in the then thriving Anglo-Papalist parishes and also in giving the community a sense of purpose. For example, it is unlikely Gregory Dix would have remained an Anglican, let alone continued to be associated with Nashdom, had Denys's policy of concentrating on Benedictine community life continued. Martin in contrast helped convince him there was a defined path to follow of wider significance. Gregory's decision to stay was a symptom of Martin giving Nashdom a political edge in the Church that appealed to others of his persuasion. Denys's outlook and policy had been diffuse and pragmatic: live the Benedictine life and see where it takes the community. Martin was in contrast focussed and clear: the community must be an unequivocal witness to a future vision of a united Church under the Pope. At his death, the Nashdom monks therefore faced the future with confidence and a sense of security.

But the narrowing of their vision of the Benedictine life to what was essentially a more political position, and identifying so strongly with an Anglo-Papalist agenda, ironically made them vulnerable. They were staking their legitimacy and their identity on a narrow territory, one that was difficult to maintain. They kept Benedictinism away from being fully embraced by the Church of England. Potential monastic vocations among less Papalist Anglicans were inevitably discouraged. Given how Benedictine the inherited traditions of much of Anglicanism were, from the cathedrals to the Oxbridge college chapels, this was a missed opportunity, one that Abbot Denys would have rued.

Yet for this Martin must not be taken to task too hard. If he had a misunderstanding in his vision, it reflected a problem within the whole Anglo-Papalist movement. A sense of certainty that their agenda for Anglicanism could succeed, and the goal of reunion with Rome might even perhaps be achieved (God willing) in a generation, was so strong that they were unable to evaluate their own potential weakness. Like many other movements in the Church over the years – catholic, evangelical, charismatic and the like – they mistook a surge of support and enthusiasm in a particular period as a sign of the 'inevitability' of their triumph over all other opinions. A more rigorous historical sense would have informed them of the ever-present diversity in the Christian Church as a whole, not only the Anglican fold. Unity, let alone uniformity, had never been remotely approached. There was no sound evidence to imply Anglo-Papalism would ever 'capture' Anglicanism. Parts of even the Anglo-Catholic wing of the Church of England, while staunchly Catholic, remained ardently anti-Papal. Such particulars, however, did not ruffle the convinced. To the zealous and confident, the realist lacks ambition.

With Martin's resignation, the solemnly professed of Nashdom had to decide who would best lead them as they strove further forward towards their most cherished goals. The choice was simply made: Augustine Morris was elected the third abbot on 6 February 1948. Neither he nor anyone else was surprised. Alternative candidates were not conspicuous. Anselm had been away from the community for much of the previous decade: 1939–43 in the USA and 1943–47 in Oxford.[535] Gregory had too many other activities and interests, and too many sharp edges, to be the focus of unity and authority at Nashdom. So Augustine was the obvious successor to Martin and had been trained as such.

In the years before the election, the new abbot had gradually been given more responsibility. He had succeeded Gregory as parish priest at St Mary's, Beaconsfield, in 1941, when the latter had retreated to the Nashdom guest house to complete *The Shape of the Liturgy*. Augustine remained based there for two years. In 1942, he became the community's auditor; the next year novice master; in 1944, the Chapter secretary.[536] In 1945, Martin appointed him the claustral prior, his second-in-command, and Augustine expedited the moves from Malling to Brondesbury and then to Nashdom. During Martin's last years, Augustine had as good as run the community and so had already proved his leadership qualities to the monks. For himself, Augustine recalled that it was during conversations in the 1943 meeting of superiors over the Church of South India issue that he had first been made aware that others saw him as a future abbot.[537]

He was the first leader of the community whose formation not only as a monk but also as an adult had taken place within the monastic community. His father had died when he was fourteen months old and, an only child, he was raised by a devoted mother.[538] Before her marriage, she had trained to be a nurse, intending to enter a Religious community.

Meeting Augustine's father, a pharmacist, had changed the course of her life, but in widowhood she was still deeply attached to the Church. After the First World War, with her son being educated at Christ's Hospital School, she became housekeeper to a retired clergyman and his invalid wife in Droitwich. Whilst there, she took her young son (now sixteen) over to see Pershore Abbey. A connection began with the monastery. Augustine began to spend part of his school holidays there and came under the direction of Martin; his mother became an associate, then oblate, and saw Abbot Denys for advice on prayer. Martin became convinced the young man had a Religious vocation and encouraged him to make an early decision. Consequently, just before his eighteenth birthday in 1923, David Morris entered the abbey as a postulant. His academic education was in the hands of Denys and Martin. He recalled that he saw himself very much as a 'kid' for many years, even after he reached solemn profession in 1930. His ordination in the mid-1930s did not take him much out of the monastery, as he was a 'nominal' curate only of the local village of Taplow, for which he was paid an honorary one pound a year.[539] So, on his election in 1948, Augustine, while confident and authoritative about the Religious life, felt he was not experienced 'in the world'. He therefore appointed Gregory as prior, the monk he considered was the most adept at dealing with the political situations of the Church and the secular world.[540]

One of his first challenges as abbot came from the problems being experienced by the American foundation. With the two brothers running missions, the priory at Valparaiso had failed to be conducive to establishing a Benedictine community. A new Bishop of Northern Indiana, while as sympathetic as his predecessor, advised them that they would need to move if they were to realize the fullness of their Benedictine vocation. Towards the end of 1945, a 126-acre farm was acquired in southwest Michigan near Three Rivers, and here the new St Gregory's Priory was established in March 1946.[541] A new postulant arrived and it seemed at last as if the foundation would flourish.

Tragedy struck, however, on 4 November 1946. Paul, the prior, was on a train approaching New York, on his way to Ralston, NJ, to see a community of sisters for whom he acted as Warden. He suffered a brain haemorrhage that took from him his powers of speech and his ability to write. He was never to recover fully, having to spend some time in a nursing home. Eventually after a further seizure in January 1949, he was taken over the Atlantic to Nashdom where he could more easily be cared for. He died that November aged fifty-seven.

Once it became clear he would not recover, he was replaced as prior of St Gregory's by Dom Francis Hilary. But with only one novice, Joseph, the new prior would find it almost impossible to build the Benedictine life. Abbot Martin sent Gregory Dix to evaluate the situation, and later in 1947 Patrick Dalton and Maurus Benson. It was important that any new American aspirants had a community to join, and by sending some experienced monks from Nashdom, St Gregory's was being given a second chance to grow. Dom Gregory also realized that funds were as important as personnel. He organized an extensive tour, lecturing and giving retreats, to raise money. It was a sign of real hope and trust in the future, as even the Bishop Visitor of the American priory had told him that the project was 'dead beyond recovery'. But as Augustine would observe, 'in any other life, Gregory would have died leading a hopeless charge', and was not to be discouraged.[542]

This was the situation that pertained when the new abbot, Augustine, took office. He visited the United States at the end of 1948, travelling across the ocean on the liner the Queen Mary, and, like Gregory, he also then engaged in a lecture tour to raise some money. He decided to replace Francis as prior, appointing Patrick. In the years that followed, buildings were erected and a new abbey church consecrated in 1951. Father Leo Patterson returned and other novices tried their vocation, so the number of American brethren began to grow. In 1956, Augustine appointed Benedict Reid as prior, and American leadership of the foundation was restored. Throughout these years, money proved a tremendous concern, but eventually some generous donors supplemented the efforts of the monks and St Gregory's was made financially stable.

Gregory Dix made a significant contribution in raising these funds during his second visit to the USA in 1950–51, but at great personal cost. In November 1950, after seeking advice over his feeling unwell, a surgeon in New York confirmed that he had cancer; but Gregory decided not to inform Abbot Augustine, who would undoubtedly have recalled him and then the money from the lecture tour would have not been raised. So, without seeking treatment, Gregory sacrificially continued his itinerary and raised by the end of it around $130,000.[543] Only after the dedication of the priory church on 3 May 1951 did he travel home and consult doctors again on his arrival in England. Being six months after the original diagnosis, it was essentially too late to save his life. Operations and other treatments prolonged it, but on 12 May 1952 he died at the age of fifty.

Gregory's death deprived Nashdom of its most famous name in the world of academic theology and also its greatest propagandist in ecclesiastical controversy. There was no one else then in the community who could match his talents and reputation in these areas. With his death therefore, the community inevitably turned away from the higher public profile it had courted since the late 1930s. Many in the community, including the abbot, were deeply grieved at the premature loss of such a brother, who, despite his sharper side, was a loyal, wise and trusted friend. However, his death meant that the ecclesiastical agenda and style of Abbot Martin could finally be superseded.

Augustine was a more genial and outgoing abbot than Martin had been, and was as concerned to make friends for the community as to represent Anglo-Papalist ideals in Church debates. He was just as committed to Nashdom's historic positions on theological and ecumenical matters, but his style was altogether more conciliatory. Without Gregory's presence, his more consensual approach could be embraced and followed. The abbot initiated another meeting of male Religious superiors, but, in the absence of Gregory's counterbalancing influence, Raymond Raynes CR dominated the proceedings.[544] As a result, little agreement was achieved and Augustine did not revive again what seemed an unproductive format. Instead he concentrated on the Advisory Council, which included bishops representing the two archbishops, and where the main community superiors met regularly. This proved a successful forum for discussion and decision that resolved problems before they might become politicized.

Augustine's approachability and humanity in dealing with problems made him a natural choice as adviser to other communities. Through the 1950s, many superiors began to contact him to have a 'ruling' on some matter of practice, and in some ways he became an unofficial leader of the Anglican Religious communities, as at that time he was their only abbot.[545] The fact that these communities did not all share Nashdom's Anglo-Papalist outlook was irrelevant as Augustine's style meant they did not feel imposed upon. This was a significant change from the relationship under his predecessor. In the 1950s, Nashdom was therefore setting 'norms' for other communities and in this regard became as influential as Cowley and Mirfield. However, this could not have happened if Martin had not first set Nashdom's reputation high in the previous decades. Augustine was able to build upon his predecessor's legacy. He did not change the community's position, but he did make it more accessible.

A less political role went hand-in-hand with a greater concentration on the contemplative side of the Benedictine life. Amidst all the church politics, it can easily be forgotten that a monk's vocation is primarily one of prayer and worship: God, not the Church, is the focus of his calling. Throughout the controversies of the early decades of the community's history, behind the monks who were in the public eye were more who anonymously lived and prayed in the monastery. Their work was in the choir stall and the oratory, humbly and unobtrusively going about their duties in the abbey. This apostolate of prayer could easily be underval-

ued, ignored, even undermined, by the engagement with church controversy. For some monks, the strong association with the Anglo-Papalist
cause was a distraction from their real purpose. There began a definite
movement therefore to return to a less public role for the abbey.

In 1952, the abbot addressed the Chapter on this matter on more than
one occasion, and there was an effort to reduce outside engagements.[546]
This did not please all those who came to try their vocations, and some
left because of what they saw as too great a withdrawal. The number
of extern oblates grew, although not all were able to maintain the commitment. The Chapter had sought to make it even more exacting at one
point, approving a resolution that in future priests who wished to be
oblates should mirror the community in committing to celibacy,[547] but
this demand was eventually dropped.[548] In 1953, there was discussion
of some oblates, including an archdeacon and the chaplain of a school
run by the OHP sisters, founding a Benedictine community in Ghana,
an echo of Nashdom's link in the 1920s.[549] This eventually did not materialize but two Ghanaian men entered the Nashdom novitiate in the
1950s, both reaching profession, though not in the end taking solemn
vows.[550]

For the monastic community, the 1950s were a time of modest growth
in numbers, as gains outnumbered losses. In the first dozen or so years
of Augustine's abbacy, 1948–60 inclusive, there were twenty-four simple
professions at Nashdom, but only nine went on to solemn profession.
There was also a solemn profession of a Religious transferred from another community. Of those ten solemn professions, seven would perse-
vere until the end of their lives. However, four monks (who had been first
professed in the last years of Martin's abbacy) sought secularization in
the 1950s. Not counting the American brethren, Nashdom therefore had
fifteen choir monks in solemn profession at the end of 1960, with five
life professed members in the lay brotherhood. There were five in simple
profession and two novices.

The withdrawals notwithstanding, by the early 1960s there was a confidence within the community that the future was assured. The changes
being wrought in post-war society had not yet impinged strongly on
Nashdom, for it was now, more than ever before, a society apart, a world
with its own rules and values, enclosing around those who entered its
novitiate. For some their confidence was rooted still in the assumptions
of 'inevitability' about their views triumphing in the Church and society.
This outlook was exemplified by Anselm's views, which he published
in 1961 in his historical study of the Catholic revival in the Church of
England. Even its title, *Rivers of the Flood*, suggested an unstoppable
force.

But to-day the Catholic Movement in the English Church is certainly stronger than ever it was, and it shows no sign of fading away; though there will always be prophets to warn us that it has run its course. They and their predecessors were saying the same thing fifty years ago (I heard them) and they will be saying the same thing fifty years hence, no doubt.[551]

He went on to dismiss those who were detecting a frustration, even regression, in the movement. However, the growth of individualism, the rise of scientific questioning and the decline in parochial religious practice were all to have a dramatic impact on the Church. Nashdom could not remain immune from these developments. Anselm's comfortable worldview was soon to be shattered.

10

Unravelling an Identity

In May 1964, the Nashdom monks privately celebrated the fiftieth anniversary of their community's formal inauguration. In July, a series of more public celebrations followed. The mass was celebrated outdoors in marquees, with festive refreshments following, the abbey thrown open for guests to admire its library, its vestment collection and other treasures. One of these occasions, on 15 July 1964, represented something more than an anniversary, for on that day the Archbishop of Canterbury, Michael Ramsey,[552] was the president of the mass (sung in English not Latin) in the morning and after lunch gave an address on the legacy of St Benedict for the Church and ecumenism. It was an unequivocal public recognition at last of the monks' place in the mainstream of the Church of England. The community even featured in television programmes on both the BBC and an ITV channel.[553]

These occasions were all held against the background of a revolution in the ecumenical climate that followed the election of Cardinal Angelo Roncalli as Pope John XXIII in 1958. He had called a Council to meet in Rome from 1962, to which 'separated brethren' were invited to send observers, reunion being one of its objectives. He initiated a range of ecumenical contacts that astonished other Christians used to the more austere policy of his predecessor Pope Pius XII. The leaders of the Roman and Anglican obediences met for the first time since the Reformation when Pope John received a visit in late 1960 from Geoffrey Fisher,[554] the latter nearing the end of his years as Archbishop of Canterbury.[555] In 1963, following Pope John's death, his successor, Paul VI, pledged to maintain this new approach to other Christians. This change of policy was taken up by some (though not all) Roman Catholics in Britain with varying degrees of enthusiasm. The Pope's representative in Britain, Monsignor Cardinale,[556] visited Nashdom during the Jubilee celebrations, along with the Roman Catholic Bishop of Northampton[557] and two monks from Douai Abbey. Roman Catholic visitors, especially Religious, now became as frequent as Orthodox. One of the Nashdom community's strongest hopes had now become a reality – official and substantial links with the Roman Catholic Church.

In contrast to their previous position as sceptical observers, the official participation of Roman Catholics in the worldwide ecumenical movement seemed to herald a new era of striving for Christian unity. Ecumenism had made many strides in the twentieth century, but without the contribution of Rome they seemed unlikely to lead to major advances. Despite the Roman Catholic wariness of the World Council of Churches remaining, nevertheless the change of heart in the Vatican aroused optimism about the churches at last all coming together. Some of this may seem naïve in retrospect, but at the time it provided a sense of excitement and possibility that, for a few years, made denominational boundaries appear less significant than they still were. This new outlook was reflected in the events of 1964. As well as Roman Catholics, the Nashdom Jubilee celebrations drew attendance from representatives of Greek Orthodox, Russian Orthodox, Baptist, Methodist, Congregationalist, Quaker, Presbyterian and French Reformed traditions. Compared to a decade earlier, this was a striking collection of Christians to gather at an Anglo-Catholic monastery. It represented a triumph of Nashdom's principles: Catholicism could bring Christians together. The community and its historical stance now appeared prophetic instead of being on the margins. Nashdom was no longer under suspicion of disloyalty but an acknowledged part of an Anglican witness to ecumenism.

Amidst all the external praise and celebration, there was another reason for the community to feel full of hope. The novitiate at Nashdom had begun to grow as fast as it had ever done, as the figures attest.

Years	Postulants entering	Novices clothed	First professions	Percentage of postulants attaining first profession
1947–51	18	15	10	55.5%
1952–56	28	17	9	32.1%
1957–61	15	9	7	46.7%
1962–66	18	16	15	83.3%

What was unusual was, firstly, the number who stayed long enough to be first professed (that is, more than eighteen months in the monastery). In the early to mid-fifties nearly thirty men had arrived to try their vocation but barely one in three made it to first profession. In 1962–66, though fewer candidates presented themselves, only three out of eighteen did not continue to profession.

There was a second unusual feature: ten of the eighteen were twenty-two or under in age. Indeed eight were twenty or under, which at that time meant they were still technically minors rather than legally adults. The youngest four were only eighteen at entry. The influx of novices raised the numbers in the community as a whole to the highest they had ever been.

This led to a decision to build. In considering an extension to the abbey, there had long been a dream of a new monastery church,[558] and an artist's impression of the proposed Italianate chapel shows a grand porticoed entrance with a slender tower topped by an elaborate cupola. However, the increase in numbers now made monastic cells the more pressing need. Even the novices' common room had had to be divided into three spaces, an unfortunate sacrifice of a significant facility. In December 1964, a building committee was created to explore possible plans with an architect.[559] Initial planning permission was granted in the summer of 1965[560] and the Chapter formally accepted the designs for the new novitiate house in December.[561] The next year an appeal for funds was launched,[562] which eventually raised more than £30,000,[563] with the remaining £25,000 being loaned by the Edgware nuns.[564] The Bishop of Oxford laid the foundation stone on 17 June 1967 and the new building was ready for use by early the next year.[565] It was unmistakably 'modern' in its appearance and jarred somewhat with the elegant Lutyens house it augmented.

The development of Nashdom's daughter house at Three Rivers was also proceeding. Conditions were harsh and of seventy-five postulants in the 1950s and 1960s, only twenty reached simple vows. By the mid-1960s, there were nine in solemn life profession.[566] In 1968, the priory voted for independence[567] and became an abbey in its own right in April 1969 when it elected Benedict Reid as its first abbot. This was an achievement for Nashdom, as well as the American monks, for the 'mother' abbey had brought a daughter house to independence, the first such occasion in the history of Anglican Benedictine monasticism. This was another sign of progress in the community's witness and a vindication of the identity that Nashdom had established.

Yet amidst all these positive developments, there were others that were threatening to shake monastic confidence. On 10 October 1964, the abbot formally minuted in Chapter what he had been saying to the seniors for some time: that the community had to consider what was happening to the Church and monastic life in general. 'Change' was on the agenda. This was the direct consequence of the deliberations of the Second Vatican Council in Rome (1962–65). The decree on ecumenism[568] was an encouragement as it endorsed the new approach taken from 1958 by Pope John XXIII. However, the main areas of significant challenge to the Nashdom community were the Council's decree on liturgy[569] and the decree on Religious life.[570] The principles of both these documents had been debated for some time; with formal conciliar endorsement, they could not be ignored by the Nashdom monks if they wished seriously to uphold the traditional Anglo-Papalist line of their identity.

One of the issues to be faced was the status of the five lay brothers in the monastery, who while vowed for life nevertheless were not members of the community's Chapter and could not even vote in abbatial elections. The origin of this second-class status was the admittance to communities in centuries past of those with little education, or aptitude for learning the Latin necessary for full participation in the Divine Office. In the twentieth century, it now looked more like the perpetuation of a 'servant' class. The new Visitor of Nashdom[571] raised the issue of lay brothers voting in abbatial elections in his first charge to the community in December 1963.[572] Yet among the choir monks, there proved a 'wide difference of opinion' on any general change to the status of the brothers.[573] However, the Vatican Council's decree was unambiguous in its direction to integrate,

> To strengthen the bond of brotherhood between members of a community, those who are called lay brothers, assistant, or some other name, should be brought into the heart of its life and activities.[574]

Abbot Augustine pursued the matter with some persistence, met separately with the lay brothers themselves, and the Chapter gradually was won round to integration in principle. The unanimous decision was taken no longer to admit postulants into the lay status. The statutes were to be changed to reflect non-ordained choir monks as a norm rather than an exception.[575] The formal vote on changing the constitution over the brothers, allowing them to have a seat and vote in Chapter for abbatial elections, was reached in December 1967, with only one vote against and one abstention.[576] However, it was 1971 before full equality was reached and they had a seat on Chapter for all meetings.[577]

One of the stumbling blocks to the process was the issue of Latin. As the abbot made clear in April 1965, the equality of all within the community was an ideal that could not be realised unless the vernacular was used in chapel.[578] This proved a divisive issue for the community. On one side, there were those who felt it impossible to sing plainsong in any other language but Latin, while others, having experienced plainsong in English in their parish backgrounds, disagreed. At first, the traditionalists seemed to have the edge in the debate, especially as Pope Paul had expressed a wish that Benedictines retain Latin for their Divine Office.

Abbot Augustine and Dom Anthony Williams went to Rome in March 1965 at the invitation of the Abbot Primate of the Benedictines, Benno

Gut,[579] a trip that also included meeting Cardinal Bea[580] at the Secretariat for Unity[581] and ended with an audience with Pope Paul VI. From this trip, the abbot gained insights into the general direction in which renewal was heading among Benedictines. Subsequent invitations to the Benedictine Abbots' congresses of 1967 (he was to be the only non-Roman Catholic there), 1970 and 1973 maintained this link.

In general, in the second half of the 1960s, about one-fifth of the Roman Catholic Benedictine monasteries remained unchanged, keeping Latin for example; a third were pushing ahead with more radical reforms, while the remainder were making changes cautiously and gradually. Augustine believed that Nashdom, being Anglican, had to be in the 'centre ground' or 'mainstream', so he returned from Rome with a conviction that his community should embrace change but only slowly. He was in any case unconvinced plainsong would sound right in English, a matter in which therefore he was more sympathetic to the traditionalists in the monastery. Therefore, there was no immediate abandonment of Latin, but he did ask in 1965 that scripture readings at the mass should be in English.[582]

It was to be alterations in the liturgy of the mass that made overall change more likely. The new Roman Catholic rites that arose from Vatican II had the priest facing west, towards the congregation, and were to be in the vernacular. There was a new concentration on simplicity and directness, with the congregation participating, as against the old style of mystique and performance, with the congregation more like an audience. Much of the ceremonial associated with the old Latin Tridentine mass was discarded, as were some items of the traditional vesture. For those who were inspired by the visual imagery of the 'back to baroque' movement, it must have seemed that all for which they had fought so valiantly was being taken away from them – and by the very institution they had assumed they were serving in that struggle, the Roman Catholic Church. There was some suggestion that the community now change to the Anglican rite, and indeed eventually there was a week of experiment with the new Series II service, but despite Augustine's support, this change was not implemented.[583] The Roman rite remained the liturgy of Nashdom, even if it were now in English.

Nashdom had to face change in the chapel, in any case, as the new novitiate building had its entrance connected to the house via a loggia to the left of the high altar in the existing chapel. The old baroque altar designed by Martin Travers had to be moved to the Lady Chapel. So as early as 1967, the community were discussing a possible new arrangement with a central altar and the choir seated at either end.[584] By March 1968, a majority was in favour of a central 'free-standing' altar.[585]

The dismantling of the traditional chapel arrangements came swiftly but the new were 'temporary' as the community had not the funds to make the transformation all at once. A sacristy altar was substituted until such time as a new purpose-made altar could be commissioned. This aggravated the pain of the change, as it made the 'new' seem impermanent and shoddy in comparison with the familiar grandeur of the 'old'. It was 1972 before the decision to have a hexagonal altar was made and April 1973 before it was in place.[586] The new arrangements when finally completed provided a beautiful and visually appealing space for worship, but photographs of the chapel taken during the interim years show a more bland and uncertain aesthetic.

As the new mass was in English, the issue of the vernacular in the Office had now to be faced again. St Gregory's in the USA was given permission by Augustine to use English for both mass and Office in April 1967.[587] The Roman Catholic Benedictines of the English congregation received permission from Rome to do the same later that year.[588] To remain 'mainstream', Augustine was now persuaded that Latin should be abandoned. He pushed forward and, after much discussion, the decision to do so gained a majority in April 1968. But the opposition from some was vocal and anguished. From others, it was registered through silence and outward indifference, the pain internalised and brooding. The abbot recorded in the Chapter minutes that his monks 'must face the problems which this involved' and 'be prepared for change'. He asked that all stay 'open-minded' and that no one should 'follow what was he judged useful to himself'.[589] For this to be formally recorded was a sign of how controversial and divisive an issue this was, whichever path had been taken.

The transformation began with compline, the last prayers of the day, being put into English. By January 1969, all the minor offices except terce were in the vernacular, but the two major Offices, lauds and vespers remained in Latin.[590] Only in 1970 was lauds prepared in English.[591] The pace was in accord with Augustine's policy of gradual change, but in some ways this merely prolonged the pain. Those who had no desire for Latin were still having to sing it at some points in the day, while the more traditional had still parts of the Office 'to defend', so that the argument seemed not to be finally resolved. In addition, just as with the temporary altar arrangements, the replacement of the sturdy traditional Office books by, initially, sheets of paper and loose-leaf folders gave a sense of provisionality that was disturbing for some of the monks.

The strains were not only over the new liturgy stemming from the Vatican Council's decrees but more seriously over the theology that lay behind those changes, especially with respect to the mass. In addition to the conventual high mass that all monks attended, the old pattern was for each priest to say a low mass every day. This was part of his duty to the Church, and his daily celebration had to be served, usually by one of the non-ordained brothers. Traditionally, most monks took the sacrament at these low masses and the conventual mass was 'non-communicating'. The new pattern established by Vatican II was to have a conventual mass, concelebrated by all the priest monks, at which the whole community received the sacrament. Each priest monk was therefore no longer required to say mass daily himself. For some of Nashdom's monks, this attacked a significant element of their vocation, at least their own interpretation of it. Several priest brethren were unable to change their practice, and continued to say their own mass.[592] This caused further tension, as they needed a server. Some lay brethren began to refuse to receive the sacrament when serving low masses; then they began to refuse to serve at all. Following Rome and being obedient to Rome, which had been a unifying force in the community for decades, now became the source of aggravation and division.

All these arguments and developments cut at the heart of the community's identity. The narrowness and brittleness of Nashdom's position, as established by Martin, was now exposed. The concentration on a more political agenda seemed now to have left the community side-lined. If the Vatican reforms meant that Canterbury and Rome could talk to each other directly and comfortably at episcopal level, the role of being a 'bridge' had been surpassed. The community was no longer required for that work. Making the Church of England more like Rome was no longer relevant either, as Vatican II had changed Roman Catholic liturgy and shifted its theological position to such an extent that the two communions were (it seemed then) converging. Nashdom's traditional Anglo-Papalist approach therefore had been overtaken. So what could its monks do now? What were they for? For some the answer was to seize the golden opportunity to maintain the 'old religion'. This seemed perfectly justifiable to those monks in particular whose ecumenical sympathies were more towards the 'unchanging' Eastern Orthodox than with Rome. However, by taking that option, they would be out on a limb in the Western Church, an anachronism from the past, and the kind of 'museum religion' they had so derided. For others, following Rome was still paramount; they must renew the life along the lines of the Benedictines in the Roman Catholic Church. Yet by doing that they were dismantling all that they had struggled to maintain over the previous decades in the face of ridicule and obstruction. It was a conundrum: they had to abandon the community's liturgical and theological tradition in order to follow its political and ecclesiastical one. Martin's vision of being Papalist Benedictines could only have come to fruition if Anglo-Papalist goals for the Church of England had been achieved. But that had not happened. Instead, Rome itself had now changed many of the rules. Nashdom was left behind. The wisdom and merit of Denys's vision of being Anglican Benedictines was now more evident, but could the monks find their way back to it?

If change in the Roman Catholic Church challenged the Nashdom community, parallel upheavals in the Church of England meant their own communion could not be a shelter from the storm of change. Among Anglicans, liturgical reform, with various experimental rites, was introduced to supersede the 1662 *Book of Common Prayer*, the latter's traditional language to be replaced by modern English. The compromise between traditions that is Anglicanism, and the autonomy of its provinces, necessitated a more piecemeal and tortuous process than that followed in the Roman communion, but the direction was nevertheless the same. The same sociological and cultural changes that prompted reform in Rome were the same that affected Anglicans. If the Church was to connect with modern society, its interactions could not remain governed by the style and customs of a previous generation. The beliefs at the heart of the faith had to be presented in a renewed guise. For some this meant radical thinking, such as John Robinson's 1963 book *Honest to God*, which attacked traditional ways of thinking about God, and created widespread debate in newspapers as well as learned journals. In some ways, however, theological debates were an easier challenge for Nashdom monks, as they had a tradition of discussing ideas openly, from Abbot Denys to Gregory Dix. It was liturgy – what they 'did' and what they 'experienced' – where they were more rigid and defended in their views.

Yet the theological ferment in the newspapers over Robinson's book was a signal of a sharp shift in the fortunes of the Church of England. There had been a modest revival in the post-war years and, in general, up to 1963–64, the Church was still experiencing a steady increase in vocations to the priesthood. But all this saw an abrupt reversal in the next few years. The spirit of change and rebellion against tradition that would give the 1960s its future reputation quickly overwhelmed any earlier optimism on the part of the Church. Statistics for confirmations, vocations to the priesthood, and general attendance began to spiral down from 1964 onwards. This downturn of interest was illustrated in, for example, what happened at the University of Cambridge. Christian teaching, both in theology and ethics, had been widely discussed in the 1950s at many lively meetings and gatherings in the university context. Religious debates and events drew large student audiences. From the mid-1960s, however, the atmosphere began to transform rapidly to one of lack of interest. There was no longer an automatic engagement with established beliefs and practices. Chapel attendance plummeted. Traditional religion was for many students now a sideline, safe to ignore and leave to others: questioning about it had been replaced by indifference.

Abbot Augustine had been clear about the new spirit even within the bulging novitiate of Nashdom's jubilee year of 1964. At a meeting of Religious concerning renewal in August 1964 in Oxford, he said,

> Are our days so different? In support of the belief that they are, I would point to one factor only: the spread of scientific education. ... The student, even the young student, is taught **not** to accept a statement on authority but to test it for himself by personal experiment. ... 'Find out for yourself: do it for yourself: look it up for yourself': these ... are the biddings of the modern educator. ... How different this is from the education of the past!
>
> Perhaps this new mental climate is the chief cause of the difference which is supposed to exist between the novice of to-day and the novice of yesterday or the day before. The novice of the past – so the story goes – did as he or she was told without reflecting or questioning why: the novice of to-day needs to know the reason for fulfilling the command or observing the custom.
>
> This questioning analytical spirit is abroad to-day and will have its influence on the monasticism of to-morrow. Venerable theories will be called into question; established practices subjected to criticism.[593]

Could Nashdom's training of monks respond to the new spirit? Since the community had arrived back at the monastery in 1945, after the wanderings of the war years, the novices had been kept separate from the solemnly professed[594] and all resided on the top floor of the abbey. This was a sparse location, originally designed for unconsidered servants and for box rooms. One new postulant remembered his arrival and the shock of his small room with an army bed, an orange-box for a desk, no carpet and no heating. Nevertheless, the youthful idealism of some of the new entrants meant they were thrilled by the sheer asceticism this represented. In Dom Anthony they had a quiet, somewhat austere, novice master, who was nevertheless kind and thoughtful, but also very clear about the rules and customs of the life. He had absorbed the tradition and intended to pass this on to his charges. His was a contemplative spirituality with a Cistercian emphasis on prayer and silence, informed by study and reading. All was directed towards God rather than community. Interaction with other monks was a necessity for the running of the monastery but was not the purpose of the Religious life. Hence Anthony judged that psychology had nothing to say to the monastic life as the purpose of the latter was about the vertical relationship with God and not the horizontal with a monk's brothers. Joining a contemplative order was about seeking God not 'community'.

Apart from their novice master and his assistant, and occasionally the abbot, the novices' interactions with the seniors were few. The whole community all gathered together in chapel for the liturgy and the Office every day, and were present at silent meals in the refectory, but otherwise the novitiate life was distinct from the senior community. Novices could only speak to seniors with permission, and never to guests. They had always to use the 'back stairs' of the house, once the preserve of Princess Dolgorouki's servants, and not the grand staircase. Only perhaps through conversation when working in the laundry or the kitchen, or on Sunday walks, did they engage more closely with the world of their seniors.[595]

Even after first vows, this same situation continued for two years, as the juniors were considered a part of the novitiate still. In the third and last year of simple profession, the junior monk transferred to be under the 'Master of Juniors' rather than the novice master. He was then allowed to join the seniors for recreation so that the latter could become acquainted with him before the vote on allowing his solemn profession. For a year he was in a 'halfway house', no longer living as a novice, but not yet properly integrated into the senior community.

In other communities, this pattern was considered inappropriate. How could novices learn the Religious life in general and the charism of the particular community unless they lived the life fully alongside the seniors from the beginning? Yet, for the Nashdom monks, this initial separation was part of their interpretation of the Benedictine tradition, canonically laid down in the Roman Catholic Church. The rationale was that the novice had to be inculcated with certain disciplines and prove faithful to them before full entry, as otherwise the contemplative atmosphere and purpose of the community could be disturbed. The risk, however, was that the junior monk had only a year in which to taste the full life of a senior before his decision over taking a solemn vow, which was meant to be irrevocable.

The practical consequence of this division was that the junior monks lived in a novitiate world, with their own recreation time, and developed a kind of camaraderie based on their shared status within the monastery. In the days when few stayed the course, and many aspirants were resident for only a short time, this had less significance; but, in the first half of the 1960s, with new arrivals staying longer, the enlarged novitiate at Nashdom began to develop a culture more its own. Talking was not allowed, except on feast days and in the kitchen, but it happened irrespective of the rules. The relative youth of many of the novices also created another layer of division with the seniors, one of age as well as that of status. This in turn gradually led in some to an instinctive feeling of rebellion, especially against what might be perceived to be pointless traditions and restrictions, such as the regulations about personal letters and not passing on the stairs. Even those who outwardly conformed, even perfectly so, were inwardly questioning aspects of the life.

This glut of generally young monks then had to cross to the world of the seniors. The slightly 'gossipy' atmosphere and camaraderie of the separate novitiate was not fully preparing them for the drier, more socially distant, world of their seniors. There are indications that it had not done so in earlier years either. Of thirty-two monks first professed in the years 1945 to 1961, only fifteen, less than half, had gone on to take solemn life vows. Some of the candidates were rejected by the votes of the senior brethren, but most of the withdrawals came from the decision of the junior monks themselves. Among the fifteen who did proceed, four had withdrawn by 1964. These statistics posed a question that caused 'disquietude', which could be put down by some to 'the unsettlement of the post-war years'.[596] The overall scheme of training was not in the event judged to be at fault and therefore was not altered. With fifteen first professions in the period 1963–68, there seemed no need.

However, the promising growth of the community in the mid-1960s was not to be sustained. A sea-change seemed to occur in 1967. From that year, the glut of young professed began to leave: of the fifteen mentioned, only six made it to life profession, and of these only four remained in the community by the end of 1971. Each of those who left had their own individual story, their own personal reasons for leaving, and none would perhaps define themselves as a part of a trend. Yet, the decisions of individuals are influenced in no small measure by the actions and atmosphere of the group. It must be assumed that the turmoil within the community over changes in monastic life, and the liturgy in particular, caused some of the unsettlement. The tension among the seniors made a commitment to the community less attractive, even if only at a subconscious level. Someone making a life vow in the early 1960s was reasonably clear on the life to which they were committing, whereas later in the decade the sweeping changes taking place made this unpredictable.

Then there was the issue of hierarchy. Outside the monastery, the old class distinctions in society were being eroded and the automatic respect once given to those in positions of power no longer could be assumed. Inside there was still much formality about monks addressing each other, with titles of Dom, Father and Brother, and even postulants referred to with the prefix Mr. This was a sign of the deference and hierarchic structure of the community. The abbot himself was like a prelate: his table at the head of the refectory was of polished wood, and he used more elaborate cutlery than the other monks. He entered by a separate door. He had someone to act as a 'batman' or valet, and others to clean his room. He was certainly not living the same life as those he led.

Obedience to the customary, a document that governed the minutiae of monastic life, such as how to behave if a mistake was made in the Office or a monk was late for chapel or the details of interactions within the refectory, was no longer easy to maintain. The generation entering the monastery in the 1940s and 1950s had nearly all been in the armed forces, either during the war or else via national service. They were used to unquestioning adherence to rules, however bizarre, and the immediate obedience to superiors inculcated in all those subject to military training. Those entering later in contrast were not so prepared to follow without reason. By the late 1960s observance of the customary was comparatively lax, and a more individualistic approach was being allowed to flourish. Some seniors complained that this was the root cause of tension in the community.

Yet the seniors' example was not necessarily helpful. For all the simplicity of life of some, others were more flamboyant and individual. The contemplative austerity of the life Dom Anthony tried to teach could seem at odds with the privileges, sometimes eccentric, that were enjoyed by some of the senior monks. The Nashdom community was not, even at the top, a community of conformists. Dom Maurus, the prior, had once been in the army in India, and still strode out into the grounds with a gun to shoot squirrels, or (his heart condition notwithstanding) energetically saw logs for the wood fire he was allowed to light in his room. He also partook of a shot of whisky and several pinches of snuff every day. Dom Anselm had accumulated an extensive and valuable music library and had his own sphere of influence. He was shy and increasingly deaf, resulting in gruffness, even rudeness, towards his brothers: hardly a model for fraternal harmony. Dom Robert had many outside engagements from his work in ecumenism and a growing interest in exorcism, so was regularly away, culminating in two years' exclaustration from the monastery. Other seniors had 'health reasons' for exemptions from the rigours of the customary. Anthony insisted to the novices that these monks were holy men, despite the diversions that some might judge at odds with their calling, and he was right. They were holy. Yet denying the same individual expression to the juniors seemed perverse in view of this.

Most marked of all the emerging tensions perhaps was the growing unease about communication and relationship. For many of the juniors, the world of the seniors seemed distant and cool, like a group of business colleagues, who might discuss work or ideas, but never anything emotional. The defence would be that one did not join a monastery to make friends but instead to pursue holiness and a relationship with God. Yet, even one of the most conservative monks admitted the problem in 1969, when he agreed the 'present rules' were 'too strict', and that under the novice mastership of Dom Benedict in the mid-1950s 'an impenetrable barrier between the professed and the novices' had been established. Another monk asked whether the community was not in practice one of hermits, while a junior noted that 'we do keep each other at as great a distance as possible'.[597] Maurus summoned up the problem in another discussion,

> The customary perhaps tends to have an inhibiting effect on our happiness. Then some people have a barbed wire fence around them ... One member testified to having been here two and a half years and only been spoken to by a certain person once, and that was when he spoke to him. There is undoubtedly tension in the community.
>
> The trouble is that we have been living to rules and now all these rules are breaking up revealing that there is nothing behind them and nothing to take their place ...[598]

This painfully honest assessment illustrates the background against which juniors and novices began to leave the monastery, and even some in solemn vows asked for release. The new novitiate block, ready early in 1968, was virtually empty, destined never to be used as originally envisaged. The irony was that in seeking to address the problem of relationship within the community, this awakened an expectation in some monks that could only be addressed by leaving. The greater the interaction, the more some realised their need for closer and freer companionship available only outside the monastery. A sense of loss about the purpose of the life undermined too the point of the sacrifice of celibacy: to find a life partner became a reason for moving on. It was very painful for those left behind. As Benedict Reid, soon to be abbot of St Gregory's put it,

> ... I think we all have to recognize that vows are not the iron-bound, static box that we often considered them to be but rather a stable process whereby a person can live out his baptism until extreme impediments appear. Today they appear more than in the past. ... It is a time of great suffering and deep questioning.[599]

In the centre of this suffering and questioning was the abbot, Augustine, who had the unenviable task of keeping the community together amidst the confusion. The Episcopal Visitor – since 1966, the suffragan Bishop of Willesden[600] – made the quinquennial Visitation in 1968, and the main recommendations of his January 1969 charge were that the customary should be revised and that the monks needed to discuss more with each other the issues of their life together. The abbot organized discussions in the March and again in the June following. He also tackled the issue of hierarchy from the top by announcing changes in his own routine. He was to cut down outside engagements so as to have more time for the brethren, and also to teach more. He was determined that his abbacy should be regarded from now on as an act of service not one of sovereignty, and hence he made a symbolic gesture.

> ... I am going to take a step which will demonstrate exteriorly that I desire that abbacy may be seen rather in its essence than in its trappings. For a year from now I shall not use the mitre. This is my personal decision ...[601]

For Augustine, this gesture was also a sign of his suffering at being the centre of all the community's turmoil. He was increasingly isolated. His theoretical power in the monastery was great, but in practice he was trapped by the competing expectations of the conservative and progressive groups of monks. He was inevitably the target of resentments and had to carry the burden of the anxiety and frustration among his monks. Despite their affection and gratitude for his long years at their helm, many monks now were dissatisfied as it was impossible for him to remove their fears and concerns. Whatever he did or suggested was open to attack from one group or another.

The death of his mother in the early 1960s had left Augustine without close family and his warm personality was not made for lofty detachment. He wanted to foster companionship and connection amidst the monks, as he needed that reassurance personally. Sometimes he longed to be just 'Gus' rather than 'Father'. However, the situation of tension militated against him; whatever his own emotional needs, he was the abbot, the leader, the centre of authority and he was forced to carry the burden. He had ever suffered a tendency to periods of depression: now, despite his outward affability, this began to surface more frequently. Some of his strongest support also began to disappear. In 1969, Anthony, unable any longer to cope with the challenging and questioning approach of the novices and unsure of the 'new monasticism' he was expected to teach, asked to be relieved of his duties as novice master. The abbot tried to retain his participation in leadership by appointing him sub-prior. Dom David Morgan, who had long been the sacristan, was given leave to live with his widowed mother, who had moved to Burnham, and consequently he came to the monastery only during the day. Whilst this was a charitable concession to an elderly woman, it meant that another of the community's powerful personalities was now living a more detached monastic life. An even greater blow fell in August 1969 when Maurus, Augustine's loyal prior since 1955, died of a heart attack during a trip to Edinburgh. At the moment of immense pressure, the abbot had lost one of his most dependable and experienced brothers.

Augustine had been elected for life, but in the early 1960s had gained the Chapter's agreement that he could offer his resignation when he reached sixty-five and, if re-affirmed in office, at five-yearly intervals thereafter. The Chapter could accept or reject the offer as it saw fit. In 1970, Augustine approached his sixty-fifth birthday and there were some on both sides of the community divide who might have favoured a change in leadership. But both sides knew any election would be divisive in itself, and there seemed to be no possible candidate who could unite the sides any better than Augustine. A younger monk who the abbot had seen as his possible successor, and so had appointed sub-prior in 1967, had broken down in 1969 amidst the stress. Although this monk did not leave the community for some time, nevertheless he had begun to suffer the personal and health difficulties that would end in his secularization a decade later. He was no longer a possible abbatial candidate. In May 1970, the Chapter duly refused Augustine's offer of resignation.[602]

A change of leadership was not going to be a route out of the impasse, in any case, as the problems went so much deeper. The detailed notes of the community discussions in 1969 reveal a frank exchange. Yet they also reveal the difficulty of making any decision. For example, the conversations about using titles resulted only in the adjustment that postulants would be referred to by their Christian names rather than as 'Mr'. No other change was agreed. The stalemate was such that movement even on something quite minor became an issue of struggle. In the mind of the more conservative members, the glory of the old Latin liturgy had been snatched from them and so now they were determined to give no further ground to the reformers; while the reformers, full of excitement at the possibilities thrown up by the monastic renewal movement, were becoming frustrated and disenchanted at the slow pace of change. Others, often remaining silent, were those who merely longed for an end to the turmoil and were prepared to accept anything that would mean dissension ceased.

Sadly, these discussions, instead of leading to a way forward, only made the divide more glaring. Augustine noted in another memorandum how dangerous this split was for the future of the community.

Nashdom suffers from being based on a monastic theology that is pre-Vatican II and pre-Abbots' Congress. ... All would in some sense be well if everyone were happy to go on as if nothing had changed, but it has to be admitted that there are in the community those who feel it to be essential to face up to these issues, in the belief that there has been under the guidance of the Spirit, a real theological breakthrough resulting largely from a better understanding of the meaning of the Gospel. ...

If Nashdom is to survive, and if men are to continue to seek and find God there, it is essential that a real effort be made to face the matter squarely. ... The degree of disenchantment sometimes shown by the younger members of the community is alarming, though this is less alarming than the determined efforts of more senior brethren to resist change at all costs. ...

There is a less hopeful attitude towards discussion now that it has been seen how little is effected. Discussion needs to be accompanied by experimentation to show that we mean business. At present discussion seems only to have prestige value, 'the best communities do it', and the function of allowing people to let off steam.

The suggestion was then made that the community had help from outside. SSJE had spent a year in the mid-1960s receiving outside speakers to inform their internal debates. Nashdom now did the same in 1971 in what was termed the 'renewal year'. There were four 'terms' with a series of talks covering all aspects of monastic life, with speakers drawn from the Roman Catholic as well as Anglican churches. Dom Jean Leclercq OSB was one of the prominent Roman Catholic guests and he gave in all five lectures. He urged the monks to take seriously their Anglican identity and express it, as this would be an ecumenical contribution of far greater witness than simply imitating Roman Catholic Benedictines. The talks were certainly informative for the monks in the maelstrom of ideas swirling through the contemporary Church, but votes counted from an informal questionnaire show that the renewal year did not shift opinions. On most issues, the community remained deadlocked on possible changes.

The question has to be asked as to why no compromise could be found after so many years of discussion. Partly this was because some of the monks had originally felt drawn to the life precisely because the old monasticism had a certainty and regularity. Their vocations were therefore built to some extent on the monastery being a refuge, a safe place where they would always know 'what' would happen and 'when' and that it would remain the same into the future. In the traditional model, their ambivalence about social interaction was protected from challenge by the formal style of monastic interchange and the long periods of silences. A relationship with God celebrated by a rich and sensuous liturgical round was the focus for their life. The traditional theology saw this monastic life as a way of perfection, a higher way of holiness far removed from the ordinary life outside. The traditional rules protected them while the traditional theology, in exchange for all they gave up, affirmed their way of life as in some way superior to that of other paths for Christian life.

Vatican II blew away all this security. The monastic way of life was no longer seen theologically as 'higher', only as an alternative. The rules were relaxed. Everything from liturgy to personal interaction was open to change. The traditionalists had to tolerate their guarded lives being open to scrutiny. They faced questions in discussion groups and the challenging of their motivations. Change was thrust upon them. Guests were allowed in chapel instead of being confined to a gallery. Monks went out on visits more often. Wilfrid, the new novice master, was one of a group of young novice guardians in Anglican communities, both men and women, who were in regular contact and encouraged links between Religious. Monk novices were now allowed to visit convents, and sisters visited Nashdom. Some of these sisters were no longer clothed in traditional habits. There was open conversation on topics once seen as taboo. There was no longer a bar on physical contact and Religious even began to hug each other when greeting.

To anyone wedded to the conventions of the old tradition, all of this was psychologically traumatic as well as spiritually undermining. The traditionalists could have been reassured if they had known where and when the boundaries of the experimentation would be drawn. Then they might have seen some value in compromise. But the great difficulty with the movement of monastic renewal was that it was an exploration, and no one could be sure where precisely it would end, or indeed for how long it would continue before a new settlement was reached. The conservative group were mainly older in age. They had nowhere to go if they left the monastery, and besides they took seriously their solemn vow of stability. Younger more radical monks had the option to leave; they could not. Trapped as they were, their only means of protest was a refusal to change. Yet because they were also of a generation of men for whom making themselves vulnerable in an emotional conversation was difficult, they could not easily communicate the fear and confusion they experienced. They felt bereaved without any obvious means to mourn. Too often therefore their judgement of new ideas came out as contemptuous or dismissive, as if they were not prepared to listen.

For the pro-reform monks, the very potential of change was what made the monastic life relevant and worthwhile. It was exciting to build something new. They had the same thrill of being pioneers that a previous generation had experienced in defying the Church of England to build an Anglo-Papalist community. Someone like Dom Anselm had been a rebel, his attitudes defying the bishops of the Church, when he joined the monks at Pershore in the 1920s. Now he was faced in his old age with a dismissal and defiance of much for which he had fought. Such is the irony of the conservative/progressive divide in any age. One generation's rebellion against tradition becomes the next's tradition against which to rebel. Yet, this was not easy for the pro-reform monks to grasp, and too often they in turn reacted to their traditionalist critics with exasperation and irritation. They did not always recognize that their freedom to experiment was possible precisely because they had been trained in the old-style disciplines. If these underpinnings were not taught to the next generation in some form or other, then the new monasticism might disintegrate. The traditionalists did have something important to contribute here.

But the question was how to bring these two approaches to an appreciation of each other's strengths, especially when there were hurt and damaged personalities on both sides. The failure of the year of renewal to achieve any consensus deprived the abbot of much of his energy to continue. Augustine had been an effective abbot when young and running an ongoing concern, but now he was exhausted after such a long abbacy and he found the ongoing conflict sapped his morale. In 1971, two of the monks solemnly professed in 1969–70 were secularized, while Gregory, the monk lent to the American foundation in 1963, also requested release from Religious life. At the same time, David, his mother having died, resumed life in the monastery but soon after, in 1973, he decided to leave in order to marry. Every one of the eight postulants in the years 1969–71 left within fifteen months of arrival. Augustine was seeing his life's work crumbling. At times, he was reduced to lethargy. Already in January 1972, Godfrey, backed by most of Chapter, suggested the abbot had an extended rest.[603] The abbot did have times away but decided to continue in office in an attempt to complete some of the reforms. This way he felt he would 'take the blame' for the changes, and his successor, whoever that was, would have a fresh start instead of dealing with a previous agenda.[604]

By this time, the successor was obvious. Dom Wilfrid Weston had been the prior since 1971 and, by the end of Augustine's abbacy, he had already shouldered a considerable amount of the administration of the monastery. When Augustine finally resigned in the summer of 1974,[605] Wilfrid was elected in the September. Only thirty-six, he was young for a superior, and for many of the monks he promised a new era. His inauguration was a time of hope and renewed confidence. He had an appealing charisma and had made a mark already outside the abbey as well as within. A nephew of the famous Anglo-Catholic Bishop Weston of Zanzibar,[606] a connection which was evocative for many Catholic Anglicans, he had overcome his initial diffidence to become an effective preacher and teacher. Well-known to other Anglican communities, he was one of the main movers behind the 1974 conference in York that inaugurated the Communities Consultative Council. He had an energy and optimism that promised a new beginning.

At the outset, Abbot Wilfrid sensed that the crisis in the monastery was partly theological. If the brethren had lost their sense of why they were monks, they would inevitably defend practices with intransigent passion, as only the structure was left holding their vocation together. In his first year as abbot, he therefore gave a series of lectures on monastic principles to anchor the community's outlook. But the monks' main work, praying the Office, still remained in flux. The revision of liturgy both in Roman Catholic and Anglican churches was continuing unabated, and so the round of change for the monks had by no means ended. For example, in June 1975, the experimental form of matins was now to be 'regarded as definitive', though terce and compline were still being revised.[607] Yet, in 1976, a new Roman Catholic breviary was issued and therefore adaptation had to begin all over again for Nashdom. A revised form of matins then came into practice from Advent Sunday 1976.[608] In September 1977, the revision of the Office was yet again minuted in Chapter, this time 'to keep in touch with the rest of the Benedictine Order'.[609] This began with the abolition of the Office of prime.[610] Nashdom was still running to 'keep up with Rome' and it was proving exhausting.

In retrospect, one can not help but feel sympathy for those who wanted more stability: it was now ten years since the revision of the Divine Office had begun and no end seemed in sight. The Chapter minutes reflect the inevitable weariness.

> In regard to renewal, Father Abbot said that an unduly conservative attitude should be avoided, as well as pessimism and superficiality. The office and timetable revision is in hand.[611]

Wilfrid in the early part of his abbacy also attempted to delegate authority. This was both a desire to share decision-making and also an attempt to reduce the stress on the abbot. On his election, he had announced that he did not believe he should stay in office longer than ten years, and this had much to do with his realization that, at a time of transition, one monk could not continue to be effective in the position for a long period. Delegation was another possible solution. However, the 'heads of department' he appointed did not always receive the recognition of their delegated authority.[612] The culture of 'Father Abbot' having the sole responsibility was still strong.

By 1979, Abbot Wilfrid had not been able to shift the dynamic of the community divide. Each side of any disagreement thought he was too close to the opposing view. That year's Episcopal Visitation was an opportunity for a re-think: even solutions such as moving from Nashdom, or founding a small branch house where a more radical monastic life could be tried, or making a foundation overseas, were put forward as possible initiatives to break the deadlock.

> Father Abbot said that he felt the community must face radical change. ... To continue as at present was not a possible way forward, with its increasing evidence of non-co-operation and the repudiation of authority.[613]

When no progress was made after the Visitation, the reforming group looked outside to implement their ideas. The novitiate of the 1970s had produced only three professions, of whom only one went on to life profession. Another novice at the end of the 1970s was professed in 1980 and subsequently life professed. Both were young priests in their early thirties, and keen to explore new forms of monastic life. But their ideas created alarm among their brethren. The former was considered too influenced by radical theology, and too caught up in a non-realist version of the faith that appeared to its critics to make a life of prayer redundant. The latter was involved in links with lay people, including a charismatic renewal group in the diocese. He wanted an 'alongside' group of laity to live at the monastery, but some brethren worried that while he was good at initiating projects, he might well then move on to the next new idea. So, asked the sceptics, who would look after this lay community in the long run? The suggestions of these young monks caused only more suspicion to grow in the minds of others.

Allowing lay people to participate more fully in the monastic experience was beginning to be a distinct trend among Religious. There were two particular projects in which Wilfrid encouraged Nashdom monks to participate. The first was in the parish of north Lambeth, south of the river in London. The team rector there, known to one of the monks, was willing that one of the churches in it, St Peter's, Vauxhall, and its empty vicarage, could be used for an experiment in community. The idea was for monks and nuns to join priests and lay people in living together for a week, thereby exploring whether there was a contribution this life-style could make to the problems of a deprived urban area. There would be exhibitions and activities to involve the local people. The project was arranged for early October 1980 to be part of the 1,500[th] anniversary celebrations of the birth of St Benedict. Predictably, the Chapter was suspicious of such innovation and gave 'no great support',[614] barely finding a majority to donate money to it. In the end, the abbot sidestepped dissension by making a financial contribution from the funds at his own personal disposal instead.[615] Wilfrid was one of the brethren who participated, and then reported back on the numbers attending the project and the enthusiasm it had generated.[616] The other project was St Gregory's Retreat in rural Wales, where a group of lay people, three of whom were oblates of Nashdom, were living a community life and providing retreat space for others to join them. Although they took on no responsibility for it, the monks agreed this retreat house could be affiliated with Nashdom,[617] and monks could visit it for periods of time.

If new ideas were to be explored away from the monastery, the abbot believed Nashdom itself could have a future as a retreat centre, providing a place of quiet and spiritual inspiration. Therefore the abbey had to renovate its facilities to create more and better guest accommodation. Moves were made to try to raise the necessary money, for example, by selling the late Dom Anselm's music library and other valuables.[618] But there was anxiety again about the responsibility for running the centre, especially as numbers were declining, with few joining to replace those who left or died.[619] Work outside the monastery was also drawing monks away. Placid was lent to a new Benedictine community in Australia early in the 1980s, and did not return, finally translating his stability to the new venture in 1986. William, one of the older monks, joined him in 1984 and remained there until his death in 1995. Aidan was accepted for ordination and went to serve a curacy in a parish in 1982. Basil was accepted to do a degree at Exeter University, so was to be away during term time for three academic years from September 1983. Others had their own routines, work and friends, who were not shared with the rest of the community. Unable to find common ground, the monks were becoming busy in independent ways.

The abbot too was busy with many outside engagements, not just sermons and talks, but also occasions such as being a principal speaker at the Anglo-Catholic gatherings at Loughborough, and ecumenical visits to Roman Catholic gatherings. Thorough and conscientious in preparing for such events, Wilfrid was an attractive and impressive representative of the community to the outside world, so that few appreciated the extent of the anxiety and uncertainty that gripped the monks back at Nashdom. Nevertheless, one of the most critical elements of the unsettlement going on was within the abbot himself. At the Vauxhall project, Wilfrid had met Helen, a sister in simple vows, who was in the process of realizing she should leave her community, and her challenging questions had made him admit his own, as yet unmet, emotional needs. It was the beginning of a significant connection that developed into a deep and abiding love. The ups and downs of their relationship, as they tried to resolve the conflicts and decide between the potential outcomes of their feelings, have been movingly told elsewhere.[620] Suffice it to say here, that this development meant that the abbot was torn between trying to resolve both the community's and his own inner turmoil. Consequently, Wilfrid offered his resignation to the community in the autumn of 1982, but, in some personal confusion, he drew back from the step and intimated that he would carry on if they wished him to do so. The resignation was not accepted.[621] However a year later, he was granted a period of leave[622] that he spent at St Gregory's in Wales, following which he offered his resignation as abbot once again, this time so unequivocally that it was accepted.[623] Few of the community were aware of his relationship with Helen and so his application for secularization some weeks later,[624] and their decision to marry, came as a shock.

Wilfrid's withdrawal left the community with all its tensions unresolved and now with the added uncertainty of who could possibly lead it. There began to be a real prospect that just twenty years after the high point of the Golden Jubilee, the Nashdom community was facing its own demise.

A New Beginning

Nashdom's problems were not without parallel elsewhere. The 1970s and 1980s were difficult decades for Religious communities in the developed world, and the membership of almost all fell markedly. To begin with, the generation lost through death in those years had been numerous, having joined between the world wars when the attraction of the vowed life was strong. Vocations had begun to be fewer in many communities in the post-1945 world and the changes of the 1960s were in part an attempt to revitalize Religious life in the face of this ongoing gradual decline. But the sociological factors were not helpful and not only did the number of vocations dwindle even further, but many who had joined in earlier decades sought secularization. With all these factors, many communities, even the large congregations of the Roman Catholic Church, faced the pain of giving up long-cherished works, closing houses and embracing change. Smaller communities faced extinction. The threat to Nashdom was therefore part of a powerful and widespread trend.

In any circumstances, the monks would have been hard pressed to respond successfully to this scenario, but the deterioration of relationships within the monastery meant their task was all the more arduous. Suspicion was rife and trust had utterly broken down in some quarters. This was the sad atmosphere the Bishop Visitor found when he came to talk to the community soon after Wilfrid's resignation. He was understanding in his address to them, yet frank about the situation.

> You have told me about the weakness of love for one another in your community ... I have discovered a community which is very near to just survival level, spiritually, and which is riddled with fear. ... Some of you think it already too late to save the community ...
>
> ... the very thought of what a community means is something of which several of you have spoken to me. The community is not what you joined, but that is not your fault. The world and the Church have changed. ...

And yet you have not been able to adopt the new ways. You are not talking to one another enough. You are frightened of one another because you get angry with one another; and I've heard a lot about that.

He went on to note the fragmentation that was the consequence of this isolating anger.

... most of you are working at things which are yours and are not shared with the rest of the community. ... One thing I will say, just to show that I understand about this private nature of so much of the life of the monks [,] is that I know this is a compensation. It is something you take to because of other disappointments ...[625]

He went on to suggest the community must have a 'work' they could share, which could act as a focus to bring them together. He suggested postponing the election of a new abbot for some months. Under the Benedictine rule, when there is no superior in the monastery, the three Religious who are most senior in profession share the authority. The bishop saw in the way Augustine, Patrick and Cuthbert were working together the beginnings of a more positive way forward.

The community did leave an abbatial election for some weeks, but in the second half of March they voted in a secret ballot to hold one.[626] The choice was limited, not least because the abbot had to be a priest. There were ten priests in all, seven over the age of seventy, in a community of sixteen life professed.[627] One of the younger priests was in his late forties, the other two a decade younger. None of these three, however, could command the trust of the older generation. So one of the seniors had therefore to be chosen. Of that older generation, however, Patrick died on 6 March, Augustine produced a medical certificate to ensure he was not a candidate, and therefore the only possibility in terms of leadership potential was Dom Godfrey Stokes, still active in his eightieth year. He was elected on the second ballot for a limited term of two years.

Godfrey had long been a significant presence in the community. Committed and disciplined, he was certainly a godly, even saintly, man. He had no pretensions and would not wear the silver abbatial cross, but instead used a much simpler one. He had joined the community during the Second World War after parochial experience and also six years with the Delhi Brotherhood[628] in India during the 1930s. He had served as novice master and master of juniors at different times. He valued enclosure and was not attracted by activities outside the monastery. Nevertheless, he had an extensive external apostolate, particularly by letter, and, as oblate master, had fostered a remarkable growth in the number of extern oblates; by 1984 there were 390.[629]

Although he was in many ways wedded to a traditional view of monasticism, his conservatism was much more about values than externals or particular practices. So he was able to embrace some change when he judged it compatible with safeguarding the life. For example, he became the first abbot to appoint a non-ordained monk as prior: Dom Francis Hutchison. During his abbacy, he advocated the community changing to use the Anglican liturgy of the *Alternative Service Book*.[630] Although this was not adopted, it is an example of how Godfrey could not be considered an unbending conservative. However, the younger monks were not all happy with what they saw as the election of a 'stop-gap'. The bishop in his January address had warned that electing an older monk would mean an abbot who 'would not have the sense that he would be able to carry anything through'. The difficulty was that the younger contingent (which included one junior and two novices) had no alternative vision common to them all. Abbot Benedict Reid from Three Rivers visiting later in 1984 noted this fact in his journal.

> ... I had a meeting with the younger ones, that is, those under age 50, professed and novices. I tried to cheer them up and encourage them to ask for access to a trained outside person to help them learn how to talk openly with each other. Also, it was obvious that these brethren didn't have too much in common. I could see that pulling this group together was going to be hard work.[631]

The option of using outside help was one the new abbot was willing to try. On the way back from the Abbots' Congress in Rome, Godfrey had spoken to a Roman Catholic abbot of the English Congregation, who had told him of an Anglican priest who had helped his own community.[632] As a consequence, Godfrey wrote to Father Peter Lang, and the community then agreed that this priest and an assistant could guide the community through some painful discussions.[633] Some progress was undoubtedly made but insufficient to hold the younger members. In 1985 and 1986, one by one the majority of them left the community; of the leavers, two were to try their vocation at another Anglican abbey, another two went to Roman Catholic monasteries. With younger priest brethren leaving, there was some discussion as to whether a lay monk could be elected as abbot, but this was rejected in January 1986. Hence, Godfrey had to continue but warned he would only do so for a maximum of a further two years.[634] By the autumn of 1986, with two monks living in Australia and one in residential care, the community living at Nashdom, and still committed to its future, consisted of nine life professed and one intern oblate. There was one novice. Dom Francis and Dom Basil, in their forties, and the novice, were the only monks under the age of sixty-five; four monks were over eighty. With such an age structure, it was now no longer physically possible to maintain such a large plant as Nashdom. Its maintenance had long stretched their financial means, now it was becoming beyond their human resources too.

The decision to move therefore came swiftly, the discussions beforehand again skilfully facilitated by someone from outside. The secret ballot on moving held on 25 October 1986 resulted in unanimous agreement to do so.[635] The idea of moving was not entirely novel. It had been put to the Chapter as early as 1976 by Dom Robert, but rejected after discussion.[636] Abbot Wilfrid had not felt there was any compelling reason to leave Nashdom at that stage, and he believed that the large premises gave scope for any future developments. The emotional attachment to the place also kept the monks rooted. 'Nashdom' meant their name, their identity. But with that identity now in pieces, the only way to forge a new sense of purpose was to start again somewhere else. However, it was the practical reasons that finally convinced the monks that moving would provide the only chance of the community's survival.

The hunt for an alternative site for the monastery cast the net wide: from Newcastle to Cornwall, from a redundant care home in Brize Norton to a property in Stevenage. In January 1987, Basil and Francis went to see a house near Speen, a village on the outskirts of Newbury. Near to the ancient parish church, it had a quiet location in attractive countryside, and yet was easily accessible for oblates and guests to reach, being near to a town and within reach of a railway station. The Bernardine sisters of St Mary's Convent, Slough, loaned the monks a school bus so that all could go and view the property. On the 10 February, the Chapter formally voted to buy it. There were some months of negotiations and financial transactions before the monks could move and establish Elmore Abbey. Just weeks beforehand, death watch beetles were found in some rooms on the ground floor, and this caused a further few weeks' delay, but the move finally took place on 2–4 September 1987.[637] (Nashdom, which they left behind, was sold to a developer, who intended to create a health spa, but in the end this idea was not realized. After a few years it was converted into residential apartments.)

Abbot Godfrey can be credited with leading the community in this momentous decision, and in doing so made its survival a possibility. He was senior enough and sufficiently respected to gain the support for this decision from all the monks. He was conservative enough to reassure the traditionally-minded, open enough to know the community had to take a risk. As his successor noted, Godfrey made the transition possible by holding the whole community to it.[638] He was able to do this because, by the mid-1980s, it was evident that the old Benedictine patterns would not be reinstated. The deep values of the Benedictine life remained the same, but a new expression had now been established. The period of seemingly continual upheaval was now coming to a close. Even in the Roman Catholic Church, where there had been a move to more conservative positions after the election of a Polish Cardinal as Pope John Paul II in 1978, there had not been a restoration of the old Latin Tridentine liturgy or the elaborate ceremonial customs that accompanied it, nor had the theological shifts of the Second Vatican Council been abandoned. The interpretation of them was now more cautious but they were not overturned. Godfrey had therefore an ecclesiastical climate in which agreement to make a transition was easier to reach. It was his achievement that he did not miss this opportunity. Defying the Bishop Visitor's prediction, he had, despite his age, 'carried it through'.

Nevertheless, on moving to Elmore, it was apparent that a successor had to be found, as the abbot was now eighty-three. However, the only two life professed monks of the younger generation (the last survivors of the glut of novices from the 1960s) were both not ordained. Soon after the physical move, the Chapter voted in a secret ballot to abandon the regulation that an abbot had to be a priest.[639] This opened the way for Dom Basil Matthews to be elected Abbot of Elmore on 28 June 1988, taking office on 3 July.

Basil had grown up in London and had come fully to the faith at the church of Our Most Holy Redeemer, Clerkenwell, famous as a bastion of Anglo-Papalism. He had joined Nashdom in 1964 and had for many years held the crucial role of clerk of works: that is, he oversaw the upkeep of the building, organizing repairs, painting and decorating, and maintaining the garden. As for many of his generation, the novitiate programme under Anthony provided him with a good education in history and theology, and encouraged him to read and study. In the 1980s, the community allowed Basil to read for a degree and gave permission for him to be away from the monastery during the academic terms. He attended Exeter University and graduated in theology in 1986. He had therefore a variety of skills, knowledge and experience to offer as a leader.

He was faced with the challenge of leading in essence a new foundation. Elmore had to become a monastery in its own right and not merely a house for a remnant of Nashdom monks. The task was particularly daunting because no one had stayed in the community since his own profession in 1965. The fifteen men who had taken vows in the years since had all left.[640] It was heartening therefore that the years 1989–91 saw four professions, among them three of the monks living at Elmore at the time of writing. These committed vocations ensured the community could survive into the twenty-first century.

By the time Basil became abbot, the Roman Catholic Benedictines, both in Britain and outside, had embraced Anglican Benedictine communities as part of the Benedictine family. The *Benedictine Year Book*, published by the English Benedictine Congregation every year, included the Anglicans from its 1971 edition. By the 1980s, this was not merely an ecumenical gesture of friendship, but a strong indication that the bonds of Benedictine vows transcended denomination. The Abbot of Nashdom and then Elmore was routinely invited to attend the congresses of Roman Catholic Benedictine leaders held every few years in Rome. The old Roman Catholic view that Anglo-Papalists were merely Protestants pretending to be Roman Catholics had long been abandoned. There was now a genuine respect for the achievements of Anglican Benedictines and a delight in the adoption of the *Rule of St Benedict* in sister churches. It was therefore puzzling to Roman Catholic abbots in Britain that Anglicans should still use the Roman rite for their Eucharist. From their perspective, the strength of the ecumenical bond was greater if Anglican monks and nuns used the rites of their own church. Friendships would then more clearly be seen to cross boundaries. The goal of reunion, in their view, was not best served by uniformity.

Basil was influenced by this point of view as he attended Benedictine conferences over the years of his abbacy. Finally, an opportunity for change sprang from a development within the community. The need for another monk to be a priest, in order more easily to maintain daily Eucharistic celebration within the abbey, led to the abbot offering himself for ordination. He was made deacon on 30 June 2002. His ordination to the priesthood by the Bishop Visitor followed on 10 July. He felt strongly that he could only preside using rites authorized by the Church of England. In preparation for these events therefore, the community agreed to use *Common Worship* for their daily Eucharist starting on 13 June 2002. This was a momentous change and revealed how far the ecumenical approach had changed from the thinking that dominated their predecessors.

If there was change in their worship, there was also much to be done practically to create the abbey. Gradually the house was adapted to the needs of the community. Guest accommodation was created, rooms in the attic, a library, and finally in 2001 a well-proportioned refectory. Most stunning of all was the new oratory, built at the back of the abbey in 1994–95. Principally constructed in wood, with great care for texture and balance, the oak-stalled choir is on the far side to the entrance, a sacristy to the left and a Blessed Sacrament chapel to the right, and in the centre under the lantern of the cruciform building stands a square altar of beige limestone. As Dom Augustine put it, the community during his monastic life had worshipped in a bedroom (Pershore), a ballroom (Nashdom) and a dining room (Elmore), and now at last it had its own oratory. It represented a rooting of the community in its new home. No longer was the new monastery a retreat from Nashdom, a refuge from the pain and defeat that some saw in the withdrawal from the latter's grandeur. Instead, Elmore had become a bold celebratory statement of Benedictine stability in a new place. It was a distinct foundation.

With the monks finally settled, the older generation, so faithful for so long, one by one slipped away. It is salutary to consider that if they had each died at seventy years of age, there would have been only three monks, an intern oblate and a novice to move to Elmore in 1987. Longevity and good health into their eighties allowed the older monks to contribute crucially to the outpouring of their venerable tradition into the life of the new monastery. Without that witness, Elmore would have had perhaps too little strength in its early years. Andrew died in 1992 aged eighty-nine. Anthony, Augustine and Godfrey all became nonagenarians. The first died in 1995, the other two in 1997. Augustine had also lived to see his platinum jubilee of profession in 1994; he was the last of those who could remember Abbot Denys and Pershore. Mark Alberic and Boniface died in 2001, and were the last of those who had entered in the days of Abbot Martin.

Their personal histories were interwoven with the hopes and dreams that had forged the old Nashdom identity. For many of these monks had been dedicated to the cause above all others of the reunion of Christendom. For them, reunion would bring such energy to the Christian witness as a whole that the power of the faith would be immeasurably strengthened. All the other goals of the Christian life – spiritual, social, political, ecclesiastical – could accordingly be subsumed within the reunion agenda. For them, the path to its achievement was difficult to tread but clear in direction: union with Rome. This Anglo-Papalism was an ecclesiastical response that belonged to a time when Roman Catholicism claimed to be immovable and unchangeable, liturgically and theologically. Potential unity meant conforming absolutely to the Roman system and disciplines, not only to its theological views. The Nashdom monks had followed this logic impeccably.

From it flowed achievements. First, they demonstrated that ecumenism is a life not just an institutional goal. It is about prayer and worship, as well as meetings and negotiations. The emphasis on living a holy, spiritual life was an ecumenical witness even to those who would not step inside an Anglican church or join in the Lord's Prayer with anyone outside their own communion. The Nashdom monks had been a point of contact to Roman Catholics in particular and provided a strong link to the latter at a time when the Vatican was cool to ecumenical conversations. For the Orthodox too, Nashdom demonstrated the potential of Anglicanism as an ecumenical partner. All of this flowed from the priority for a spiritual and liturgical outlook. The theological discussions could follow later. There were others who advocated this path, but it was rare for a community as a whole to have such an outlook. Parishes inevitably were more mixed and could not be so focussed on one ecclesiastical goal. Nashdom as a monastic community had the freedom to live out this vision.

Most tellingly, the monks had expressed in their life that a contemplative vocation does not have to mean being hidden and unobtrusive. Nashdom had maintained a contemplative charism with a strong public profile in the Church. It was expected that so-called active communities, committed to social work, would be a voice in the Church. The idea that a contemplative monk would be equally powerful in being heard was significant. Most contemplatives in the Church of England were, like Father William of Glasshampton,[641] convinced that their vocation could only flourish if they 'retired' from the world and they had a profound distrust of 'publicity'. Some of Nashdom's monks had no such inhibitions. Indeed, they had courted publicity and emerged as leaders of particular constituencies in the Church.

The weakness in this achievement was that they confused the principle with the policy. To commit to ecumenism was not the same as committing to a particular way of pursuing it. When the ecclesiastical landscape changed, many monks were unable to separate one from the other, so that as the policy became redundant, they felt they had lost their purpose. Some Nashdom monks became too rigid in their interpretation of how to pursue their aspirations. Other monks were able to see the difference but too few to allow the community to adapt, and they were not united in advocating one alternative policy. Consequently, it might be observed that the vocal arguments were over liturgy and practices, but the real debate was about how to pursue the community's objectives. Since the days of Abbot Martin and Gregory Dix, Nashdom had lost flexibility in its vision and become too associated with that one interpretation. When this profile did not survive the renewal movement of the 1960s, the community lost its clarity. Its achievements were in the past and its stance seemed no longer relevant.

By the 1990s, the specifically Anglo-Papalist cause among Catholic-minded Anglicans as a whole could be viewed as a fascinating historical interlude rather than a vibrant element in the future. In any case, the Church of England was by then more attentive to a revived Evangelical wing. The Anglo-Catholic movement in its wider sense retained influence but it was divided by issues such as the ordination of women and attitudes towards sexual morality. It was quite possible for some Anglo-Catholics to be deeply conservative about one issue and yet liberal about another. A lack of consensus was the hallmark of Anglican Catholics through the last decades of the twentieth century. In the face of innovation and experiment among Roman Catholics, and a variety of expressions of spirituality ranging from the charismatic to the silent, the ceremonially intense to the unadorned minimalist, the remaining Anglo-Papalists had no unequivocal Roman pattern to which to conform either. Some gave up and became Roman Catholic or Orthodox, an individual conversion that represented the ultimate betrayal of the most basic principle of Anglo-Papalism: that only *corporate* reunion would suffice. Whatever the frustration for the individual, the whole point of being Anglo-Papalist was patiently to labour for that. For those who remained loyal to Anglicanism, the goal of reunion would always remain, but the path of imitation as a way to get there was now confused. If we judge Nashdom by the test of Anglo-Papalism, it rises and falls with that movement. As the Anglo-Papalists failed to achieve their objectives, so too then did Nashdom.

However, in uncovering the history of the community from its inception, and especially in re-examining the teachings of its first abbot, a broader perspective can be gained. Pershore was not an Anglo-Papalist foundation, certainly not once Anselm Mardon had left in 1915. Denys believed in reunion and worked for it when he could, but he did not see the purpose of his monks as being a political one. His aim was simply to restore the Benedictine way of life to the Church of England. The *Rule of St Benedict* was not a Roman Catholic document but one belonging to all those who aspired to live a Christian life. To live its monastic expression was to show others a way to Christ, to inspire them to follow a Christian commitment, and encourage a revival in Christian living. It was a way to renew the Church, a way to spread the Gospel, 'propagation by cloisters' as Denys termed it. His Benedictine challenge was to revive the life among Anglicans so that it in turn could challenge the Church to live a more holy life. The monastic enterprise was therefore about values not political goals. Many had not understood the thrust – let alone the nuances – of Denys's vision, not least because he was so limited in being able to articulate it plainly. Under Martin, they had seen a much clearer and more defined goal, and this (as Denys in the 1920s had fearfully predicted it might) swamped his founding principles. Yet as the Anglo-Papalist dream dissolved, the underlying Benedictine values had a chance to be reaffirmed.

At the heart of the Benedictine life is the *Opus Dei*, the work of God, the praise and worship of the Divine Office. This is the prime responsibility of any monastic community and throughout the events recounted in this book, the community said and sang their prayers, worship was offered throughout each day and God was at the centre of the lives of all its members. This must be emphasized as being the underlying motivation of the foundation. A history of a community's prayer and worship life is impossible to capture in words, as it is a story of liturgy, silence and repetition, and the inner life of members that by its very nature is hidden from others. Yet none of what is told in this book would have happened without the underpinning of spiritual practice that is intrinsic to Religious life.

This in turn led to many outside the community seeking spiritual companionship and counsel from those within it. This too is a story hard to relate as it is manifest, usually only in hidden ways, in countless individuals' lives. It is not possible to gather historical evidence of this influence, except through anecdote, or weigh its effects accurately. Therefore, while we cannot judge the community's historical role solely on its political dimensions, yet its spiritual role is impossible to quantify. What can be said is that, whatever the perceived successes and failures of its ecclesiastical dealings, the monks of Pershore, Nashdom and Elmore have touched many lives spiritually over ninety years.

Consequently, it is no coincidence that even as the vowed monastic community has weakened numerically, the external oblature of the monastery has grown into a group of several hundred. This growth would have gladdened Abbot Denys's heart. For him, the monastery was not an end in itself but an inspiration to a wider community. The steady stream of visitors and retreatants to Elmore is another witness to the community's role in the Church as a centre of prayer and spiritual sustenance. Despite its small numbers, the community is as near now to Denys's original vision as it was at its numerical height at Nashdom. Maintaining an Anglican Benedictine community in the wider Church remains the cornerstone of the monks' charism, the rich inheritance that belongs to the handful of monks now at Elmore.

The years from the mid-1990s have not been easy ones for the community. Although a dozen or so men came to try their vocations, and there were several first professions, none stayed. The sense of frailty was further emphasized when Abbot Basil resigned in October 2005. Exhausted by seventeen years as leader, a sabbatical away from the monastery had led him to realize he was being called to a vocation away from Elmore. He left the Religious life. With too few monks remaining to make an abbatial election appropriate, Dom Simon was elected on 13 December

2005 as Conventual Prior, and formally installed the following month. History has come full circle in just under one hundred years. The Benedictine challenge that faced the handful of aspirants in 1913–14 still gently beckons the small group of brethren who currently live at Elmore Abbey and any, in whatever location, who may wish to lead the monastic life in the future.

List of Superiors and Departed Brethren at Pershore, Nashdom and Elmore

Superiors

1914–15	Dom Anselm Mardon *(superior)*
1915–22	Father Denys Prideaux *(warden)*
1922–34	Abbot Denys Prideaux
1934–48	Abbot Martin Collett
1948–74	Abbot Augustine Morris
1974–84	Abbot Wilfrid Weston
1984–88	Abbot Godfrey Stokes
1988–2005	Abbot Basil Matthews
2005–	Dom Simon Jarratt *(Conventual Prior)*

Claustral Priors

1923–26	Dom Bernard Clements
1936–45	Dom Anselm Hughes
1945–48	Dom Augustine Morris
1948–52	Dom Gregory Dix
1955–69	Dom Maurus Benson
1971–74	Dom Wilfrid Weston
1974–79	Dom Anthony Williams
1979–82	Dom Cyprian Martin
1984–2001	Dom Francis Hutchison
2001–06	Dom Kenneth Newing

Sub-Priors

1967–69	Dom Bernard Mincher
1969–74	Dom Anthony Williams
1999–2005	Dom Simon Jarratt

Bishops Visitor

1914–18	Huyshe Yeatman-Biggs, Bishop of Worcester
1919–26	Ernest Pearce, Bishop of Worcester
1928–38	Walter Frere CR, Bishop of Truro (retired 1935)
1940–44	Frederick Western, former Bishop of Tinnevelly, Madura & Ramnad
1944–62	Vibert Jackson, former Bishop of Honduras & the Windward Islands
1962–66	Nathaniel Newnham Davis, former Bishop of Antigua
1967–74	Graham Leonard, suffragan Bishop of Willesden, from 1973 Bishop of Truro
1974–90	Richard Rutt, suffragan Bishop of St Germans, from 1979 Bishop of Leicester
1990–95	Timothy Bavin, Bishop of Portsmouth
1995–2002	Rowan Williams, Bishop of Monmouth
2002–	Dominic Walker OGS, Bishop of Monmouth

Superiors of the American foundation of St Gregory's, Conventual priors under the Abbot of Nashdom

1939–47	Dom Paul Severance
1947–49	Dom Francis Hilary Bacon
1949–56	Dom Patrick Dalton
1956–69	Dom Benedict Reid

St Gregory's became an independent abbey in 1969.

Abbots

1969–89	Abbot Benedict Reid
1989–	Abbot Andrew Marr

Members of the Pershore, Nashdom, Elmore community who died in vows

	profession in OSB	date of death
Denys Prideaux	1922	29 Nov 1934, aged 70
Martin Collett	1922	12 Mar 1948, aged 68
Bernard Clements	1923	13 Sep 1942, aged 62
Anselm Hughes	1923	8 Oct 1974, aged 85
Michael Warner	1923	20 Jun 1972, aged 71
Augustine Morris	1924	20 Jan 1997, aged 91
Benedict Ley	1925	4 Feb 1964, aged 68
Dunstan Bailey	1930	15 Aug 1952, aged 67
Christopher Bowen	1930	3 May 1972, aged 66
Patrick Dalton	1932	6 Mar 1984, aged 72
Joseph Sylvester	1933	26 Feb 1947, aged 45
Cuthbert Fearon	1936	21 Jan 1989, aged 76
Gregory Dix	1937	12 May 1952, aged 50
Maurus Benson	1937	10 Aug 1969, aged 66
Andrew Beard	1938	19 Sep 1992, aged 89
Thomas More Bishop	1939	12 Oct 1942, aged 44
Godfrey Stokes	1942	19 Jul 1997, aged 93
Boniface Nielsen	1947	12 Aug 2001, aged 92
Robert Petitpierre	1948	20 Dec 1982, aged 79
Mark Alberic Brierley	1949	22 May 2001, aged 82
Anthony Williams	1950	1 Oct 1995, aged 91
Edward Breach	1953	26 Jan 1982, aged 75
Dunstan Morrell	1953	1 Nov 1986, aged 77
John of the Cross Howton	1957	7 Aug 1977, aged 47
William Cove	1960	14 Feb 1995, aged 85
Cyprian Martin	1961	23 Jan 1982, aged 61

American Foundation of St Gregory's Abbey

Paul Severance	1937	2 Nov 1949, aged 57
Francis Hilary Bacon	1938	4 Sep 1967, aged 63
Joseph Scott	1948	9 Oct 1981, aged 59
Leo Patterson	1950	3 Apr 1994, aged 81

Anthony Damron	1955	10 Nov 1989, aged 64
Wilfrid Braidi	1958	9 Oct 1997, aged 85
David Rogers	1966	14 Sep 1994, aged 61

Intern Oblates of Pershore, Nashdom, Elmore
Charles Hutson, died 7 Jun 1938, aged 77
Hugh Hiscocks, died 1 Aug 1949, aged 51
Alban Oliver, died 24 Jul 1950, aged 79
Charles Burgess, died 16 Feb 1953, aged 85
Edward Cryer, died 9 Oct 1954, aged 71
Raphael Tidd, died 9 Sep 1957, aged 80

Notes

1. This and some of the events detailed in the succeeding paragraphs are considered in more detail in *Kollar1*; see also in the books of Peter Anson, one of the monks who converted in 1913: *Anson1, Anson2* and *Anson3*.

2. Aelred's family had considered sending him to Oxford but his widowed mother had insufficient funds to do so, *Anson2*, p. 25.

3. Faith Press, London, 1961, p. 149.

4. It should be stressed that the term Anglo-Papalist is used in this book without any derogatory intention.

5. See Petà Dunstan, 'Bishops and Religious 1897–1914', *Anglican Religious Life Journal 1* (March 2004), pp. 41–8; also, Rene Kollar, 'The 1897 Lambeth Conference and the Question of Religious Life in the Anglican Communion', in *Kollar2*.

6. NC to DP, 26 February 1912, EA.

7. A more detailed discussion of this and related points can be found in *Kollar1*, pp. 227–8.

8. A start later than intended and a period of illness in the middle, when he went to London for two months, meant that Aelred's canonical novitiate at Maredsous was nearly three months short of the normal minimum, and certainly not 'an entire and uninterrupted year in the novitiate house' usually expected by Roman Catholic canon law.

9. Randall Thomas Davidson (1848–1930), Bishop of Rochester 1891–95, Bishop of Winchester 1895–1903, Archbishop of Canterbury 1903–28.

10. Charles Gore (1853–1932), Bishop of Worcester 1902–05, Bishop of Birmingham 1905–11, Bishop of Oxford 1911–19.

11. Founded in 1891 by Jessie Park Moncrief (1853–1933), who later became Mother Agatha, this was at first an active community called the Community of the Holy Comforter, working in Edmonton. They moved to Baltonsborough in 1906 and adopted a cloistered Benedictine rule.

12. This community was founded in Feltham in 1868, under the leadership of Mother Hilda Stewart (1828–1906). She had been Sister Ella SSM, and then a Third Order sister SHT, prior to the Feltham foundation. After Feltham, the community moved to Twickenham in 1889, Malling Abbey in 1893 and to St Bride's, Milford Haven, in 1911.

13. Mary Jane Ewart (1852–1927), who was Sister Mary Pauline of All Saints 1883–1907, after which she transferred to the Benedictine community then at Malling and was immediately elected Abbess.

14. *Doing the Impossible: A Short Historical Sketch of St Margaret's Convent, East Grinstead*, privately published, SSM, East Grinstead, 2nd edn, 1984, p. 36.

15. The Society of the Atonement; see *CC*, pp. 547–8; also, Titus Cranny (ed.), *Father Paul and Christian Unity*, Chair of Unity Apostolate, Graymoor, Garrison, NY, 1963.

16. Elizabeth CSF, *Corn of Wheat*, Becket Publications, Oxford, 1981, pp. 17–18.

17. Detailed accounts of Father Ignatius (1837–1908) can be found in: *CC*, pp. 51–72; Baroness de Barouch, *The Life of Father Ignatius OSB, the Monk of Llanthony*, Methuen & Co, London, 1904; Arthur Calder-Marshall, *The Enthusiast*, Faber & Faber, London, 1962.

18. This is the same community that was at Malling Abbey in Kent 1893–1911 and then at Milford Haven, where most of the community converted to Roman Catholicism in 1913.

19. Its last members were absorbed into the Caldey community, although only Dom Asaph Harris persevered, remaining a Benedictine monk until his death in 1967. Dom Gildas left and returned after some years, dying at Caldey as a simply professed monk in 1918. See *Anson3*, p. 217, note 48.

20. Niall Diarmid Campbell (1872–1949), 10th Duke of Argyll 1914–49.

21. John Athelstan Laurie Riley (1859–1945), sometime on the London Board of Schools and the National Assembly of the Church of England; also the Chairman of the Anglican and Eastern Churches Association.

22. Dr Darwell Stone (1859–1941), Principal of Pusey House, Oxford, 1909–34.

23. Charles Lindley Wood (1839–1934), 2nd Viscount Halifax 1885–1934.

24. Henry Falconar Barclay Mackay (1864–1936), Vicar of All Saints', Margaret Street, 1908–34.

25. Sir C. J. Hubert Miller (1859–1940), 8th baronet 1868–1940, of Froyle, Hampshire. He was a gentleman collector and ecclesiologist. Upper Froyle was known as the 'Village of Saints' as a result of the profusion of statues he brought back from Italy and set up there.

26. John Cyril Howell (1873–1916), Vicar of St Mary's, Graham Street, 1909–16.

27. Samuel Gurney (1885–1968), Anglo-Catholic man-about-town, a founder of the Nikaean Club and sometime member of the Archbishops' Council on Foreign Relations.

28. NC to AR, 7 March 1913, MS 251, Nos 139–40, LPL.

29. DS to CG, 4 March 1913, copy in the papers of Dav, Vol. 240, Nos 214–15, LPL. This letter also provides details of the subsequent narrative.

30. AC to CG, 25 February 1913, quoted in Aelred Carlyle and others, *A Correspondence*, Caldey Island, 1913, pp. 75–6; and also in *Anson1*, pp. 179–80.

31. John Ludlow Lopes (1882–1961), curate-in-charge of St Francis, Saltley, 1912–14. He subsequently converted to Roman Catholicism.

32. PA to AidH, 24 April 1972, EA. See also, *Anson2*, p. 128, which quotes from an article by Mgr Ronald Knox in *Pax* (March 1938), p. 278.

33. Frederick Penny Vasey (1867–1931).

34. AM to FV, 18 April 1913, MA, copy in EA.

35. FV to AM, 19 April 1913, MA, copy in EA.

36. Harry Bertram Jones. He was received into the Roman Catholic Church at Downside Abbey on 1 April 1913.

37. Gordon Humphrey Tugwell (1885–1960) joined the community 1902. Abbot Aelred had sent him to Scotland to be ordained and he served as a curate at St Peter's, Kirkcaldy, from 1910 to 1912. Back at the monastery for the crucial meetings in February 1913, he did not follow the majority and was the priest brother who removed the reserved sacrament from the monastery chapel to the parish church at the time of the 'conversion'. He held a series of parochial appointments in the Church of England in the next forty years, his last being as Vicar of Hindringham in Norfolk from 1947 to 1959.

38. PA to AidH, 14 August 1972, EA.

39. Michael Cooper, member of the Caldey community 1900–13. In his clerical career, he was employed as a teacher and chaplain, and then had two parishes, first in Illinois and then in Kansas during the 1920s/1930s.

40. Michael Roy Frederick Barton (1889–1964). Among a series of parochial appointments in ECUSA, he was also assistant chaplain to the Community of St Mary at Peekskill, NY, 1919–22. He married in 1924.

41. AC to AM, 8 March 1913 and 20 March 1913, EA.

42. Aubrey Campbell Blaker (1855–1918), oblate of Caldey 1902–13. During his life in community, he served for periods as guest master, editor of *Pax*, and as the priest of the small island church, where he used the Book of Common Prayer. After leaving Caldey, he lived with the Society of the Divine Compassion in Plaistow for some years.

43. PA to AidH, 14 August 1972, EA.

44. The others were Henrietta Rose Dyne (1862–1944), Charles Tylden (1865–1877), Mabel Teresa Susan (1869–1960) and Ada Winifred Miles (1871–1949). Ada was the only one to marry and have children and grandchildren.

45. Reverend Gostwyck Prideaux (1797–1880). He married Lucretia Castle (*c*. 1797–1857).

46. Susan Jackson (died 1854).

47. Henrietta Camilla Jenkin (1807–85).

48. A detailed account of DP's family background and upbringing can be found in Aidan Harker, *Anglican Abbot: Dom Denys Prideaux*, an unpublished manuscript in EA.

49. Paper by Anthony Payne (Denys's nephew), with letter to AidH, 30 August 1967, EA.

50. Charles Jean Marie Loyson (1827–1912). He was successively a Sulpician, a Dominican and a Carmelite friar, but left the Roman Catholic Church in 1871.

51. Henry Pelham Archibald Douglas Pelham-Clinton (1864–1928), 7th Duke of Newcastle 1879–1928.

52. DP to JP, 16 October 1899, EA.

53. James Bell Cox (1837–1923), priest-in-charge of St Margaret's, Princes Road (or Toxteth Park), Liverpool, 1876–1921.

54. DP to JP, 16 May 1899, EA.

55. DP to JP, 21 May 1900, EA.

56. This included the founder, Richard Meux Benson. 'Last Thursday, I had a long talk with Father Benson who has just come over from America. He is quite fully persuaded the end of the world is at hand ... he is intellectually wonderful

for his age. He belongs to the aging Giants, Gladstone, Newman, and age apparently cannot impair their intellect.' DP to JP, 7 November 1899, EA.

57. DP to JP, 14 October 1898, EA.

58. Paper by Anthony Payne (Denys's nephew), with letter to AidH, 30 August 1967, EA.

59. Ada married John Melvin Payne in 1901 and had three children: Anne Teresa (1906–99) later Mrs Maher, Anthony Charles (1908–85) and Joscelyne Henrietta (1910–95), later Mrs Finberg.

60. Anne Maher (née Payne) to AidH, 12 November [1964], EA.

61. DP to JP, 23 April 1900, EA.

62. His health may have been impaired by smoking, a habit he regarded as beneficial: 'my safe guard ag[ain]st the "flue"', DP to JP, 26 January 1900, EA.

63. Henry Westall (1838–1924), curate of St Cuthbert's, Philbeach Gardens, 1882–96, Vicar 1896–1924.

64. Morley John Beaver Richards (1872–1907), Curate of St Thomas's, Huddersfield, 1896–97. After his time at Malling as chaplain, he went to the diocese of Zanzibar, before converting to Roman Catholicism. He became a Dominican friar.

65. PA to AH, 11 February 1956, EA. He expounded the view in print in 'Dom Denys Prideaux (1864–1934)', *Church Quarterly Review* (January 1965), p. 47: 'His health improved rapidly as the result of the Abbot's somewhat amateurish psychiatry, which was largely a mixture of stimulation by verbal suggestions and hypnotism. In most cases the Abbot relied on his instincts and natural psychic gifts.'

66. George Bennet Chambers (1881–1969). After his Caldey years, he served as a parish priest in the Church of England.

67. Samuel Gurney, who was a friend of Aelred's, commented, 'Aelred was psychic and could sense spiritual presences. ... He shared with spiritualists some of their beliefs ...', Samuel Gurney, 'Aelred Carlyle', in *Pax* (Spring 1956), Vol. 46, No. 277, p. 20.

68. PA to AidH, 16 October 1973, EA. Similar sentiments are found in a previous letter to the same correspondent, dated Good Friday 1972, EA.

69. DP to JP, 30 May 1908, EA.

70. NC to AR, 23 April 1911, MS 2351, 137–8, LPL.

71. Peter Anson, 'Dom Denys Prideaux (1864–1934)', *Church Quarterly Review* (January 1965), p. 49.

72. Ronald Arbuthnott Knox (1888–1957), Fellow of Trinity College, Oxford, 1910–17 (chaplain 1912–17). He converted to Roman Catholicism in 1917.

73. Ronald Knox, 'Dom Aelred Carlyle: a memoir', in *Pax* (Spring 1956), Vol. 46, No. 277, p. 30.

74. The SSPP was amalgamated into the Anglo-Catholic Conference in the 1920s and was wound up at the end of 1929. A more detailed account of the society can be found in Rodney Warrener and Michael Yelton, *Martin Travers 1886–1948*, Unicorn Press, London, 2003, pp. 34–45. Also, for its work on the aesthetic front, see *Anson4*, pp. 316–27. The founders of SSPP included Samuel Gurney (1885–1968), Maurice Child (1884–1950) and Ronald Knox (1888–1957). They had all taken a vacation together in Belgium in the summer of 1910

and were much influenced by Catholic practice there. Ronald Knox, *A Spiritual Aeneid*, Longmans, London, 1918, pp. 83–4.

75. It may have been Peter Anson who coined the phrase 'Back to Baroque' for the wider movement of which the SSPP was a part. The Anglo-Papalists saw the Baroque as going forward in contrast to the Gothic which they saw as backward, so Anson's wry phrase could be judged as a 'back-handed compliment' from an Anglo-Catholic turned Roman Catholic. In *Anson4*, p. 327, Anson judged the movement 'not only unreal but unhealthy'.

76. *Pax* (June 1909).

77. *Anson3*, p. 251.

78. DP to JP, 23 July 1912, EA.

79. There is some suggestion that he may have wished to leave much earlier, especially had he known that the particular funds that sustained him were running out. In a letter to his mother in 1914, he was complaining about her handling of his money and added, 'had I left Caldey when I wished ... all this would never have happened'. DP to JP, 21 August 1914, EA, which echoes similar sentiments in a previous letter of 8 January 1914. Presumably his mother had encouraged him to stay on at Caldey when he first indicated he wanted to move.

80. AC to DP, 15 November 1912, PA, copy in EA.

81. DS, diary, 2–3 January 1913, PH.

82. NC to DP, 26 February 1912, EA.

83. DP to JP, 28 April 1913, EA.

84. Henry Wise (1856–1923) lived at Leamington. He had a degree from Magdalen College, Oxford, and had studied for the bar, but lived as a gentleman with private means. He bought the Pershore property for £7,000. It is important to stress that this property only *bordered* the old Abbey church and was a nineteenth-century structure, not a part of any surviving medieval buildings. The monks would not be able to use the medieval church. Even Abbot Aelred had originally made the error of thinking that the property given to his community in 1910 was the old abbey itself. 'I received a letter from a friend to say that the ancient Benedictine Abbey of Pershore having come onto the market, he had purchased it; and he wrote to offer it to me as a free gift ...' AC to SG, MS 2238 16–17, LPL.

85. Society of St John the Evangelist, a men's community based at Cowley in Oxford, and referred to as 'The Cowley Fathers'.

86. DP to JP, 5 August 1913, EA.

87. Huyshe Wolcott Yeatman-Biggs (1845–1922), suffragan Bishop of Southwark 1891–1905, Bishop of Worcester 1905–18, Bishop of Coventry 1918–22.

88. James Hamilton Francis Peile (1863–1940), Vicar of All Saints, Ennismore Gardens, Kensington, 1907–10, Archdeacon of Warwick 1910–20, Archdeacon of Worcester 1921–38.

89. See NC to AR, 6 October 1913, MS 2351, No. 142, LPL.

90. *Jub*, pp. 23–4; BKB, memorandum, EA; Penelope Lawson CSMV to AugM, 14 June 1964, EA.

91. DP to JP, 4 December 1913, EA.

92. DP to JP, 7 December 1913, EA. In a subsequent letter of 8 January 1914, he begged his mother to send money regularly: 'You also seem to imagine we can live on air here.'

93. AM to LH, 11 February 1914, Dav, Vol. 240, Nos 264–5, LPL.

94. Memorandum by RD, Dav, Vol. 240 No. 263, LPL.

95. The response 'ora pro nobis' was to be replaced with 'oret pro nobis'.

96. Bishop of Worcester's memorandum of the meeting of 13 January 1914 with AM and DP, Dav, Vol. 240, Nos 271–80, LPL.

97. This was the name given to agents of the Protestant Truth Society, founded in 1890 by John Kensit to resist 'ritualism' in the Church of England.

98. The story is related in *Jub*, p. 12, quoting *Berrow's Worcester Journal*, 8 May 1914.

99. This argument is more fully delineated in Denys's article 'Pershore Abbey and the Benedictine Life', published in *Caritas*, Vol. 3, No. 11 (May 1914), pp. 5–13.

100. DP, memorandum of 23 August 1915, EA. This is also the source of subsequent quotations from DP in this section.

101. Richard Meux Benson (1824–1915) founded SSJE 1866, Superior 1866–90.

102. DP to JP, 30 June 1915, EA.

103. DP to JP, 8 January 1914, EA.

104. DP to JP, 21 August 1914, EA.

105. Philip Barrett, *The Book of Pershore*, Baron, Buckingham, 1980, 2nd edn, 2000, p. 85; also Marion Freeman (ed.), *Pershore*, Images of England Series, Tempus, Stroud, 1997, p. 55.

106. Gerald Speirs Maxwell (1858–1915), Superior SSJE 1907–15.

107. Brother Martin N/OSB (Thomas Chaplin) to GM, 24 August 1915, EA.

108. Geoffrey Curtis, *William of Glasshampton: Friar: Monk: Solitary 1862–1937*, SPCK, London, 1947, p. 46 and pp. 104–5.

109. DP to JP, 30 June 1915, EA.

110. Clement Carter became a private in the 3rd Battalion of the Worcestershire Regiment, and was killed in action in France on 21 July 1917. It is not certain what happened to Thomas G. Chaplin, but it is possible he may have been a soldier by that name listed in the Commonwealth War Graves Commission registers as killed on 8 January 1917. But this is far from certain. Another aspirant, Edward Charles Daun (1885–1914), volunteered on the outbreak of war and, as a lieutenant in the Royal Sussex Regiment, was killed on 14 September 1914.

111. Anselm was received into the Roman Catholic Church and entered the Caldey community's novitiate on 1 September 1915, being professed in simple vows on 24 September 1916. He was one of the monks who subsequently became disillusioned with Abbot Aelred's leadership and he decided not to take solemn vows. He left the community in 1919 and returned to Birmingham, where he ran a fruiterer's, later a greengrocer's, shop. On 2 August 1920, aged 40, he married Edith Gertrude Humphreyson. He died on 26 November 1961, four days after his 82nd birthday.

112. FV, memoranda to the Baltonsborough nuns, August 1915, MA, copies in EA.

113. PA to AH, 7 April 1956, EA.

114. PA to AidH, 24 April 1972, EA.

115. Bernard Evelyn Kenworthy Browne (1889–1979), curate of Monmouth 1912–15.

116. BKB, memorandum, EA.

117. BKB to GM, 21 August 1915, EA.

118. Alban Henry Baverstock (1871–1950), Rector and Vicar of Hintell Martel, Wimborne, in Dorset, 1899–1930.

119. Alban Baverstock to FV, 26 August 1915, MA, copy in EA.

120. J. Cyril Howell to FV, 26 August 1915, MA, copy in EA.

121. BKB to GM, 24 August 1915, EA.

122. The nuns at Baltonsborough moved to Malling Abbey in Kent in 1916, where they came under the sympathetic Bishop of Rochester. As the bishop was willing to authorize professions, the community no longer required a male Benedictine community to provide oversight or a focus for canonical obedience. The 'congregational' idea faded away. The community still lives there today.

123. DP to J[ames] Fleming Stark, 10 October 1915, EA. Stark was the first lay extern oblate of the community. Although an extern, he lived at the monastery in 1916 for a while. He died on 12 June 1919.

124. BKB to GM, 7 September 1915, EA.

125. BKB to GM, 4 October 1915, EA.

126. BKB to GM, 24 October 1915, EA.

127. His services may have been dispensed with in October 1916, partly because Bernard objected to so many 'seculars' living in the house, House chapter, 3 and 4 October 1916.

128. The donkey (Jenny) was much loved in the community. Denys said the animal was his companion, once the 22-year-old bulldog had had to be put down. See DP to JP, 17 October 1915, EA.

129. DP to JP, 19 March 1918, EA.

130. See daily Chapter minutes between 16 September 1916 and 23 September 1916.

131. This daily 'chapter' began to be recorded on 15 September 1916.

132. George Montagu Withers (1874–1943). He had served various curacies in London, the last in St Stephen's, Haggerston, before trying his vocation. He left in 1917 to become a chaplain to the forces. His last appointment was as Rector of St Leon, Colchester, 1934–39.

133. When Abbot Denys died in 1934, George Withers wrote the community a letter of condolence: 'I was one of those who was with him at Pershore in the difficult days of 1916, when I was honoured quite undeservedly with the friendship of one whom I really came to Pershore to obey.

His intense humility often made me feel ashamed, his astounding wisdom in the addresses on Recollection and Solitude remain with me, and above all his readiness to place himself at the mercy of others, if only he could secure their obedience – those who very often were too small-minded and impatient to recognize his greatness.' George Withers to MC, 4 December 1934, EA.

134. Charles Frederick Hrauda (1881–1945).

135. Francis W. Engleheart to AH, 30 July 1962, EA.

136. Robert Surtees Thornewill (1875–1950).

137. Daily Chapter minutes, 30 December 1916 and 24 January 1917.

138. 'Hrauda ... taught me my present faith, the faith I have lived in since 1918 without one doubt.' BKB to AH, 9 June 1962, EA.

139. Hrauda spent the rest of his life in the Chichester diocese, living in Hove, until his sudden death early in 1945 aged 63. He helped out at various churches, and spent time as a chaplain at the retreat house of the Community of the Holy Cross, Haywards Heath.

140. DP to JP, 19 March 1918, EA.

141. RD to LH, 5 May 1917, Dav, Vol. 342, Nos 217–18, LPL.

142. DP to RD, 18 July 1917, Dav, Vol. 342, Nos 227–8, LPL.

143. Lord Hugh Cecil to RD, 31 July 1917, Dav, Vol. 342, Nos 237–8, LPL.

144. Francis Alphonsus Bourne (1861–1935), Roman Catholic Archbishop of Westminster 1903–35, Cardinal 1911.

145. RD to Lord Hugh Cecil, 4 August 1917, Dav, Vol. 342, No. 239, LPL.

146. H. J. Creedy to RD, 27 August 1917, Dav, Vol. 342, No. 249, LPL.

147. This comment is from his memorandum. In a separate letter he wrote, 'There was ... no obedience to anyone, just an unnamed loyal tradition, which we had managed to keep going, while Bro Denys still kept in the background.' BKB to AH, 9 June 1962, EA.

148. This was one of several orphanages/homes inaugurated by Alban Baverstock, the Rector of Hinton Martel.

149. After a very short time, however, Bernard converted to Roman Catholicism, taught at Stonyhurst for a year and then tried a vocation with the Jesuits. After two years he realized he had no vocation to either Religious life or priesthood, going on instead to found and run a preparatory school. He married and had five children. See BKB to AH, 9 June 1962, EA.

150. In 1918, Coventry became a separate diocese and Huyshe Yeatman-Biggs translated from the See of Worcester to be its first bishop.

151. DP to JP, 14 November 1917, EA.

152. DP to JP, 6 November 1918, EA.

153. DP to JP, 6 November 1918, EA.

154. DP to JP, 3 December 1919, EA.

155. DP to JP, 13 April 1920, EA.

156. DP to JP, 13 April 1920, EA.

157. BKB to AH, 9 June 1962, EA.

158. AugM, memorandum on DP, no date, EA.

159. From a series of letters, BC to WW, 4 April, 6 April, 29 August, 2 September 1920, 8 April 1921, EA.

160. AugM, memorandum on DP, no date, EA.

161. Leighton Sandys Wason (1867–1950), perpetual curate of Cury with Gunwalloe, Cornwall, 1905–19. His story can be found in Roy Tricker, *Mr Wason ... I Think*, Gracewing, Leominster, 1994.

162. *Jub*, p. 20.

163. DP to JP, Ash Wednesday 1914 and 13 April 1920, EA.

164. DP to JP, 14 March 1921, EA.

165. Ernest Harold Pearce (1865–1930), Bishop of Worcester 1919–1930.

166. EP, memorandum, 13 September 1919, Dav, Vol. 240, Nos 294–7, LPL.

167. EP to RD, 10 October 1919, Dav, Vol. 240, Nos 285–7, LPL.

168. RD to EP, 29 November 1919, Dav, Vol 240 Nos 288–292, LPL.

169. It had been issued by Bishop Yeatman-Biggs on 21 January 1915.

170. Arthur Chandler (1860–1939), Bishop of Bloemfontein 1901–20, Rector of Bentley in Hampshire 1921–37.

171. BC to WW, 19 February 1922, EA.

172. EP to RD, 22 February, 1 March and 2 March 1922, Dav, Vol. 240, Nos 309–13, LPL.

173. Arthur Chandler to RD, 4 March 1922, Dav, Vol. 240, No. 317, LPL.

174. EP to DP, 22 October 1921, Dav, Vol. 240, Nos 312–16, LPL.

175. DP to Ada Payne, 14 February 1922, EA.

176. DP to JP, 14 February 1922, EA.

177. Philip Mandeville Bartlett (1884–1958), Vicar of St Saviour's, Poplar, 1919–58.

178. CM 11 July 1922. Bernard had been granted *one* visit away per year. Other monks had to apply on a case-by-case basis to the Abbot for such a privilege, which might be refused.

179. VR, statement to WF, 3 October 1928, MS 3067, Nos 248–62, LPL.

180. CM, 21 August 1921.

181. VR's various statements about these events can be found in his statements and letters in MS 3067, LPL, particularly Nos 240–62.

182. BC to DP, 28 October 1926, EA.

183. ConfM, 6 October 1922, 21 November 1922, 10 March 1923.

184. ConfM, 26 August 1922.

185. CM, 27 March 1922.

186. CM, 2 March 1922.

187. CM, 29 June 1921.

188. BC to WW, 27 November 1921, EA.

189. In mid-1922, the work was divided as follows: Martin was in charge of the gardens, helped by Mr Marton the part-time gardener and any postulants; Bernard ran the kitchen, helped by Francis and Dominic; Peter was the sacristan and supervised the laundry; Victor and Michael looked after the pantry and provisions; Cyril (when he returned) looked after the animals; Francis ran the refectory; Anselm was the choir master and infirmarian; and Victor was the guestmaster, the only monk other than the Abbot allowed to converse with guests. CM, 11 July 1922 and ConfM, 11–12 December 1922.

190. ConfM, 8 October 1922.

191. Martin Boyd, *Day of My Delight*, Lansdowne, Melbourne and London, 1966, pp. 135–6; The passage is very similar (sometimes word for word) to the equivalent narrative in his earlier autobiography, *A Single Flame*, J M Dent & Sons, London, 1939, p. 188.

192. *James*, p. 39.

193. Nina Smith to the editor of the *NAR*, 22 July 1962, EA.

194. *Jub*, pp. 30–1.

195. *Jub*, p. 31.

196. BC to WW, 20 April 1922, EA.

197. AH, memorandum, 1974, EA.

198. BC to WW, 23 April 1922, EA.

199. DP to JP, 20 December 1921, EA.

200. AH, memorandum 1974, EA.

201. AugM, interview with author, 22 July 1995.

202. AugM, memorandum, EA.

203. E. M. Almedingen, *Dom Bernard Clements: A Portrait*, John Lane, London, 1945, p. 31.

204. ConfM, 22 May 1923.

205. Victor Roberts, statement to WF, 3 October 1928, MS 3067, Nos 28–262, LPL.

206. CM, 13 April 1924.

207. CM, 2 June 1925.

208. DP, memorandum to GB, 2 May 1930, MS 3066, Nos 178–82, LPL.

209. AugM, interview with author, 15 June 1996.

210. Boyd, *Day of My Delight*, p. 136. The passage also appears in his earlier autobiography, *A Single Flame*, p. 188.

211. BC to WW, undated except for 'Thursday' but probably May 1922.

212. AH's first book was *Early English Harmony*, published in 1913. Nine more followed, the last brought out in 1967. He wrote for a variety of journals including *Musical Quarterly*, *Music and Letters*, *Musica Disciplina* and the *Proceedings of the Musical Association*. He also edited *The Bec Missal* and *The Portiforium of Wulstan* for the Henry Bradshaw Society's series of volumes of liturgical texts, and contributed articles to *Grove's Dictionary* of music. In 1926 he became Secretary of the Plainsong and Medieval Music Society (an association founded in 1888).

213. BC to WW, 26 December 1921, EA. Cyril was rearing another calf the next year, ConfM, 11 December 1922.

214. Nina Smith to editor of the *NAR*, 22 July 1962, EA.

215. BC to WW, 23 November 1928, EA, and *James*, p. 41.

216. DP to JP, 17 May 1923, EA.

217. DP to Ada Payne, 11 June 1923, EA.

218. DP to Ada Payne, 11 June 1923, EA.

219. Marcus Ethelbert Atlay (1881–1934), Vicar of St Matthew's, Westminster, 1914–22, Canon Treasurer of Gloucester Cathedral 1923–34.

220. DP to JP, 20 July 1922, EA.

221. Francis Underhill and Charles Scott Gillett, introduction to *Report of the First Anglo-Catholic Priests' Convention*, Society of St Peter and St Paul, London, 1921.

222. EP to RD, 7 June 1923, Dav, Vol. 240, No. 330, LPL.

223. RD to EP, 25 June 1923, Dav, Vol. 240 No. 331, LPL.

224. EP to RD, 26 October 1923, Dav, Vol. 240, Nos 337–9, LPL.

225. DP to JP, 17 May 1923, EA.

226. RD, memorandum, Dav, Vol. 240, Nos 342–4, LPL.

227. Désiré Joseph Mercier (1851–1926), Archbishop of Malines 1906–26, made Cardinal 1907.

228. See G. K. A. Bell, *Randall Davidson, Archbishop of Canterbury*, Oxford University Press, London, 2nd edn, 1938, pp. 1254–303.

229. See Petà Dunstan, 'Bishops and Religious 1897–1914', *Anglican Religious Life Journal* 1 (March 2004), pp. 41–8.

230. RD to DP, Dav, Vol. 240, No. 350, LPL.

231. DP to RD, 3 January 1924, Dav, Vol. 240, Nos 351–2, LPL.

232. DP to JP, 18 February 1924, EA.

233. The haste was probably because he had decided to send some monks to found a branch house overseas (see Chapter 6) and wanted the matter settled before their departure in March 1923.

234. CM, 1 March 1923.

235. CM, 3 March 1923.

236. RD to DP, 13 March 1925, Dav, Vol. 240, Nos 427–9, LPL.

237. Hubert Murray Burge (1862–1925), Headmaster of Winchester College 1901–11, Bishop of Southwark 1911–19, Bishop of Oxford 1919–25.

238. Walter Howard Frere (1863–1938), Bishop of Truro 1923–35.

239. DP to Henrietta Prideaux, 14 June 1923, EA.

240. DP to WS, 20 June 1924, EA.

241. DP to WS, 13 March 1924, EA.

242. DP to JP, 17 May 1923, EA.

243. *Laudate* Vol. 1, No. 1 (March 1923), pp. 3–4.

244. CM, 30 September 1924.

245. Herbert Brisbane Ewart (1863–1947).

246. Frances Fleetwood Pellew Wilson (1850–1919), who inherited a large fortune from her father, a Lancashire mill owner, married Prince Alexis Dolgorouki in 1898. Her husband died in 1915 aged 68. Both are buried at Hitcham, near Taplow.

247. Being in her mid-fifties, the princess expected to need the house for no more than twenty years, so she is said to have tried to have the house constructed as cheaply as possible; as a result, among the decorative features, what looked like mahogany was in fact stained deal. Clive Aslet, *The Last Country Houses*, Yale University Press, New Haven, 1982, p. 40.

248. H. Basil Harrison to WS, 5 May 1924, EA.

249. DP to WS, 5 May 1924, EA.

250. This was what the room was called when the monks saw the house, but originally it was designed as an 'entertaining' room, with several possible uses. Lutyens' plans call it the 'big room'.

251. DP to WS, 5 May 1924, EA.

252. HB to RD, 2 August 1924, Dav, Vol. 240, Nos 403–4, LPL; RD to HB, 9 August 1924, Dav, Vol. 240, No. 405, LPL.

253. The reasons for this are discussed later.

254. Herbert Basil Harrison, who resided at the Manor House, Pershore.

255. Some of the furniture and art works had been sold off in earlier years. However, the auction of the remainder of the Louis and Empire furniture, and other contents, took place at Nashdom during the rest of that same week.

256. *Laudate*, Vol. 2, No. 32 (June 1924).

257. Walter Warren Seton (1882–1927).

258. DP to WS, 13 March 1924, EA.

259. WS to DP, 19 May 1924, EA.

260. Charles Henry Bickerton Hudson (1861–1937).

261. CHBH to WS, 2 June 1924, EA.

262. CHBH to WS, 6 June 1924, EA.

263. CHBH to WS, 24 June 1924 and 30 October 1924, EA.

264. Ernest Hermitage Day (1866–1946).

265. E. Hermitage Day to WS, 13 June 1924, EA.

266. Thomas Dyer Edwardes (1847–1926). He became a Roman Catholic the same year that he offered the property to the Benedictines.

267. AR to WS, 9 June 1924, EA.

268. Aelred Carlyle was no longer the abbot, however. He had resigned in 1921, left the Religious life and subsequently worked as a secular priest in Canada.

269. WS to Charles Freeman, 19 June 1924, EA.

270. *Jub*, pp. 39–40.

271. DP to WS, 20 June 1924, EA.

272. HB to RD, 6 May 1925, Dav, Vol. 240, Nos 431–2, LPL.

273. *Jub*, p. 39.

274. DP to WS, 30 September 1924, EA.

275. WS to DP, 18 January 1927, EA.

276. Society of St John the Evangelist (Cowley), Community of the Resurrection (Mirfield) and Community of St Mary the Virgin (Wantage).

277. LH to WS, 1 November 1924, copy in EA.

278. *Laudate*, Vol. 2, No. 4 (December 1924).

279. WS to Sidney Dark, editor of the *Church Times*, 19 January 1925, copy in EA.

280. DP to WS, 20 June 1924, EA.

281. DP to JP, 1 September 1924, EA.

282. Henry Power Bull (1858–1947), Superior SSJE 1916–31.

283. HB to RD, 6 May 1925, Dav, Vol. 240, Nos 431–2, LPL.

284. H. P. Bull to RD, 29 June 1925, Dav, Vol. 240, Nos 442–4, LPL.

285. Thomas Banks Strong (1861–1944), Dean of Christ Church, Oxford, 1901–20, Bishop of Ripon 1920–25, Bishop of Oxford 1925–37.

286. TS to Revd Mervyn Haigh, 3 October 1930, Lan, Vol. 102, No. 263, LPL. Soon after this, Strong was replaced as committee chair by George Bell, Bishop of Chichester.

287. RD to TS, 14 July 1925, Dav, Vol. 240, No. 446, LPL.

288. *Laudate*, Vol. 4, No. 15 (September 1926), p. 124, and Vol. 4, No. 16 (December 1926), p. 193.

289. AH, memorandum 1974, EA.

290. Mowbray Stephen O'Rorke (1869–1953), Bishop of Accra 1913–24.

291. Paul Jenkins, 'The Anglican Church in Ghana, 1905–1924, (II)', *Transactions of the Historical Society of Ghana*, Vol. XV, No. 2 (December 1974), p. 193.

292. The first two Ghanaians were ordained in 1916, and there were three Anglican Ghanaian priests at the end of 1924.

293. BC to WW, 27 April 1922, EA.

294. *Jub*, p. 35.

295. DP to JP, 20 July 1922, EA.

296. CM, 1 March 1923.

297. CM, 2 March 1923.

298. EP to DP, 22 October 1921, Dav, Vol. 240, Nos 315–16, LPL.

299. *Laudate*, Vol. 1, No. 1 (March 1923).

300. For this and other details in this section, see Paul Jenkins, 'The Anglican Church in Ghana, 1905–1924', *Transactions of the Historical Society of Ghana*, Vol. XV, No. 1 (June 1974), and Vol. XV, No. 2 (December 1974).

301. B. Sundkler and C. Steed, *A History of Christianity in Africa*, Cambridge University Press, Cambridge, 2000, p. 725.

302. For this, and some of the subsequent information, *Laudate*, Vol. 1, No. 2 (June 1923).

303. *Laudate*, Vol. 1, No. 3 (September 1923) and Vol. 1, No. 4 (December 1923).

304. *Laudate*, Vol. 2, No. 1 (March 1924), Vol. 2, No. 3 (September 1924) and Vol. 2, No. 4 (December 1924).

305. O'Rorke became the incumbent of some villages in Norfolk for ten years, then a school chaplain in Somerset, and spent some of his retirement years with the Community of the Companions of Jesus the Good Shepherd in Devon.

306. John Orfeur Aglionby (1883–1963), Bishop of Accra 1924–51.

307. *Laudate*, Vol. 2, No. 2 (June 1924).

308. And (more trivially) the monks approved of his *very* purple cassock and biretta. PH to Winifride SPB (Winifred Wilkinson), 18 July 1924, EA.

309. PH to Winifride SPB (Winifred Wilkinson), 11 April 1924, EA.

310. PH to Winifride SPB (Winifred Wilkinson), 18 July 1924, EA.

311. CM, 3 October 1916.

312. *Laudate*, Vol. IV, No. 13 (March 1926) and Vol. IV, No. 14 (June 1926).

313. JA to DP, 19 May 1926, EA.

314. PH to Winifride SPB (Winifred Wilkinson), 18 July 1924, EA.

315. CM, 21 May 1929.

316. BC to DP, 28 October 1926, EA. This letter is the source of quotations in the section that follows, unless otherwise sourced.

317. PH to MC, 10 November 1925, EA.

318. MC to PH, 13 November 1925, EA.

319. PH to MC, 15 November 1925, EA.

320. JA to DP, 19 May 1926, EA.

321. Richard Lloyd Langford-James (1873–1948), Vicar of St James, Edgbaston, 1923–41.

322. Richard Langford-James to VR, 4 January 1927.

323. *Laudate*, Vol. V, No. 17 (March 1927) and Vol. V, No. 18 (June 1927).

324. He returned to the Church of England and spent the rest of his life as a parish priest, and published a number of books on prayer and spirituality.

325. CM, 8 February 1936 and 12 August 1936.

326. *Laudate*, Vol. V, No. 19 (September 1927), Vol. V, No. 20 (December 1927) and Vol. VI, No. 23 (September 1928); *Bailey*, pp. 43–6.

327. For details in this paragraph and the following, see *Laing*, and also Bernard Clements, *A Monk in Margaret Street*, Mowbray, London, 1941, pp. 98–105.

328. Bengt Sundkler, *The Christian Ministry in Africa*, SCM Press, London, 1960, p. 199.

329. *Laing*, p. 23.

330. *Laudate*, Vol. VII, No. 28 (December 1929).

331. PH to DP, 12 November 1929, EA.

332. JA to DP, 11 July 1930, EA.

333. BC to DP, 16 September 1930, EA.

334. It is interesting that the Jubilee book of 1964 said only that Abbot Denys had 'recalled' the *three* brethren to England in 1931, without mentioning that two of them had gone over to Rome and there was in fact only one to recall. Perhaps this illustrated that the remembrance of the secessions still caused some pain among the senior brethren. *Jub*, p. 36.

335. *Laing*, p. 31.

336. Although for a while it was successful: one rabbit won second prize at shows in August 1933 at Loudwater and Sandy, *NAL* (September 1933).

337. The community also held a market (confusingly in the 1930s still called the Pershore Market) in a parish hall in London once a year. There was usually a prominent Anglo-Catholic speaker. This market was usually opened formally by Princess Marie Louise, a good friend to the Anglican Benedictines, and one of whose ladies-in-waiting was a neighbour of the community at Nashdom. Members of the community on occasions dined with the Princess there. Through her mother, Princess Helena (1846–1923), Princess Marie Louise (1872–1956) was a granddaughter of Queen Victoria. She also visited the monastery on several occasions, and, with the Prince of Wales, visited St Cyprian's, Kumasi, in 1925. *Laudate*, Vol. III, No. 10 (June 1925).

338. *James*, p. 39.

339. AugM, interview with author, 15 June 1996.

340. Columba (Joseph Aloysius) Marmion (1858–1923), Abbot of Maredsous 1909–23. He was the abbot who was involved in the 1913 conversion from Anglicanism of the Caldey community, allowing Aelred Carlyle to do a 'novitiate' at Maredsous and for the other monks in the first instance to be oblates of that monastery, so that their eventual recognition as a Roman Catholic community was greatly facilitated. See Mark Tierney, *Dom Columba Marmion: A Biography*, Columba Press, Dublin, 1994, pp. 141–56.

341. This was explicitly stated by Anselm and minuted in the CM of 13 April 1924.

342. *James*, p. 42.

343. Certainly one other Anglican community (Community of St Peter) finally split into two in the early 1930s partly owing to the introduction by the chaplain and Mother Superior of particular ascetic practices gleaned from French Roman Catholic sources.

344. Elizabeth Georgina Slater (1867–1949), professed 1893, Mother Elizabeth SC 1897–1949.

345. AugM, interview with author, 28 October 1995.

346. *James*, p. 46.

347. Richard Langford-James to VR, 4 January 1927, EA: 'I know the horror the Abbot has o[f] anything like "sloppiness" and sentimentality. But I think he sometimes carries that horror too far ...'

348. CM, 27 June 1928.

349. Albert Ernest Frost (1876–1961), oblate 1928 as Bede, chaplain to SSM (East Grinstead) 1940–57.

350. CM, 29 November 1928.

351. RD to TS, 10 May 1927, Dav, Vol. 217, No. 37, LPL.

352. William Cosmo Gordon Lang (1864–1945), Bishop of Stepney 1901–08, Archbishop of York 1908–28, Archbishop of Canterbury 1928–42.

353. CM, 29 November 1926.

354. *A Valiant Victorian: The Life and Times of Mother Emily Ayckbowm* ... , Mowbray, London, 1964, p. 233.

355. Mother Raphael Mary Augustine Roberts (1885–1981), professed 1909, Mother Superior, later Abbess, of Edgware Abbey 1926–81.

356. *NAL* (June 1932).

357. This arrangement lasted until 1965, when the sisters decided to elect a bishop as Visitor.

358. Note that the word 'Congregation' was mentioned in *Laudate*, Vol. VII, No. 25 (March 1929) in reporting the first of these developments.

359. CM, 2 November 1928.

360. *Laudate*, Vol. VI, No. 24 (December 1928).

361. *Laudate*, Vol. VII, No. 25 (March 1929), No. 26 (June 1929) and No. 27 (September 1929).

362. GD, memorandum, 20 November 1930, EA.

363. CM, 31 October 1929.

364. *Bailey*, pp. 47–9.

365. Guy Warman, Bishop of Manchester, to KK, undated, included in KK to MC, 27 October 1938.

366. CM, 17 November 1931.

367. CM, 30 September 1924.

368. CM, 13 April 1924.

369. CM, 7 April 1925.

370. CM, 2 June 1925.

371. CM, 7 June 1925.

372. AugM, interview with author, 15 June 1996.

373. CM, 14 June 1925.

374. CM, 31 October 1928, 16 November 1931, 6 November 1936, 15 and 23 February 1937 and 9 December 1937. The Pershore and Nashdom Trust Ltd was finally incorporated on 16 November 1937.

375. Visitation injunctions of Bishop Frere, 2 January 1933.

376. *The History of the Benedictine Community of St Mary's Abbey, West Malling, Kent*, unpublished manuscript in Malling Abbey archives, p. 336. This gives some detail (gleaned from day books) of the approach by a group at Nashdom.

377. Between 1927 and 1934, five solemnly professed monks left the community: Francis, Victor, Peter, Dominic and Mark (the last three to become Roman Catholics). In the same period, thirteen simply professed withdrew: Cyprian, Wulstan, Bruno, Hugh, Gabriel, Joseph, John Baptist, Edmund, Leo, Paulinus, Ignatius, Philip and Francis Xavier, of whom four are known to have become Roman Catholics, though one of them returned very quickly to the Anglican fold.

378. For this paragraph and other particulars of Denys's viewpoint in the later text, see Dav, MS 3066, Nos 178–82 and 195–222, LPL.

379. For this paragraph and other particulars of Victor's viewpoint in the later text, see Dav, MS 3066, Nos 240–62, 294–304 and 334–7, LPL.

380. Ralph Nattress to GB, 1 January 1939, Bel, MS 3068, No. 105, LPL.

381. For these letters, see Dav, MS 3069, pp. 98–102, LPL.

382. AugM, interview with author, 22 July 1995.

383. CM, 12 November 1928.

384. CM, 20 December 1928.

385. Winfrid Oldfield Burrows (1858–1929), Bishop of Truro 1912–19, Bishop of Chichester 1919–29.

386. George Kennedy Allen Bell (1883–1958), Bishop of Chichester 1929–58.

387. Bel, MS 3067, Nos 99–103, LPL.

388. In the years that followed, Victor quarrelled once too often with Bishop Bell on other matters and, by the end of the 1930s, his licence was revoked. However, the sisters stood by him, and he remained the Warden of CHC until his death in 1954. He destroyed all his own papers before his death so that nothing survives in the CHC archive to elucidate further the account that emerges from the Bell papers.

389. The Chapter were still discussing Victor's vows and minuting the issue as late as 1941. See CM, 17 September 1941. There was no reconciliation with Victor Roberts, and only after his death in 1954 were relations between the Community of the Holy Cross and Nashdom restored. As late as 1947, Martin wrote to one of his spiritual directees, who had asked him if she could go for a retreat at CHC, warning her about Roberts, 'I don't see that a short visit can do you any great harm, so long as you do not come in close contact with what I call "The Head". Don't allow yourself to come in close contact with any of them.' MC to Miss E. Hogben, 26 January 1947, EA.

390. AugM, memorandum on Denys, no date, EA.

391. *Laudate* Vol. IV, No. 14 (June 1926).

392. In 1928, he visited Italy, including the new headquarters of the Carthusian Order at Fameta, near Lucca, and also Monte Cassino, where St Benedict founded his monastery. *Laudate*, Vol. VI, No. 22 (June 1928). In 1929, he visited Italy and France, including the Benedictine hermits at Camoldoli, the Basilian monks at Grotta Ferata, the Carthusians at Grand Chartreuse, and the shrines of St Francis de Sales and Jeanne Françoise de Chantal at Annecy. *Laudate*, Vol. VII, No. 26 (June 1929).

393. The Confraternity of Our Lady and the League of Our Lady.

394. *James*, p. 46.

395. Many of the stories related about him are apocryphal but for some that are true see *Jub*, p. 47.

396. AugM, memorandum on Denys, no date, EA.

397. CM, 4 August 1932.

398. CM, 23 March 1933.

399. DP to family, 18 December 1933, EA.

400. AugM, interview with author, 22 July 1995.

401. Martin Collett, Bernard Clements, Michael Warner, Augustine Morris, Benedict Ley and Dunstan Bailey.

402. Bernard Horner CR (1873–1960), Superior CR 1940–43.

403. CM, 6 December 1934.

404. CM, 9 January 1935.

405. All Saints', Margaret Street, parish papers, August 1935, quoted in P. Galloway and C. Rawll, *Good and Faithful Servants: All Saints' Margaret Street and Its Incumbents*, Churchman Publishing, Worthing, 1988, p. 128.

406. More detail on Bernard Clements can be found in Almedingen, *Dom Bernard Clements*. Also, Galloway and Rawll, *Good and Faithful Servants*, pp. 114–36.

407. *NAL* (August 1948).

408. *Laudate*, Vol. VII, No. 28 (December 1929).

409. AugM, interview with author, 28 October 1995.

410. *Jub*, p. 65.

411. *Jub*, p. 66.

412. *Bailey*, p. 52.

413. CM, 19 December 1934 and *Jub*, pp. 42–43.

414. CM, 22 April 1935.

415. *NAL* (September 1935).

416. CM, 6 August 1935.

417. *NAL* (June 1936).

418. *NAL* (December 1935).

419. CM, 4 August 1932 and 23 November 1932.

420. Lilian Mary G. Bond (1887–1980) was sometimes known as Nashdom's 'eldest daughter'.

421. CM, 25 February 1936. A few years later, the Chapter altered the status of these women. This was all part of an Anglo-Papalist desire to follow Rome in all matters. So in 1938, it was formally pronounced that women could not be under vows of any sort (with respect to a men's community), and women oblates of Nashdom 'had executed a Life promise only, at the most' (CM 11 November 1938). They were still called oblates but did not have the same status within the community fold as their male counterparts. This was a somewhat begrudging attitude towards a group of women who had been some of the staunchest friends the monks had ever had. In time, the distinction was dropped. Years later, Augustine Morris expressed much regret when he recalled what he referred to as the 'masculinist supremacist' attitudes of his earlier days in the community. AugM, interview with author, 28 October 1995.

422. *Jub*, p. 66.

423. For the text, see Roger Coleman (ed.), *Resolutions of the Twelve Lambeth Conferences 1867–1988*, Anglican Book Centre, Toronto, 1992, pp. 45–54.

424. DP to Mabel Prideaux, 17 July 1917, EA.

425. C. F. Hrauda to DP, 8 August 1921, EA.

426. DP to JP, 30 July 1923, EA.

427. Serge (Sergius) Nikolaevich Bolshakoff (1901–90). Ecumenism and issues of social justice were the main topics of his research work and writings in later years. He later received a doctorate in philosophy at Christ Church, Oxford, in 1943. Of his many books, the most notable is probably *Russian Mystics*. He lived at the Swiss abbey of Hauterive from 1974 until his death in 1990.

428. In 1933–34, Bolshakoff founded an international academy for the study of economic and social problems on the lines of Christian principles as defined in papal encyclicals to provide a counterweight to Marxism. The preliminary meeting was held at Nashdom, with further conferences in London and Oxford, and, according to *NAL* (December 1934), Nashdom was the site for the fledgling organization's headquarters. Both Denys and Martin were supporters of the aims of the idea.

429. Alexis Khrapovitsky (1863–1936), professed as Anthony 1885, Russian Orthodox Bishop of Cheboksarsk 1897–1900; Archbishop of Ufimsk 1900–02, of Volinsk 1902–13, of Kharkov 1913–17; Metropolitan of Kiev and Galich 1917–36.

430. Tikhon Lysshenko or Liashenko (died 1945).

431. *Laudate*, Vol. VII, No. 25 (March 1929).

432. Nikolai Karpov (1890–1931), Russian Orthodox Bishop of London 1929–31.

433. Denys and Martin attended the consecration, held at St Philip's, Buckingham Palace Road, a former Anglican church given over to the Orthodox in London. *Laudate*, Vol. VII, No. 27 (September 1929). Note that there were two Russian Orthodox communities in London after a split occurred in 1927: those of the Russian Church Abroad (or 'of the Exile'), whose allegiance was to Metropolitan Anthony of Kiev, and those of the Russian Patriarchal Church, still loyal to the leadership in Russia, which the Church Abroad disowned as collaborators with the (atheist) Bolshevik revolutionary government in Moscow. St Philip's had been used since 1923, but after the split, the two communities worshipped there on alternate Sundays. The building, in increasing disrepair, had eventually to be demolished – and made way for Victoria coach station. The Patriarchal Orthodox moved to another former Anglican parish church, All Saints, Ennismore Gardens, in 1956, but the Church Abroad refused to share this and found their own premises elsewhere.

The complicated allegiances within Orthodoxy are also shown by the fact that Bolshakoff's Benedictine confraternity was 'decreed closed' by the Russian Orthodox Abroad at their Synod in August 1938, and then came under the jurisdiction of the Rumanian Patriarch. See Protopriest M. Polski to MC, 14 December 1938, and MC to Protopriest M. Polski, 20 December 1938, EA.

434. AugM, interview with author, 15 June 1996.

435. Keith F. E. Winslow (1888–1959), professed as Bede 1915.

436. Maurice Bévenot SJ (1897–1980), professed as a Jesuit 1914. It should be added that Bévenot was one of five Jesuits who did visit Nashdom in June 1938 for theological conversations, but this face-to-face meeting was the exception to the usual pattern of relations with Roman Catholics.

437. Augustine Morris remembered visiting Prinknash Abbey during the Second World War, as he knew Bede Griffiths, and that Benedict Ley knew two monks at Downside Abbey. These and Gregory Dix's contacts with some Jesuits in the 1930s were the only substantial links that Augustine could recall between Nashdom and English Roman Catholic communities before the 1950s. AugM, interview with author, 15 June 1996.

438. That is, between the (then) Feast of the Chair of St Peter (18 January) and the Conversion of St Paul (25 January).

439. Lewis Thomas Wattson (1863–1940), later Father Paul James Francis SA.

440. Spencer John Jones (1857–1943), Rector of Batsford with Moreton-le-Marsh, Gloucestershire, from 1887. A sermon he preached at St Matthew's, Westminster, on 29 June 1900, was so praised that it was expanded to become the book *England and the Holy See*, Longmans, London, 1902, which became the best-known fluent exposition of the Anglo-Papalist position. This book was the reason the transatlantic correspondence with Father Wattson began.

441. For more information, see Titus Cranny, *Father Paul and Christian Unity*, Chair of Unity Apostolate, Graymoor, Garrison, NY, 1963, especially pp. 79–131, and Geoffrey Curtis, *Paul Couturier and Unity in Christ*, SCM Press, London, 1964, especially pp. 52–68 and 132–47.

442. For the text, see Coleman (ed.), *Resolutions*, p. 6.

443. Paul Irénée Couturier (1881–1953), on the staff of the Institut des Chartreux, Lyon, 1909–51.

444. Lambert Beauduin (1873–1960). He was a monk of the Abbey of Mont César at Louvain before moving to Amay.

445. *NAL* (September 1934).

446. See *Laudate*, Vol. XIV, No. 55 (September 1936), pp. 126–37, for his article about the pilgrimage. Couturier would call Benedict his first Anglican friend and his 'guardian angel' and gave him his crucifix containing a fragment of the cross.

447. Henry Joy Fynes-Clinton (1875–1959), Rector of St Magnus the Martyr, City of London, 1921–59.

448. Curtis, *Paul Couturier*, p. 171.

449. Pierre-Marie Gerlier (1880–1965), Bishop of Tarbes et Lourdes 1929–37, Archbishop of Lyon 1937–65, Cardinal 1937.

450. Maria Pia Gullini (1892–1959), Abbess of Grottaferrata 1931–40, 1946–51.

451. Paul B Quattrocchi OCSO, *La beata Maria Gabriella d'Unità*, Monasterio Trappiste, Vitorchiano, 1960, 2nd edn 1980; 2nd edn trans. Mary Jeremiah OP, as *A Life for Unity: Sr Maria Gabriella*, New City Press, New York, 1990, p. 76.

452. BL to Abbess Maria Pia, 15 July 1938, quoted in Quattrochi, *A Life for Unity*, p. 83.

453. Maria Sagheddu (1914–39), born in Dorgali, Sardinia, professed as Maria Gabriella, 31 October 1937.

454. Mother Sarah SSP (1871–1962), professed 1897.

455. Mother Janet Mary SGS (1860–1938), professed in life vows as a sister SSM (Haggerston) 1890, founded SGS 1909 and served as its Reverend Mother until her death.

456. This community had been founded by a Mother Everilda, who left the Benedictines of West Malling (see chapter 1) around 1900 in protest at Mother Hilda remaining in office. She was joined by Mother Mildred. When the West Malling community left for Milford Haven in 1911, one of their number, Mother Margaret, did not wish to move to Wales and so joined Everilda's small group. The three then tried to claim tenancy of the vacant Malling Abbey in 1913 as the 'heirs' of the original Anglican community there, but without success. Eventually,

Mother Mildred continued with a few new sisters at Plaxted and then at Kettle-baston near Ipswich. Sister Scholastica transferred to SGS in 1935 (and died the following year); another sister died at Christmas 1937. Mildred's death in 1938 brought the community to an end.

457. In 1935, Martin had outlined a proposal to Chapter for a congregation to include Edgware, SSP Laleham and Malling Abbey, but this did not materialize. CM, 9 January 1935.

458. The Benedictine CHC sisters at Haywards Heath were totally ruled out of the equation by the continued presence there as Warden of Victor Roberts. As for Alton Abbey, this was not then formally following the *Rule of St Benedict* and was, unusually for the time, a mixed community of brothers and sisters. Indeed the superior from 1922 to 1932 was one of the sisters; at the death of the last surviving of the sisters in 1951, the community became just for men.

459. Maud Euan-Smith (1873–1966), professed as Magdalen Mary 1904, Abbess 1928–51.

460. For a more detailed account, see Petà Dunstan, 'Who's Taking Advice: The Founding of the Advisory Council', in *The Anglican Religious Communities Year Book 2004–2005*, Canterbury Press, Norwich, 2003, pp. 26–8. The same essay is also published as the 'Historical Summary' in *A Handbook of the Religious Life*, 5th edn, Canterbury Press, Norwich, 2004, pp. vi–viii.

461. *Laudate*, Vol. VIII, No. 29 (March 1930), Vol. IX, No. 33 (March 1931) and Vol. IX, No. 35 (September 1931).

462. CM, 9 January 1935.

463. William Braithwaite O'Brien (1874–1960), Superior SSJE 1931–49.

464. *A Directory of the Religious Life*, SPCK, London, 1943, pp. 42–4.

465. WF to CGL, 17 October 1936, Lan, Vol. 145, No. 103, LPL.

466. For a fuller treatment of this subject, see *Marr*.

467. Vivan Albertus Peterson (1892–1966), Rector of St James's, Cleveland, from 1919.

468. The next solemn professions did not take place until 1937.

469. *Benedicite* (December 1938). Paul Severance to MC, 25 October 1938, EA.

470. John T. Dallas, Bishop of New Hampshire to CGL, 16 September 1938, Lan, Vol. 163, No. 200, LPL.

471. CGL to John T. Dallas, Bishop of New Hampshire, 29 September 1938, Lan, Vol. 163, No. 201, LPL.

472. Kenneth Escott Kirk (1886–1954), Regius Professor of Moral and Pastoral Theology, University of Oxford, 1933–37, Bishop of Oxford 1937–54.

473. KK to CGL, 4 July 1938, Lan, Vol. 163, No. 197, LPL.

474. Alan Don (CGL's secretary) to WF, 20 October 1936, Lan, Vol. 145, No. 104, LPL.

475. CM, 13 March 1940.

476. *NAL* (June 1939).

477. CM, 22 May 1940.

478. After several years at a parish in New Jersey, Father Meinrad worked in the Diocese of Nassau, the Bahamas, for over twenty years. In 1965, he returned to the USA to live as an Oblate of the Society of St Paul. In 1977, he first took

annual vows as a member of that Religious community and continued to do so until his death in 1995.

479. CM, 31 January 1941.

480. This was possible because Anselm, having been lecturing in the USA when war broke out in Europe, had found it difficult to get passage home. In 1941, he was still stranded and would not return home until 1943. While in the USA, he spent two years as Rector of Fredonia, NY.

481. *NAL* (June 1939).

482. *NAL* (September 1939).

483. He and Gregory would take solemn vows together on 11 October 1940. Note that Maurus's assistance was as 'housekeeper', as he was not yet ordained in 1939.

484. Note that Bernard remained as Vicar at All Saints', Margaret Street, and Anselm was stranded in the USA, being halfway through a lecture tour.

485. This part of the Malling property would be the home of a small community of Cistercian monks from 1966 to 2004, and would be known in those later years as Ewell Monastery.

486. *NAL* (September 1939).

487. Quoted in Eric Fenn's foreword to Bernard Clements, *Speaking in Parables*, SCM Press, London, 1943, p. 4.

488. Later published as Bernard Clements, *When Ye Pray*, SCM Press, London, 1936.

489. Christened Herbert Francis, and known as Frank by his family, he had been given the name Adrian as a school nickname. It stuck and he was known as Adrian until he entered the Nashdom community in 1937.

490. 'Adrian' Bishop to 'Dadie' Rylands, 28 June 1923, GHWR/3/47, KCA.

491. Cyril Connolly on p. 46 and Noel Annan on p. 79 of Hugh Lloyd-Jones (ed.), *Maurice Bowra: A Celebration*, Duckworth, London, 1974.

492. C. M. Bowra, *Memories 1898–1939*, Weidenfeld and Nicolson, London, 1966, p. 273.

493. Bowra, *Memories*, p. 325.

494. The monks were suspicious about the circumstances of his death, even after the war ended: 'This seems to have been the work of fifth columnists, for the news of it was published in Italy before it was received in England.' *NAL* (1946). This was also the view of his friend, Bowra: see Maurice Bowra to Sebastian Sprott, 18 June [1943], WSHS/1/9, KCA.

495. *Jub*, p. 61.

496. *NAL* (December 1940).

497. MC to Miss E. S. Hogben, 26 June [1942], EA.

498. Maurus Benson to Miss E. S. Hogben, 24 October 1944, EA.

499. Abbess Raphael's exacting standards meant the house was 'cleaner than the monks had ever seen it'. *NAL* (Pentecost 1946).

500. *Bailey.*

501. Gregory Dix, *The Shape of the Liturgy*, Dacre Press, Westminster, 1945.

502. AugM, interview with author, 28 October 1995.

503. Lesslie Newbiggin, *Unfinished Agenda*, SPCK, London, 1985, pp. 86–7. This quotation referred to a meeting in 1946.

504. William Temple (1881–1944), Bishop of Manchester 1921–28, Archbishop of York 1928–42, Archbishop of Canterbury 1942–44.

505. Edward Keble Talbot (1877–1949), Superior CR 1922–40.

506. CR, OSB Nashdom, SSF, SSJE, SSM.

507. Richard Elliott Raynes (1903–58), Superior CR 1943–58.

508. AugM, interviews with author, 22 July 1995 and 15 June 1996. Augustine's memories, even in old age, proved accurate where verification from another source was possible, so it seems reasonable to trust his verbal account. The author went through the events of the conference with Augustine on two occasions, almost a year apart, and his report of it was the same on each occasion.

509. William Robert Mounsey (1867–1952), Bishop of Labuan and Sarawak 1909–16, Vicar of St Mark's, Regent Park, 1921–24.

510. Raynes's forcefulness was illustrated at the end of this gathering. He expressed dismay at finding an 'English' altar in the chapel of the CR retreat house, one not furnished in the baroque style of continental Roman Catholicism. He accordingly had the altar demolished after compline on the last evening.

511. *Kemp*, p. 155.

512. Frederick Burstal Bedale (1888–1961), Director SSM 1943–52.

513. GD to KK, 20 November 1943, Kirk Papers, MS 4346, No. 17, LPL.

514. Reginald Richard Roseveare (1902–72), Bishop of Accra 1956–67.

515. Augustine remembered clearly that he and Roseveare were late returning and Bishop Mounsey had jokingly reprimanded them, 'You're late for school', to which Augustine had replied, 'We were doing our homework.' AugM, interview with author, 22 July 1995.

516. *Bailey*, p. 124.

517. GD to KK, 28 November 1943, Kirk Papers, MS 4346, No. 18, LPL.

518. Gregory's admission of his own lack of effectiveness can be seen in a letter to Bishop Kirk: ' ... on reflection I am quite sure that you brought us out of the business last week better than could have been hoped. (I put it that way because I think that is how the credit lies. Certainly not with me. I was tired & far from well & could not weigh things at all fairly ...)' GD to KK, 24 April 1950, Kirk Papers, MS 4346, No. 64, LPL.

519. KK to CGL 4 July 1938, Lan, Vol. 163, Nos 197–8, LPL.

520. He was indisposed for most of 1939 with chest problems, pneumonia (from which he nearly died) and then phlebitis. *Kemp*, p. 82.

521. KK to CGL, 8 April 1940, Lan, Vol. 178, Nos 270–2, LPL.

522. CGL to KK, April 1940, Lan, Vol. 178, Nos 273–4, LPL.

523. KK to CGL, 26 April 1940, Lan, Vol. 178, No. 273, LPL.

524. Frederick James Western (1880–1951), Bishop of Tinnevelly, Madura and Ramnad 1929–38. He was elected Visitor by the Nashdom Chapter on 25 September 1940.

525. KK to WT, 31 May 1944, Tem, Vol. 35, No. 201, LPL.

526. Vibert Jackson (1874–1963), Bishop of Honduras 1921–27, then the Windward Islands 1930–36, Vicar of South Ascot 1940–63. The Chapter elected him as Visitor on 10 July 1944.

527. WT to KK, 2 June 1944, Tem, Vol. 35, No. 202, LPL.

528. Maurus Benson to Miss E. S. Hogben, 21 June 1945, EA: 'The South India scheme is making a lot of extra work for him [the Abbot].'

529. MC to Miss E. S. Hogben, 14 November 1944, EA.

530. MC to Miss E. S. Hogben, 16 December 1939 and 22 February 1940, EA.

531. MC to Miss E. S. Hogben, 30 July 1942, EA.

532. MC to Miss E. S. Hogben, 17 June 1945, and Maurus Benson to the same, 21 June 1945 and 10 July 1945, EA.

533. The resignation was formally accepted at an Extraordinary meeting of Chapter the following day.

534. *Jub*, p. 64.

535. Anselm held the position of claustral prior, the Abbot's deputy, from very early in 1936, but stepped down in 1945, when he had been granted leave of absence to live in Oxford and edit the two volumes of the *New Oxford History of Music*.

536. CM, 30 May 1942 and 24 February 1944.

537. AugM, interview with author, 15 June 1996.

538. Louisa Florence Morris (1872–1961). The information on Augustine's background is entertainingly told in Louisa Morris, 'Thou hast kept the good wine until now', an unpublished autobiography by Augustine's mother, copy in EA.

539. AugM, interview with author, 15 June 1996.

540. AugM, interview with author, 28 October 1995.

541. More details of this story, and those that follow, can be found in *Marr*.

542. AugM, interview with author, 28 October 1995.

543. *Bailey*, pp. 239–40.

544. CM, 23 February 1955, and AugM, interview with author, 22 July 1995.

545. Augustine recalled how Bishop Vibert Jackson, in view of this, referred to him as 'a bigger man than the rest'. AugM, interview with author, 28 October 1995.

546. CM, 9 July 1952 and 3 October 1952.

547. CM, 2 April 1954. The advisability of admitting married men as priest-oblates had been an issue even in the 1930s. CM, 4 March 1938.

548. CM, 4 December 1956.

549. CM, 15 August 1953. However, the chaplain mentioned, Father Henry Martin (1920–82), would join the Nashdom community and was professed as Cyprian in 1961.

550. One of them, Francis Thompson, later became the Bishop of Accra.

551. Anselm Hughes, *The Rivers of the Flood*, The Faith Press, London, 1961, p. 16.

552. Arthur Michael Ramsey (1904–88), Bishop of Durham 1952–56, Archbishop of York 1956–61, Archbishop of Canterbury 1961–74.

553. *NAR*, No. 30 (Autumn 1964), pp. 2–3.

554. Geoffrey Francis Fisher (1887–1972), Bishop of Chester 1932–39, Bishop of London 1939–45, Archbishop of Canterbury 1945–61. The Archbishop visited the Pope on 2 December 1960, following visits to the Holy Land and a meeting with Athenagoras I, the Orthodox Patriarch in Istanbul.

555. After her state visit to Italy, Queen Elizabeth II called on the Pope on 5 May 1961. Queen Elizabeth, the Queen Mother, and Princess Margaret had an audience with him the previous year on 22 April 1960.

556. Igino Eugenio Cardinale (1916–83), Titular Archbishop of Nepte 1963–83, Apostolic Delegate (from the Vatican) to Great Britain 1963–69.

557. Thomas Leo Parker (1887–1975), Roman Catholic Bishop of Northampton 1940–67.

558. CM, 13 July 1956 and 8 November 1956.

559. CM, 1 December 1964.

560. CM, 24 August 1965.

561. CM, 15 December 1965.

562. This was notable for having a Roman Catholic among the more than thirty patrons. Cardinal Bea, head of the Vatican's Secretariat for Promoting Christian Unity, had refused the position (CM, 3 June 1966) but the Cistercian Abbot of Caldey did agree (CM, 20 July 1966).

563. CM, 16 February 1967.

564. CM, 12 December 1966. The loan was repaid within ten years. CM, 16 December 1976.

565. CM, 18 January 1968.

566. Dom Patrick Dalton had returned to Nashdom in 1965 and transferred his stability to his original monastery. Another Nashdom monk, Dom Gregory Silver, had resided at St Gregory's since 1963, being given the position of novice master there.

567. The Nashdom Chapter noted its assent to this process in CM, 20 February 1968.

568. *Unitatis Redintegratio* (21 November 1964).

569. *Sacrosanctum Concilium* (4 December 1963).

570. *Perfectae Caritas* (28 October 1965).

571. Nathaniel William Newnham Davis (1903–66), Bishop of Antigua 1944–52. Bishop Vibert Jackson had resigned as Visitor in the autumn of 1962 on grounds of age and frailty. The Chapter elected Bishop Newnham Davis as his successor on 27 December 1962.

572. CM, 4 December 1963 and 11 December 1963.

573. CM, 12 February 1964.

574. Walter M Abbott (ed.), *The Documents of Vatican II*, Geoffrey Chapman, London and Dublin, 1966, pp. 477–8.

575. CM, 27 September 1965.

576. CM, 20 December 1967 and 30 December 1967.

577. CM, 8 April 1970, 5 May 1970, 14 May 1971, 8 June 1971, 6 July 1971. The brothers first attended Chapter in full (as distinct from participating in some particular discussions) on 13 November 1971.

578. CM, 7 April 1965.

579. Benno Gut OSB (1897–1970), professed 1918 at Einsiedeln, Abbot Primate of the Benedictine Confederation 1959–67, Cardinal 1967.

580. Augustin Bea SJ (1881–1968), entered the Jesuit order 1922, Cardinal 1959, President of the Vatican Secretariat for Christian Unity 1962–68.

581. In the meeting, the Cardinal told Abbot Augustine that the revival of the Religious life among Anglicans was an 'ecumenical' fact. AugM, interview with author, 15 June 1996.

582. CM, 7 April 1965.

583. AugM, interview with author, 28 October 1995.

584. CM, 12 June 1967.

585. CM, 11 March 1968.

586. CM, 28 September 1972 and 8 March 1973.

587. CM, 24 April 1967.

588. CM, 20 October 1967.

589. CM, 23 March 1968.

590. CM, 14 January 1969.

591. CM, 6 March 1970.

592. One priest monk would say his own daily mass until he died in the 1990s. Another did the same – and in Latin – until his death in the 1980s.

593. *NAR*, No. 30 (Autumn 1964).

594. *Jub*, p. 67.

595. For help with the details in this and subsequent paragraphs, I am grateful for interviews with the following members and former members of the community: Aidan (Harold) Harker, in community 1953–86, Basil (Alan) Matthews, in community 1964–2005, Bruno (Christopher) Mackenna, in community 1963–67, Francis Hutchison, in community since 1962, Hugh Kelly, in community since 1957, Wilfrid (David) Weston, in community 1960–84. However, none of these interviewees are responsible for the opinions expressed herein, for which responsibility is entirely the author's.

596. *Jub*, pp. 69–70.

597. Community discussion, No. 4, 2 June 1969, EA.

598. Community discussion, No. 6, no specific date but June 1969, EA.

599. BR to AugM, 3 February 1969, EA.

600. Graham Leonard, suffragan Bishop of Willesden 1964–73, Bishop of Truro 1973–81, Bishop of London 1981–91.

601. AugM, address to community, 30 May 1969.

602. CM, 19 May 1970.

603. CM, 12 January 1972.

604. AugM, interview with author, 28 October 1995.

605. He recalled that he had made the decision to resign while presiding at mass in Newcastle Cathedral on 11 July 1974. On his return to the monastery, he told the monks at compline that evening. AugM, interview with author, 28 October 1995.

606. Frank Weston (1871–1924), Bishop of Zanzibar and East Africa 1908–24.

607. CM, 19 June 1975.

608. CM, 25 November 1976.

609. CM, 30 September 1977.

610. CM, 7 December 1977.

611. CM, 27 October 1977.

612. CM, 18 October 1978.

613. CM, 16 May 1979.

614. CM, 14 March 1980.

615. CM, 28 August 1980.

616. CM, 9 October 1980.

617. CM, 8 July 1982.

618. CM, 11 November 1982.

619. Christopher and Michael had died in 1972, Anselm two years later, and then John in 1977 at the young age of 47. In January 1982, Cyprian, who had been appointed Prior in 1979, died of a heart attack aged 61. Edward and Robert died the same year, and Patrick in March 1984.

620. Helen Weston, *The Winter is Past*, Triangle (SPCK), London, 1995.

621. CM, 7 October 1982.

622. CM, 13 September 1983.

623. CM, 4 January 1984.

624. CM, 25 January 1984.

625. Address to the community by the Visitor, Richard Rutt, Bishop of Leicester, 18 January 1984, EA.

626. CM, 20 March 1984.

627. Although one, Placid, was 'on loan' and resident in an Australian abbey. Although technically still a monk of Nashdom, he was in practice a member of his new monastery, to which he would formally transfer stability in 1986.

628. This had originally been the Cambridge University Mission to Delhi, founded in 1877; after the Second World War it became more formally a Religious community, the Brotherhood of the Ascended Christ, with a predominately Indian membership.

629. CM, 6 February 1984.

630. The committee to look into this was finally discontinued in January 1987. CM, 9 January 1987.

631. Benedict Reid, *A Spirit Loose in the World*, Harbor House (West), Summerland, CA, 1993, p. 180.

632. GS to Peter Lang, 3 October 1984, copy EA.

633. CM, 8 October 1984.

634. CM, 31 January, 14 April and 17 April 1986. The vote on lay abbacy was 3 for, 8 against and 1 abstention.

635. Dom Dunstan Morrell was the only probable opponent of the decision but he decided to vote with the rest of the community so that there would be unanimity. Ironically, he would not have to move as he died on 1 November, a week after the formal decision had been taken.

636. CM, 12 August and 23 September 1976.

637. The Bishop of Reading blessed the monastery on 14 September, and the Archbishop of Canterbury blessed the chapel on 8 October.

638. Basil Matthews, interview with author, 10 February 2002.

639. CM, 21 December 1987.

640. Three, however, were still monks elsewhere at that time: two in other Anglican communities and one a Roman Catholic.

641. See Curtis, *William of Glasshampton*.

Index